Christian Freedom

American University Studies

Series VII
Theology and Religion
Vol. 144

PETER LANG
New York • San Francisco • Bern • Baltimore
Frankfurt am Main • Berlin • Wien • Paris

Christian Freedom

Essays by the Faculty of the Saint Meinrad School of Theology

Edited by
Clayton N. Jefford

PETER LANG
New York • San Francisco • Bern • Baltimore
Frankfurt am Main • Berlin • Wien • Paris

Library of Congress Cataloging-in-Publication Data

Christian freedom : essays by the faculty of the Saint Meinrad School of Theology / [edited by] Clayton N. Jefford.
p. cm. — (American university studies. Series VII, Theology and religion ; vol. 144)
Includes bibliographical references and indexes.
1. Freedom (Theology) 2. Liberty—Religious aspects—Catholic Church. 3. Liberty—Religious aspects—Christianity. 4. Sociology, Christian (Catholic) I. Saint Meinrad School of Theology. II. Jefford, Clayton N. III. Series.
BT810.2.C477 1993 261.7'2—dc20 92-30406
ISBN 0-8204-2061-1 CIP
ISSN 0740-0446

Die Deutsche Bibliothek-CIP-Einheitsaufnahme

Jefford, Clayton N.:
Christian freedom : essays by the Faculty of the Saint Meinrad School of Theology / Clayton N. Jefford.—New York; Berlin; Bern; Frankfurt/M.; Paris; Wien: Lang, 1993
(American university studies : Ser. 7, Theology and religion ; Vol. 144)
ISBN 0-8204-2061-1
NE: American university studies/07

The author's photo on the back cover is by Mark Bettinger.

The paper in this book meets the guidelines for permanence and durability of the Committee on Production Guidelines for Book Longevity of the Council on Library Resources.

Printed in the United States of America.

Contents

Acknowledgments

In the Fall of 1989 the faculty of the Saint Meinrad School of Theology agreed to produce a single volume of essays that would be devoted to the theme of "Christian freedom". There has been much enthusiasm for the project within the faculty—an enthusiasm which inspired the composition of the individual essays, offered support during the editorial process and encouraged the completion of the final volume. Numerous persons who have been involved at different stages along the path to publication need to be acknowledged here.

A special thanks is extended to the many contributors to the book whose names appear on the "Contents" page. Each has submitted an essay from their field of expertise which demonstrates both scholarly competence and personal interest. Needless to say, without their quality work and patience, no such volume could be possible. Another faculty member, Fr. Damien Dietlein, OSB, has been of invaluable assistance in his role as assistant editor and proof reader for the manuscript. I am especially grateful for the insightful correctives and comments which he has offered at each stage of the production.

In addition, a word of appreciation is due to the Saint Meinrad School of Theology for its collective support of the project. Dr. Thomas P. Walters, Academic Dean of the school, has been particularly helpful in his efforts to secure financial resources in support of the volume. Ms. Ava Gehlhausen, secretary for the faculty, has faithfully assembled the individual essays into the format that was needed for publication. And numerous other members of the faculty and staff have offered their support and appreciation for the book as it has progressed toward its final form.

Finally, I would like to thank Mr. Michael J. Flamini, Senior Acquisitions Editor for Peter Lang Publishing, Inc. His work and the courteous efficiency of the Peter Lang staff have made the task of publication as painless as could be hoped. There is no editor who could not appreciate such cooperation and assistance.

Clayton N. Jefford

Saint Meinrad, Indiana
September, 1992

Abbreviations

Ancient Sources

Col	Colossians
1-2 Cor	1-2 Corinthians
Deut	Deuteronomy
Eus. *HE*	Eusebius, *Ecclesiastical History*
Exod	Exodus
Gal	Galatians
Gen	Genesis
Hab	Habakkuk
Ign. *Eph.*	Ignatius, *Ephesians*
Ign. *Mag.*	Ignatius, *Magnesians*
Ign. *Phil.*	Ignatius, *Philadelphians*
Ign. *Rom.*	Ignatius, *Romans*
Ign. *Smy.*	Ignatius, *Smyrneans*
Ign. *Trall.*	Ignatius, *Trallians*
Isa	Isaiah
Jer	Jeremiah
Jos. *JW*	Josephus, *Jewish Wars*
Lev	Leviticus
Matt	Matthew
Phil	Philippians
Phlm	Philemon
Prov	Proverbs
Ps	Psalms
Rom	Romans
1 Thess	1 Thessalonians

Modern Sources

AA	Alcoholics Anonymous
AAFH	Academy of American Franciscan Histor
AER	*American Ecclesiastical Review*

AF	The Apostolic Fathers (Robert M. Grant, ed.)
AGB	Association of Governing Boards
CCD	Confraternity of Christian Doctrine
CCL	Corpus Christianorum. Latin Series
CentBNS	Century Bible. New Series
CFAT	The Carnegie Foundation for the Advancement of Teaching
CHR	*The Catholic Historical Review*
CM	*Catholic Mind*
CORE	Congress of Racial Equality
CS	*Chicago Studies*
DRE	Director of Religious Education
FKD	Forschungen zur Kirchen- und Dogmengeschichte
Gel	Leo Cunibert Mohlberg, ed. *Liber Sacramentorum Romanae Aeclesiae Ordinis Anni Circuli* (1981)
Gellone	Alexandre Dumas, ed. *Liber Sacramentorum Gellonensis* (1981)
Greg	Jean Deshusses, ed. *Le sacramentaire grégorien* (1979)
HDR	Harvard Dissertations in Religion
ICC	International Critical Commentary
ICEL	International Commission on English in the Liturgy
ICR	Interreligious Committee on Race Relations
ITQ	*Irish Theological Quarterly*
JNTSSup	Journal of New Testament Studies. Supplement Series
LMD	*La Maison-Dieu*
MHR	*Missouri Historical Review*
MNTC	Moffatt New Testament Commentary
MR	*Missale Romanum: editio typica altera* (1975)
NCCB	National Conference of Catholic Bishops
NCCIJ	National Catholic Conference for Interracial Justice
NCD	*National Catechetical Directory*
NCEA	National Catholic Educational Association
NCR	*National Catholic Reporter*

NDSCPL	*Notre Dame Study of Catholic Parish Life*
NEH	National Endowment for the Humanities
NICNT	New International Commentary on the New Testament
NPNF	Nicene and Post-Nicene Fathers
OCA	Orientalia Christiana Analecta
OR	Michel Andrieu, *Les Ordines Romani du haut moyen age* (1961-1984)
PDK	*Phi Delta Kappan*
POAU	Protestants and Other Americans United for the Separation of Church and State
QD	*Quaestiones Disputate*
RACHSP	*Records of the American Catholic Historical Society of Philadelphia*
RelEd	*Religious Education*
SBLSBS	Society of Biblical Literature Sources for Biblical Study
SC	Sacrosanctum Concilium (Constitution on the Sacred Liturgy of Vatican II)
SCLC	Southern Christian Leadership Conference
SNCC	Student Non-violent Coordinating Committee
TS	*Theological Studies*
UND	University of Notre Dame
USCC	United States Catholic Conference
VC	*Vigiliae Christianae*
Ver	Leo Cunibert Mohlberg, ed. *Sacramentarium Veronese* (1978)

This volume is dedicated to
The Right Reverend Timothy Sweeney, OSB
Archabbot of Saint Meinrad Archabbey
and to
The Most Reverend Daniel Mark Buechlein, OSB, DD
Archbishop of Indianapolis

As monks, educators and church leaders,
these two people have guided Saint Meinrad School of Theology
in the spirit of Saint Benedict's intention:
"To establish a school for the Lord's Service"
(R. B. Prol. 45)

For their leadership we are truly grateful

Introduction

Eugene Hensell, OSB

In her recent study entitled *Reason for the Hope: The Futures of Roman Catholic Theologates*, Katarina Schuth makes the following observation with regard to scholarship in these theologates: "Apart from the few schools where publishing and writing are expected, scholarship in the theologates is extremely limited, and faculty feel overwhelmed with the multiple tasks they are asked to perform.... Motivation for doing scholarly work is often low; the tangible rewards are almost nonexistent, funding for sabbaticals is usually not available, and there is little expectation at most schools that scholarly writing will be done."[1] To the degree that this observation is accurate, there is a serious challenge with regard to scholarly activity that faces Roman Catholic theologates. Many of these schools are aware of the situation and make a serious attempt to meet this challenge. They realize that at stake is the credibility of the church's competence to do serious theological education. This situation did not develop overnight, however, and it is best understood when seen within a broader context of seminary education.

Over the past forty years an important shift has taken place in Roman Catholicism wherein theological scholarship has moved from the seminary to the university.[2] No doubt part of the reason for this move has been that seminaries find it difficult to sustain the kind of funding that is necessary to attract and retain a significant number of reputable scholars and theologians. An added factor seems to be that an increasing number of scholars prefer to work in a university environment where they feel less demand upon their time and fewer restrictions on their scholarship than what they experience on seminary campuses. But while these issues sometimes attract media attention and on occasion make the seminaries appear to be anti-intellectual, they do not get to the more fundamental problem—the self-understanding of the seminary or the theologate itself.[3] This issue is complex and generates a whole series of further questions. What is the mission of a seminary or theologate that educates students for ministry in the church? What is the nature of theological education for ministry? Should every minister in some way be a theologian? Should every minister, ordained and lay, be expected to have an aptitude for theology and to collaborate competently in theological inquiry? What is the role of scholarship and teaching in a seminary context?[4]

Questions such as these become even more important as an increasing number of seminaries appear to narrow their visions and to limit their tasks to professional education and the practical training of ministers. Serious scholarship and the technical study of religion and theology are being shifted to the departments of religious studies that now are found on almost every university campus. This division of labor is praised by many and promoted as the way of the future in theological education and scholarship. Not everyone, however, is enthusiastic about this trend. Robert Wood Lynn, past senior vice-president of the Lilly Endowment and currently scholar-in-residence at Bangor Theological Seminary, recalls the challenge made in the mid-1950s by H. Richard Niebuhr that theological schools be an "intellectual center of the church". He makes the following observation: "Whenever seminaries fail to embody that vision, American churches become even more vulnerable to the temptations of an easy and finally self-destructive 'anti-intellectualism'."[5] To renew that vision will certainly be one of the major challenges to face every seminary as we quickly move into the twenty-first century.

Critical thinking and serious discussion about the church and theological issues must always be important aspects of a seminary's self-understanding. Conducted in a spirit of faith, openness and mutual respect, they can only serve to enrich the lives, commitments and understanding of both students and faculty. When this is not the case, both the intellectual life and the spiritual vibrancy of the seminary suffer malnutrition and eventually die.

Likewise, teaching and serious scholarship should not be considered to be incompatible in seminaries and theologates. Until recently, however, serious scholarship was understood to be limited to research that resulted in publication. Teaching, on the other hand, was something that had to be done as long as there were students, but it was not to consume quality time and thus prevent a serious scholar from doing his or her *real* work.[6] Those faculty members who spent time teaching, preparing class, grading papers and working closely with students claimed that there was no time left for research and publication. Thus, a dichotomy quickly arose. One either taught class or one did research and published. The idea that good teaching could lead to exciting research and that quality research, in turn, could enhance classroom activity was seldom expressed. They were treated as two separate worlds. Research was praised and rewarded while teaching oftentimes was not. Teaching became almost counter cultural in higher education.

Roman Catholic seminaries were not left untouched by the so-called "publish or perish" mentality. Along with the general church renewal that was mandated by Vatican II came increasing demands for in-depth spiritual and character formation in seminaries. Furthermore, theology courses required new content, new methodologies and more time. A greater emphasis was placed upon pastoral concerns which were sometimes misunderstood and interpreted to mean basic practical applications. As a result of these shifts in emphases and other related transitions, many serious scholars claimed to find it increasingly difficult to conduct their scholarly work in a seminary context. Gradually they began to move to larger Catholic colleges and universities and even to secular institutions of higher education where there was a rapid rise of interest in the academic study of religion.

Today the "publish or perish" attitude is being seriously challenged in many sectors of higher education. Teachers are encouraged to do research as part of responsible teaching, and researchers are challenged to relate their work more closely to what happens in the classroom and in the lives of people. Ultimately, higher education is challenged to create a new vision of scholarship. As Ernest Boyer has recently stated, "What we are faced with, today, is the need to clarify campus missions and relate the work of the academy more directly to the realities of contemporary life."[7] This is certainly the challenge that faces many seminaries and theologates in our times. We must find that balance between serious scholarship, effective teaching and the daily pastoral demands of the church. The following essays represent one faculty's attempt to recognize that challenge and, at least in part, to meet it.

This collection of essays possesses several notable and distinct features. First, all of the authors are faculty members of a freestanding Roman Catholic seminary whose primary mission is the formation of priests and ministers for pastoral service in the church. In order to complete that mission effectively, these professional educators are challenged continually by a formation process which extends far beyond the traditional demands of academia. They must strive for an academic excellence that is expected to be manifested both in classroom teaching and through research projects. They also must be able to place this academic excellence within a pastoral and ecclesial context that is constantly sensitive to the growing and shifting needs of the church. And finally, they all play a part, formally and informally, in the personal and spiritual formation of their students. This is a task that is considered to be extremely important for the quality and vitality of the church's ministry, and it is a responsibility which faculty members take very seriously.

A second feature that deserves attention is the fact that these authors form a diverse and ecumenical seminary faculty. They include Roman Catholics and Protestants, men and women, clergy, religious and laity, celibate and married. In other words, they represent the broader reality of the church as it is experienced in most sections of our country. Their theological thinking, pastoral sensitivities and faith commitment are all influenced, refined and strengthened through their mutual interactions. The insight and expertise which they bring to their research and writing are neither provincial nor untested. Their work is rooted in that solid, living Christian tradition which always strives for unity, but which thrives on the diversity of its expression.

The third notable feature of this collection of essays is the concept which guided their composition and around which they were assembled into this present volume—freedom. The concept of freedom is very appropriate as a guiding motif for a collection of primarily theological essays. It has been a central concern of Christian thought and living since the very beginning of the church. While theologians generally have agreed that freedom is essential in order to live a life of faith, they are quick to admit that the concept often is ambiguous and refuses to fit neatly into any one definition or understanding.[8] Nevertheless, freedom continues to be located at the center of humankind's religious quest for hope and meaning. Therefore, these essays bring to our attention some of the major challenges, past and present, that Christians must face as they seek the truth which will make humanity free.

Notes

1 Katarina Schuth, *Reason for the Hope: The Futures of Roman Catholic Theologates* (Wilmington, DE: Michael Glazier, 1989) 106-107.

2 Robert J. Wister, "The Teaching of Theology 1950-90: The American Catholic Experience," *America* 162 (February 1990) 88-93, 106-109.

3 A recent manifestation of this situation is the strong and often negative response from Protestant, Catholic and Jewish seminary leaders to an article which appeared recently in a popular monthly magazine and which attempted to assess the quality of seminary students throughout the country; Paul Wilkes, "The Hands That Would Shape Our Souls," *Atlantic Monthly* (December 1990) 59-88.

4 These issues are consistently the focus of the journal *Theological Education*, published semiannually by The Association of Theological Schools, the primary accreditation agency for Catholic and Protestant theology schools in the United States and Canada.

5 Robert Wood Lynn, "Coming Over the Horizon," in *Good Stewardship: A Handbook for Seminary Trustees* (eds. B.E. Taylor and M.L. Warford; Washington, DC: AGB, 1991) 58.

6 Lynne V. Cheney, *Tyrannical Machines: A Report on Educational Practices Gone Wrong and Our Best Hopes for Setting Them Right* (Washington, DC: NEH, 1990) 25-34.

7 Ernest L. Boyer, *Scholarship Reconsidered: Priorities of the Professorate* (Washington, DC: CFAT, 1990) 13.

8 Avery Dulles, *A Church to Believe In: Discipleship and the Dynamics of Freedom* (New York: Crossroad, 1982) 66-79.

Paul's Defense of Christian Liberty in Galatians*

John J. Buckel

From the very dawn of Christianity, those who have held a position of leadership within the church often have grappled with questions that relate to religious freedom. Paul's letter to the Galatians is the earliest Christian document in which such questions are addressed at some length.[1] In this epistle the apostle reflects upon the notion of Christian freedom within the context of a discussion of justification and the Mosaic law. Paul summarizes clearly and concisely the gospel message in terms of liberty: "For freedom Christ has set us free" (5:1).

Galatians is truly a remarkable piece of Christian literature. Written in a passionate style, this emotional and intensely personal epistle puts the reader in contact with some of Paul's fundamental theological insights. What is more, it gives one a glimpse of the pre-Christian days of Paul (cf. 1:13-14), his first experience of the risen Lord (cf. 1:15-16), his early years as a missionary (cf. 1:17-24) and his initial contact with the other apostles (cf. 2:1-14). From the opening comments of Galatians until its conclusion, Paul wants to jolt and challenge the recipients of this letter, and to persuade them to his way of thought.

One very quickly realizes in Galatians that the apostle is infuriated. In contrast to his normal custom, Paul offers no thanksgiving on behalf of his readers after the opening salutation,[2] and, in fact, expresses dismay at their behavior (cf. 1:6). Furthermore, Paul makes a number of fiery comments throughout the epistle which indicate that his emotions are running high. "You foolish Galatians! Who has bewitched you" (3:1). "I am perplexed about you" (4:20). The apostle's anger drives him to the point where he makes an almost obscene remark (cf. 5:12). Even the final comments of Galatians, which Paul wrote with his own hand, are those of anger and not of thanksgiving or final greetings (cf. 6:17). What were the circumstances that compelled Paul to write such a passionate letter, one that contains a fair amount of autobiographical information and that addresses fundamental elements of the Christian faith?

Chaos in Galatia

A short time after the apostle's most recent visit, the fledgling Christian communities in Galatia were in turmoil. Paul succinctly describes the cause of the confusion: "there are some who are confusing you and want to pervert the gospel of Christ" (1:7). Apparently, these "troublemakers"[3] had unnerved the Galatians by their insinuations that the Galatians had not yet fulfilled the necessary conditions by which to obtain righteousness. The opponents of Paul had coerced the Galatians into the belief that justification could *only* be obtained[4] by those Gentiles who observed at least part of the Mosaic law (cf. 3:2, 5; 5:4), in particular those precepts that concerned circumcision (cf. 5:2-3; 6:12), dietary practices (cf. 2:11-14)[5] and the observance of special days (cf. 4:10).

Composed primarily of Gentile Christians,[6] the churches of Galatia were founded by Paul himself (cf. 4:13). According to the agitators, the apostle had preached a limited and incomplete version of the gospel to the Galatians so that he might attract more converts to Christianity (cf. 1:10). These troublemakers charged that he had neglected to inform the Galatians that adherence to the Torah was a prerequisite for the obtainment of righteousness.

In all likelihood, the adversaries of Paul spoke of justification in terms of the way in which one becomes a "descendant of Abraham" (3:7).[7] Only the person who is deemed to be an offspring of the patriarch participates in the blessing that was promised to Abraham and his descendants (cf. Gen 12:3; 18:18). The main point of contention between Paul and his opponents was whether the Mosaic law was a factor in order for a person to become a descendant of Abraham, that is, to obtain righteousness.

There is within Jewish tradition a great reverence for the Torah. According to the rabbis, the Torah existed before creation. It is God's most treasured possession, and something so special that the angels tried to prevent its journey to earth. The people of Israel regard themselves as infinitely precious to God, and central to human history precisely because they have been given and have accepted the Torah.[8] There were marvelous examples of unwavering fidelity to the Mosaic law whereby faithful Jews preferred to suffer an agonizing death rather than to ignore the commandments of the Torah (cf. 2 Maccabees 7).

The opponents of Paul undoubtedly appealed to the sacred traditions of Judaism in order to substantiate their claim that the apostle had preached a corrupt rendition of the gospel.[9] First, they probably referred to the Abraham narrative, focusing their attention on the fact that God had commanded the patriarch and his male descendants to be circumcised (cf. Gen 17:10-13). Within the context of this epic it is stated explicitly that whoever is not circumcised breaks the divine covenant and is severed from the chosen people (cf. Gen 17:14). Secondly, the adversaries must have quoted Lev 18:5, a passage that contains one of the fundamental doctrines of Judaism. Here it is unequivocally affirmed that obedience to the commandments of the Mosaic law is a *sine qua non* of justification. Moreover, Paul's adversaries presumably cited Deut 27:26 in order to warn the Galatians that non-observance of the Torah results in a curse. Thirdly, the troublemakers may have referred to the two children of Abraham: Isaac, son of Sarah; and Ishmael, son of Hagar.[10] According to the agitators' way of thinking, those who failed to adhere to the law were likened to the offspring of Hagar, that is, illegitimate heirs of the blessing of Abraham. Those who observed the Torah were akin to the progeny of Sarah, namely, rightful heirs. Fourthly, the agitators seemingly indicated to the Galatians that there were numerous ordinances in the Torah which addressed the issue of morality. Hence, Paul's teaching of a "law-free" gospel gives the mistaken impression that immoral conduct is an acceptable form of behavior.

In addition to their scriptural argumentation, the agitators also have cast doubt upon Paul's account of the gospel through their denial of his apostleship. They were convinced that Paul had learned of the gospel secondhand from the authentic apostles, such as Peter, James and John, "who were acknowledged pillars" (2:9).[11] In the eyes of the troublemakers, Paul was subordinate to these real apostles. And in consideration of their allegations against Paul, his opponents may well have gone so far as to say that he in fact was an "enemy" of the Galatians (4:16).

Paul's Response

Paul reacts vehemently to the charges that are made against his gospel and his apostleship. With no concern for courtesy, the apostle condemns these troublemakers in the strongest terms (cf. 1:8-9) and wishes them bodily harm (cf. 5:12).[12] He accuses them of hypocrisy with regard to their preaching (cf. 4:17; 6:12-13), and draws attention to the fact that although the agitators persuade others to observe the law, they do not keep the law themselves (cf. 6:13). According to the apostle, his adversaries had ulterior motives for their attempts to coerce the Galatians to accept circumcision (cf. 6:12). Moreover, Paul emphatically insists that it is the agitators who preach a perverted gospel (cf. 1:7) and that all who acquiesce in this "different gospel" (1:6) turn away from God, are severed from Christ and have fallen from grace (cf. 5:4). Furthermore, the tone of admonition in the epistle and the harsh language that the apostle uses make it obvious that he is not one who "seeks to please others" (1:10).

Although Paul's anger is clearly visible in Galatians, one does, nevertheless, get the impression that he feels very close to its recipients. The apostle reminds the Galatians that it was he who first preached the gospel to them (cf. 4:13) and that they had received him "as an angel of God, as Christ Jesus" (4:14). Throughout the letter Paul addresses the Galatians in intimate terms (e.g. 1:11),[13] and on one occasion refers to them as "my little children" (4:19).[14] Moreover, Paul shares with the Galatians the deeply personal experience of his encounter with the risen Lord (cf. 1:15-16). In consideration of the affection that Paul has for the Galatians, he seems to wonder how they, perhaps at the suggestion of the trouble-makers, even could consider the possibility that the apostle had become their enemy by preaching to them the gospel which he had received from Christ himself (cf. 4:16).

The letter to the Galatians may be divided into three major sections within which the apostle wields his plan of attack.[15] Paul's fundamental objective in the first section of the epistle is to defend the authenticity of his apostleship and gospel, as well as his independence from the apostles in Jerusalem (cf. 1:6-2:14). He then demonstrates in a variety of ways that one is justified by faith in Christ apart from the law (cf. 2:15-4:31). Finally, the apostle informs the Galatians of the consequences of his teaching, demonstrating that, properly understood, his instruction does not promote a life of licentiousness (cf. 5:1-6:10). This threefold division is anticipated in 1:1-4, at which point Paul asserts that: 1) his apostleship is of divine origin; 2) salvation comes through Jesus Christ, who gave himself for the sins of humanity; and, 3) Christ died so that humankind might be delivered.

By Divine Commission

Paul wastes no time in his defense against the false accusations that are offered by the troublemakers. He makes it known in his opening comments that he has every right to be called an authentic apostle. Paul testifies that his authorization to preach the gospel does *not* stem from any human being but was granted to him by Jesus Christ and God the Father (cf. 1:1, 11). Subsequently, the apostle narrates the events that surrounded his initial contact with the risen Lord and his first years as a Christian missionary. Thus, he illustrates that he was not dependent upon the apostles for the contents of the gospel that he received. Nor was he subordinate to the other apostles.

The intimate details that Paul relates to the Galatians with respect to his life story make for fascinating reading. His autobiographical account includes elements of violence, a heavenly encounter, dramatic change, friendship, suspicion and confrontation. The apostle begins his narrative with an unashamed admission that prior to his acceptance of faith in Christ he "was violently persecuting the church of God and was trying to destroy it" (1:13).[16] Paul boasts that he was well acquainted with the sacred traditions of his Jewish ancestors, to such an extent that he was considered advanced in Judaism beyond many of his own age (cf. 1:14). Assuredly, whatever complaint one might have against Paul, one could not accuse him of ignorance of the Mosaic law and its rigorous demands. With the use of terminology that is reminiscent of the prophetic writings, the apostle's description of his initial experience of the risen Lord is profound in its simplicity. "[...He] who had set me apart before I was born, and called me through his grace, was pleased to reveal his Son to me, so that I might proclaim him among the Gentiles" (1:15-16).[17] With this testimony, Paul substantiates his manifesto in 1:1 and 1:11 with respect to the divine origin of his apostleship and his authority to preach the good news to the Gentiles.

Since his credentials as a Christian missionary now are established, Paul next responds to the accusation that he is inferior to the other apostles. First, Paul dismisses the erroneous notion that the gospel which he received came to him through the original apostles. Paul assures the Galatians that immediately after the risen Lord was revealed to him, he did not confer with those who were apostles before him. On the contrary, he was not even in the same region where they resided (cf. 1:17). Under oath Paul attests that it was not until three years later that he met any of the original apostles, that is, Cephas and James (cf. 1:18-20). The fact that he was not yet known by sight to the Christians in Judea bears witness to this sworn statement (cf. 1:22). As to the other apostles, it was only fourteen years later that Paul made their acquaintance.

Paul acknowledges that upon one occasion he went to Jerusalem to confer with the other apostles with regard to the gospel that he preached (2:1-2). Nevertheless, the apostle went there under the direction of the Spirit and not because his proclamation of the good news was under suspicion. Paul informs the Galatians of a situation in Jerusalem that was similar to their own, where the truth of the gospel was challenged. He mentions some unnamed "false believers" (2:4) who apparently had insisted upon the necessity of circumcision and perhaps also had demanded adherence to the dietary regulations of the Torah. Paul, however, had remained steadfast to the gospel that he received and did not compel Titus, his Gentile companion, to be circumcised. This decision seems to have been accepted without question by the other apostles. Paul notes triumphantly that Cephas, James and John, whom he sarcastically defines as "those who were reputed to be something" (2:6), added nothing to his understanding of the gospel and, in fact, extended to him the right hand of fellowship.

Finally, Paul makes it known that he once personally condemned Cephas to his face because this highly esteemed apostle was obviously in the wrong. While Cephas had eaten freely with the Gentiles before the arrival of "the circumcision faction" (2:12), he withdrew and separated himself from them afterwards. Before all of the other apostles, Paul scolded Cephas that such behavior was not consistent with the truth of the gospel. In addition to his previous testimony, this episode makes it abundantly clear that Paul is in no way inferior to the other apostles.[18]

Not the Law but Faith

Confident that he has defended himself successfully against all false charges with regard to his status as an apostle, Paul now takes the offensive and attacks directly the "other gospel" that was offered by the troublemakers. In stark contrast to their teaching, Paul insists that the Torah has absolutely no role in the way that one becomes a child of Abraham. In a fashion that is reminiscent of the repeated thrust of a battering ram, he again and again states the good news that one obtains righteousness through faith in Christ *alone*. Paul makes the ultimate statement as he distances himself from the mandatory observance of the Torah. As far as the apostle is concerned, he has "died to the law" (2:19).

The role of faith as an indispensable ingredient in justification was not at issue between Paul and the Galatians (cf.

2:16b).[19] The issue was whether one becomes a descendant of Abraham *exclusively* by faith. The troublemakers apparently had swayed the Galatians into the belief that, in addition to faith, at least the partial observance of the Mosaic law was a prerequisite by which righteousness is obtained. In almost every conceivable way the apostle prevails upon his readers to accept his position that Gentiles participate in the blessing of Abraham through Christ by means of faith without the observation of the Torah.

If one is to understand Paul's line of thought, one must keep in mind that he closely associates justification with those who "receive the Spirit" (3:2), are "descendants of Abraham" (3:7), "blessed with Abraham" (3:9), "redeemed" (3:13a), receive the "inheritance" (3:18), are "righteous" (3:21), "children of God" (3:26), who "belong to Christ" (3:29a), are "Abraham's offspring" (3:29b) and "heirs according to the promise" (3:29c).[20] Moreover, it should be noted that the apostle uses the expression "works of the law" as an idiom to designate the commandments of the Torah, especially those that pertain to circumcision and food regulations.[21]

Paul launches his frontal assault on the teaching of the agitators with a barrage of questions that are directed at the Galatians (cf. 3:1-5). He challenges them to recall their initial contact with the good news of Jesus Christ. Did they receive the Spirit by the performance of works of the law or, instead, by having heard with faith? In view of their own personal experience, the Galatians are compelled to admit the overriding importance of faith.

The apostle outflanks the troublemakers as he demonstrates that they have grossly misunderstood the sacred writings. Although Abraham was circumcised, scripture itself testifies that he was justified upon the basis of his faith (cf. Gal 3:6; Gen 15:6). Not only was the patriarch declared righteous *before* he was circumcised, but this also occurred 430 years before the Torah came into the possession of Israel (cf. 3:17).[22] Paul's conviction that people of faith are empowered to become children of Abraham should come as no surprise to the Galatians. After all, it was foretold by scripture (cf. 3:8).

Paul also calls into question the agitators' interpretation of a biblical text that probably served a vital role in the substantiation of their position with regard to the mandatory observance of the Torah. His opponents had pressured the Galatians into the belief that Deut 27:26 threatened damnation upon all who did not adhere to the law. Evidently the Galatians were under the impression that obedience to only a few of the precepts of the Torah constituted them as observers of the Mosaic law.[23] Paul's version of Deut 27:26 (cf. Gal 3:10b), however, sheds new light upon this passage. He accentuates the fact that if one is to avoid the law's curse, one must obey each and every precept of the Torah. According to the apostle's understanding of Deut 27:26, the full condemnation of the Torah is imposed upon all transgressors. There are no exceptions. Paul's argumentation seems to imply that no one fulfills all of the commandments of the law, since all people are sinners.[24] Subsequently, he makes the shocking declaration that "all who rely on works of the law are under a curse" (3:10a).[25]

With his demonstration that dependence upon the Torah has dire consequences, the apostle once again focuses his attention upon scripture in order to fortify his position. The prophet Habakkuk states in no uncertain terms that justification comes through faith (cf. Gal 3:11b; Hab 2:4).[26] With the aid of syllogistic reasoning, Paul illustrates that every attempt to obtain righteousness by any means other than faith, such as the law, is doomed to failure. Since one obtains righteousness by faith (major premise contained in 3:11b), and since the law has nothing whatsoever in common with faith (minor premise in Gal 3:12a as substantiated by Lev 18:5 in Gal 3:12b), then one logically must conclude that no one is justified by the law (3:11a).

Perhaps the most powerful weapon in the apostle's arsenal is his reference to the death of Christ. Paul reminds the Galatians that when he first preached the gospel to them, he proclaimed the crucified Christ (cf. 3:1). The apostle maintains that Christ died on the cross so that all people might be "redeemed from the curse of the law" (3:13a),[27] that is, delivered from sin (cf. 1:4). Without a doubt, Paul makes a strong connection between the justification of the Gentiles and the crucifixion of Christ (cf. 3:13-14).[28] For that reason, it is unthinkable that anyone is justified by means of the law. Such a belief would imply that Christ died in vain (cf. 2:21).

In his attempt to discredit the false teaching of the troublemakers, Paul also calls to mind a well-known fact from the legal realm. Once a will has been validated, no one can alter it (cf. 3:15). Just as the conditions of a person's will cannot be changed after it has been certified, neither can the conditions of the promise that was ratified by God centuries before the law was given to Israel be changed, that is, annulled, by the law. Whoever contends that the inheritance is obtained through the law suggests that it is not received by the promise, and thus, in effect, annuls the covenant that God made with Abraham. Obviously, this cannot be done.

The apostle expounds on the significance of the fact that the promises were made to Abraham and his offspring (singular and not the plural form, "offsprings"). According to Paul, the "offspring" clearly refers to Christ and only to Christ (cf. 3:16).[29] Therefore, the way that one participates in the blessing that is promised to the offspring of Abraham, namely, Christ, is through one's relationship with him. Everyone who has faith in Christ and has been baptized is united with him (cf. 3:26-28) and thus belongs to Abraham's seed (cf. 3:29), sharing in the patriarch's blessing and receiving the promise of the Spirit (cf. 3:14). It is not those who are closely bound to the Mosaic law who receive the inheritance, but those who are united with Christ. One's intimate association with Christ also unites that person with other believers. Accordingly, the apostle proudly announces that all distinctions between Jewish and Gentile Christians, slave and free, male and female, are a thing of the past (cf. 3:28).[30]

Paul seems to anticipate a reprisal against his understanding of the Torah as he offers the rhetorical question, "Why then the law?" (3:19a). As he sees it, the Mosaic law was never designed to be a means by which to obtain righteousness. It simply was *added* "because of transgressions" (3:19b). Moreover, the Torah was given only on a temporary basis (cf. 3:19c) and, unlike the promise to Abraham, which was ratified by God (cf. 3:17), it "was ordained through angels by a mediator"

(3:19d). Furthermore, the primary objective of the law was to consign "all things under the power of sin", to "imprison", to "guard" and to act as a "disciplinarian" until Christ came, so that humanity might be justified by faith (cf. 3:22-24). Even though the law has a secondary status and even though righteousness is not obtained by the law, it is not inherently evil and it does serve a purpose.[31] Consequently, Paul can say in all intellectual honesty that the Torah does not stand in opposition to the promises of God (cf. 3:21).

Paul then returns to the narrative on Abraham, where he strikes once more against the way that the troublemakers employ scripture. In sharp contrast to the heretical teaching of these troublemakers, the apostle insists that it is not the non-observers of the Torah who are children of slavery, but those who "desire to be subject to the law" (4:21). Like Ishmael, they too are excluded from the inheritance. Assuredly, it is those who believe that the inheritance comes through faith in Christ alone who are akin to Isaac, that is, are children of the promise.

Paul also calls attention to the fact that the Galatians were in bondage before they acknowledged Christ Jesus in faith (cf. 4:8). Inasmuch as the Galatians have been designated as adopted children of God (cf. 4:5) and thus are heirs to the promise, it is unthinkable that they should return to their former status as slaves (cf. 4:9).

Free to Love

Having overwhelmed the troublemakers' position with an array of arguments, the apostle now illustrates the ramifications of his teaching. He triumphantly proclaims the Christian declaration of independence: "For freedom Christ has set us free" (cf. 5:1). Paul then proceeds to demonstrate once again that the decision to accept or reject his gospel of freedom is not to be taken lightly. It is, quite literally, a matter of life and death.

From the apostle's point of view, those who accept his teaching that justification is obtained exclusively through faith are bound intimately with Christ (cf. 5:6, 24) and thus reap an abundance of benefits. They are a "new creation" (6:15), possess the "fruit of the Spirit" (5:22) and will enjoy eternal life (cf. 6:8). All who succumb to the perverted gospel of the agitators and insist that circumcision and fidelity to the Torah are obligatory in order to obtain righteousness, however, are separated from Christ (cf. 5:4). These unfortunate people are under the yoke of slavery (cf. 5:1) and are destined for corruption (cf. 6:8).

Surprisingly enough, though Paul repeatedly argues against the necessity of circumcision and of obedience to the Mosaic law (cf. e.g. 5:2-4), he nevertheless maintains that it really makes no difference whether an individual is circumcised (cf. 5:6; 6:15)! The apostle reiterates his conviction that one's commitment to the Torah is not sinful *per se*.[32] In Paul's mind, the *motive* for one's desire to comply with the commandments of the Mosaic law is fundamentally important. On the one hand, those who wish to submit themselves to the dictates of the Torah yet realize that it is *not* a means to righteousness will suffer no ill consequences (apparently the assumption in 5:6 and 6:15).[33] On the other hand, those who are faithful to the Torah because they believe that it is a prerequisite for justification are anathema.

Lest there be some skepticism about his stance on moral behavior, Paul makes it abundantly clear that his "law-free" gospel is not to be construed as a promotion of dissolute living. He sternly warns the Galatians that the gift of freedom is not to be abused by submission to the "desires of the flesh" (5:17). In order to avert any misunderstanding, the apostle lists a rather lengthy catalogue of vices that are to be avoided, for example, fornication, licentiousness, impurity, etc. (cf. 5:19-21). Paul cautions his readers that all who do such things "will not inherit the kingdom of God" (5:21).

The apostle wishes to impress upon his readers that Christian liberty must be understood within the context of love, responsibility and community. Earlier in the epistle Paul informed the Galatians that it was out of love that Christ died for all people (cf. 2:20). As Christ has given freely of himself in the service of others, so now the Galatians are called to give freely of themselves in the service of one another in a spirit of love (cf. 5:13).[34] Since they are sisters and brothers in the

Lord, Paul advises that the Galatians must realize that they have a responsibility towards each another.[35] He exhorts them to be kind, good and patient (cf. 5:22), share all good things (cf. 6:6), love one another (cf. 5:14), bear one another's burdens (cf. 6:2) and gently correct those who have wronged them (cf. 6:1).[36] The Galatians are instructed to act in a loving manner towards all people, as well as towards those who are of the "family of faith" (6:10).

Paul's concluding remarks about the troublemakers are especially bitter. He invokes judgment upon the "ringleader" of the agitators (cf. 5:10) and then expresses the hope that all of the troublemakers might castrate themselves (cf. 5:12). True to the sharp tenor of the entire epistle, the final verses also end on a sarcastic note. Evidently the opponents of Paul have focused much of their attention upon the "marks of circumcision". The apostle, however, boasts not of his own circumcision, but of the physical scars that he has endured for the sake of the gospel.[37] In view of these "marks of Jesus" (6:17), Paul adjures his readers not to bother him any more.

The final words of the letter are, in a manner of speaking, a disguised prayer that the Galatians might accept Paul's version of the gospel. He has warned them previously that all who yield to the teaching of the troublemakers have "fallen away from grace" (5:4). Now he prays that the grace of our Lord Jesus Christ might be with the Galatians (cf. 6:18).[38] Of course, this will only occur, according to Paul's argumentation, if they accept his teaching.

Paul has completed the defense of his understanding of the good news. The time is at hand for the Galatians to make a decision. They must decide for themselves whether they are to remain steadfast to the gospel that the apostle first preached to them or whether they will capitulate to the teaching of the troublemakers. Now that he has stated his case, Paul is confident that the Galatians will "not think otherwise" (5:10).

Conclusion

In effect, the apostle has confronted the Galatians with a question of tremendous importance: "Do you realize what you are doing?" Paradoxically, in their attempt to obtain something which they already possessed, that is, righteousness, the Galatians were in danger of losing it. Paul has demonstrated that to be declared as righteous is not an irreversible condition. Consequently, should the Galatians stubbornly refuse to accept his "law-free" gospel and choose instead to rely upon the Torah, they will be severed from Christ and revert to their pre-redeemed state.

Christ Makes a Difference

Paul's fundamental difficulty with the troublemakers seems to be that by their demand for obedience to the Torah they act as if the death and resurrection of Christ has had no impact upon salvation history. Nothing could be further from the truth. One of the recurring themes in Galatians is that the person of Christ has changed everything. The apostle notes the monumental transformation that took place in his life as a result of a revelation of the risen Lord. Through this experience it was made known to him that one is justified by faith in Christ alone. Henceforth, it is Christ and not the Mosaic law that plays center stage in his life. As a result the apostle reinterprets scripture in the light of Christ. Moreover, his newfound faith in Christ Jesus greatly influences the way in which he envisions society. Paul has come to realize that for those who are bound to Christ, not only are previous religious distinctions removed, but all social distinctions as well. Furthermore, even his outlook on moral behavior has undergone a dramatic change. The apostle's motivation to live a virtuous life now is understood in terms of fidelity to the reign of God instead of obedience to the Torah. Paul's reflections throughout the epistle clearly indicate that although Christians are undeniably connected to the past, they are by no means chained to it.

The Challenge of Freedom

It is not at all surprising that since the gospel was first proclaimed, questions have arisen with regard to Christian liberty. Whenever individuals confront divine realities, there will be uncertainty, challenges and mistakes. The apostle provides much needed guidance for those under his care by an appeal to the fundamental tenets of the Christian faith, as well as to scripture. He informs the Galatians that the good news which he originally preached to them takes precedence over any other gospel that is contrary to that which they initially received. In the defense of his rendition of the good news, the apostle does not hesitate to upbraid such a commanding figure of authority as Cephas himself for behavior that is contrary to the truth of the gospel.

Christ liberates all who believe in him from the shackles of sin so that they might love more fully. Indeed, love presupposes freedom. It was not for a life of unbridled passion that Christ set humankind free but for a life of love and charitable service. Christian liberty never is to be taken for granted. Rather, freedom should always be treasured as a precious gift, one that was obtained at a great price, namely, the death of Christ.

Notes

* An earlier version of this article appeared under the same title in *Louvain Studies* 17 (1992) 254-268. I wish to thank the editors of *Louvain Studies* for permission to republish this material here.

1 There is an overwhelming consensus that Galatians was written no later than CE 55. Although Paul also addresses issues that pertain to Christian freedom in the letter to the Romans, the majority of exegetes assume that Romans was composed after Galatians. Cf. e.g. Gerd Lüdemann, *Paul, Apostle to the Gentiles: Studies in Chronology* (Philadelphia: Fortress, 1984) 263.

2 Cf. e.g. Rom 1:8-15; 1 Cor 1:4-9; Phil 1:3-11; and, 1 Thess 1:2-10.

3 Henceforth, I shall use the terms "troublemakers", "agitators", "opponents of Paul" and "adversaries of Paul" interchangeably.

4 I use the expressions "to be justified" and "to obtain righteousness" synonymously.

5 Cf. F.F. Bruce, *The Epistle to the Galatians* (NIGTC; Grand Rapids, MI: Wm. B. Eerdmans, 1981) 19: "Insistence on those [Jewish] food restrictions by some Christians is implied in [Paul's] account of Peter's withdrawal from table-fellowship with Gentiles at Antioch."

6 Cf. e.g. Gal 4:8; 6:12.

7 Cf. John W. Drane, *Paul: Libertine or Legalist?* (London: S.P.C.K., 1975) 24: "The basic issue at question was not the Law and circumcision, but sonship to Abraham, and through him to God himself" (cf. also Gal 3:29; 4:7).

8 Cf. Eugene B. Borowitz, "Judaism. An Overview," *Encyclopedia of Religion* 8 (1987) 135-136 for a presentation of the rabbinic theory of Torah.

9 The apostle's numerous citations from scripture may indicate that the opponents of Paul were the first to use the sacred writings in support of their position.

10 This hypothesis has been proposed, for example, by C.K. Barrett, "The Allegory of Abraham, Sarah, and Hagar in the Argument of Galatians," in *Rechtfertigung: Festschrift für Ernst Käsemann* (eds. J. Friedrich, W. Pöhlmann and P. Stuhlmacher; Tübingen: J.C.B. Mohr, 1976) 9.

11 Cf. Ernest Burton, *A Critical and Exegetical Commentary on the Epistle to the Galatians* (ICC; Edinburgh: T. & T. Clark, 1980) liv-lv: The trouble-

makers depicted Paul as "a man who knew nothing of Christianity except what he had learned from the Twelve, and preached this in a perverted form."

12 Paul does not appear to follow the advice that he gives to the Christians in Rome. "Bless those who persecute you; bless and do not curse them" (Rom 12:14).

13 Likewise, Gal 3:15; 4:12, 28, 31; 5:11, 13; 6:1, 18.

14 Paul also refers to the recipients of his letters as "children" in 1 Cor 4:14; 1 Thess 2:11; and, Phlm 10.

15 In general terms I concur with a number of biblical scholars at this point, most notably, H.D. Betz (*Galatians: A Commentary on Paul's Letters to the Churches of Galatia* [Hermenia; Philadelphia: Fortress, 1979] 14-25), who suggest that the influence of Greco-Roman rhetoric is readily seen in the structure of Galatians.

16 Luke relates to his readers the intensity with which Paul sought after the disciples of the Lord (cf. Acts 9:1-2).

17 Cf. Isa 49:1 and Jer 1:5. Paul's allusion to these distinguished prophets may indicate the extent to which he was convinced of his special election and appointment. Cf. also Ronald Y. Fung, *The Epistle to the Galatians* (NICNT; Grand Rapids, MI: Wm. B. Eerdmans, 1988) 63-64.

18 With respect to Paul's reference to Peter in Gal 2:11-14, Donald Guthrie (*Galatians* [CentBNS; London: Thomas Nelson, 1969] 63) suggests that when the apostle "actually withstood Peter publicly before the Antioch church, there could not have been a clearer evidence of his apostolic status."

19 Paul seems to assume in Gal 2:16b that the recipients of this epistle would agree with his comment, "And we have come to believe in Christ Jesus, *so that we might be justified. . . .*"

20 In a similar fashion, cf. e.g. Jan Lambrecht, "Das Gesetzverständnis bei Paulus," in *Das Gesetz im Neuen Testament* (QD 108; ed. K. Kertelge; Freiburg: Herder, 1986) 112.

21 Cf. Gal 3:2, 5, 10. For a more in-depth discussion of "works of the law", cf. my "'Curse of the Law.' An Exegetical Investigation of Galatians 3,10-14" (PhD dissertation, Katholieke Universiteit Leuven, 1988) 213-230.

22 Cf. also Exod 12:40.

23 One receives the impression from Gal 5:2 that the recipients of the epistle were not following *all* the precepts of the Torah.

24 Paul explicitly states elsewhere that all people are sinners (cf. Rom 3:9, 23; 5:12).

25 There has been much dispute with respect to Paul's argumentation in Gal 3:10. Cf. my "Curse of the Law" 1-118, 197-236.

26 Bruce (*Galatians* 161) observes that the apostle commented on the story of Abraham in Gal 3:6-9 in order to inform the Galatians with regard to the way that one obtains justification. "It might be argued, however, that Abraham was a special case; hence Paul cites the statement of justification by faith as a permanent principle in Hab 2:4." Cf. also Rom 1:17.

27 Along with others, I am of the opinion that the Galatians probably were more apt to understand the term "redeemed" in light of manumission in antiquity. Cf. e.g. George S. Dungan, *The Epistle of Paul to the Galatians* (MNTC; London: Harper, 1934) 97; and my "Curse of the Law" 287-291.

28 Cf. W.D. Davies, "Paul and the People of Israel," in *Jewish and Pauline Studies* (Philadelphia: Fortress, 1984) 127: "In a way in which Paul does not explain, Christ by his [death on the] cross had opened the promise to Abraham to the Gentiles."

29 Cf. e.g. Robert Yates, "St. Paul and the Law in Galatians," *ITQ* 51 (1985) 112: "The rabbis would understand Paul's use of the singular of 'seed' to refer to one person, but for them that person would be Isaac."

30 Cf. Bruce, *Galatians* 187: "Paul makes a threefold affirmation which corresponds to a number of Jewish formulas in which the threefold distinction is maintained, as in the morning prayer in which the male Jew thanks God that he was not made a Gentile, a slave, or a woman."

31 Similarly, Paul claims in Rom 7:12 that "the law is holy, and the commandment is holy and just and good."

32 For an opposing hypothesis, cf. e.g. Gerhard Ebeling, *The Truth of the Gospel: An Exposition of Galatians* (Philadelphia: Fortress, 1985) 178-179.

33 Cf. also Gal 3:21.

34 Paul argues in a similar fashion in Rom 13:8-10.

35 In view of Paul's remarks in 5:15 and 5:26, one wonders whether the Galatians were in special need of such exhortation, since they already seem to have experienced some fierce dissension within their communities. Along the same lines, cf. Fung, *Galatians* 247-248.

36 From his comments in Galatians it appears that once again one has a case where Paul does not follow his own advice, e.g., to be gentle with those who have wronged oneself.

37 Paul lists some of the ways in which he has suffered for the sake of the gospel in 2 Cor 11:23-28.

38 Cf. also Gal 1:2.

Ignatius of Antioch and the Rhetoric of Christian Freedom*

Clayton N. Jefford

Ignatius of Antioch serves as a unique focus for any study that is related to the theme of Christian freedom. There is little question among church historians that his letters have come to symbolize the evolving nature of nascent Christianity during both the apostolic and post-apostolic periods. Indeed, it is just short of miraculous that the epistles of the Ignatian correspondence are not included among the texts of New Testament scripture but, instead, have been relegated to that corpus of materials which we now call the Apostolic Fathers.

As a bishop and theologian at the beginning of the second century, Ignatius manages to encapsulate the essence of many issues that challenged the rise of ecclesiastical structure and organization. Three of these issues stand apart as specific elements that typify the concerns of early Christian leaders: the relationship of Christianity to its mother religion of Judaism; the development of an institutional hierarchy; and, the position of the church with respect to secular authorities. For Ignatius in his role as bishop of Syrian Antioch, each of these elements has been interwoven into a theological matrix that holds as its foundation the very necessity of freedom within the Christian mindset. He remains a singular figure in the early history of the church because of his ability to develop a model of theology that holds the motif of freedom as its organizational premise.

The struggle of Ignatius with the restrictions of Judaism offers numerous parallels to the situation of the apostle Paul. Ignatius attempts to free Christianity from the limitations of first-century Judaism that continued to exert its influence over early Christian theological, ethical and institutional concerns.

At the same time he develops the Pauline attack upon those "Judaizers" who would argue for Christianity as a subset of the Jewish mentality, and not as a separate religious entity in and of itself.[1]

There is no great surprise that Ignatius should find himself in the middle of such controversy, since Antioch was a Hellenistic city with an unusually large Jewish population. To encourage colonization in the early third century, Seleucus I had provided various privileges to the Jewish people of the area, including the right to form a separate political body and to enjoy the status of citizenship alongside the Greeks themselves.[2] Such freedoms and favoritisms did indeed lead to an influx of diaspora Jews. But by the end of the first century CE, local jealousies and discontent had forced the Jewish community into a defensive position because of anti-semitic violence and rampant rumors that the Jews were responsible for fires that had destroyed the central market area, city archives and royal palaces.[3] In such a setting the church of Antioch no doubt was eager to establish its identity apart from the synagogue. The continuing struggle between Judaism and Christianity in Antioch, a struggle that was both political and theological in nature, most likely had a primary influence upon the perceptions of Ignatius, just as it probably is reflected within the visions of the Gospel of Matthew and the Didache.[4]

While Ignatius develops a concern for the church as an institution that needed to pull itself away from the constraints of the synagogue and Judaism, he also sees the need within Christianity to establish a standard ordering of roles and offices by which the authority of Christ could be delegated and controlled. The subsequent call to a three-tiered hierarchy of bishop, presbyter and deacon remains his most lasting imprint upon ecclesiastical structure. Of course, while one would not argue that Ignatius himself inaugurated this system,[5] there is no question that it was through his influence and direction that the structure became the dominant model for western Christianity.

Finally, the aura of Ignatius and his contributions to theology and ecclesiology are definitively shaped by the fact that his surviving letters were produced during a time of imprisonment. He is a servant of Christ who bears the shackles and chains of one whose service has led to captivity at the hands of secular authorities. What is known about Ignatius today is known primarily through the lenses of his imprisonment. As such, one comes to understand him not only as a bishop who struggled to establish an ecclesiastical character within the ranks of a religiously troubled era, but as a bishop who consistently worked to correlate the needs and goals of Christian leaders to the inevitable world of power struggles. The subsequent martyrdom that Ignatius suffered and the image of him as a servant of Christ, "faithful unto death", provides a spark for the Christian imagination which continues to color the modern understanding of his place in ecclesiastical history.

The condition of imprisonment that Ignatius portrays through his letters suggests that he naturally would have an urgent concern for the topic of freedom, both on an individual basis and as a member of the body of Christ. This perception seems reasonable in that a similar concern had been expressed previously in the thought and theology of Paul, a concern which undoubtedly developed from Paul's experiences as a prisoner "for Christ".[6] The focus of Paul's own position with regard to the theme of freedom surfaces in his letter to the Galatians. The form of that discussion centers in the typically Pauline dichotomy between freedom and slavery, spirit and flesh, faith and law. In this brief discussion he offers a wealth of terminology and images as they relate to the theme of freedom and its meaning for the development of a valid Christian theology.

Within the writings of Ignatius, however, one discovers that references to "freedom" are severely limited. Terminology such as "free", "freedom" and "to set free" appear in only three letters: once in the letter to the Magnesians (12.1); three times in the letter to Polycarp (4.3; 7.1); and, three times in the letter to the Romans (4.3). On the surface such an omission seems peculiar, especially when compared to the frequent appearance of similar terms in the letters of Paul. Indeed, in this one respect the works of Paul that were written under persecution diverge widely from the letters of Ignatius.

On the other hand, there is no similar lack of terminology among Ignatius' letters with respect to words that are related to bondage. Images such as "binding", "captivity", "slavery" and "suffering" are widespread in usage and in metaphorical intention. Examples of such "persecution terminology" occur in the letters to the Ephesians (prologue; 1.2; 3.1; 11.2; 12.1-2; 21.2), to the Magnesians (2.1; 9.1), to the Trallians (3.3; 4.1-2; 12.2-3), to the Romans (1.1; 4.1-8.3), to the Philadelphians (5.1), to the Smyrneans (4.2; 10.2; 11.1) and to the bishop Polycarp (2.3; 3.1-2). One is led to believe that the focus of Ignatius' activity and thinking is oriented toward these images or, at least, to the negative expression of the struggle between captivity and freedom as it is expressed within his own personal situation.

Most of these images of bondage and captivity are related to the suffering of Jesus and to the contemporary situation of other Christians with whom Ignatius was in contact. Thus Ignatius and others are slain "for the sake of God" (Ign. *Eph.* 12.2), suffer in order to be "disciples of Jesus Christ" (Ign. *Mag.* 9.1), carry their bonds "for the sake of Jesus Christ" (Ign. *Trall.* 12.2; *Phil.* 5.1) and endure all things "in the name of Jesus Christ alone" (Ign. *Smy.* 5.1). There is little question that Ignatius envisions the persecutions of the moment as trials and tribulations that serve to test and purify those persons who seek to be worthy participants in the life of the church.

Much of this perception consequently is offered to the readers of Ignatius' letters in the form of teachings. These teachings, and the symbols and metaphors which they employ, remain today as the primary images by which the author is known.

Perhaps the most readily recognized teaching of Ignatius in this respect is the view that bishops, presbyters and deacons must be envisioned among congregations as those persons who reside within the community in the place of God, the apostles and Jesus Christ respectively (Ign. *Mag.* 6.1-2). As he says, without some acceptance of this standard it is impossible for the title "church" to be applied to any particular congregation (Ign. *Trall.* 3.1). It also is his view that the practice of baptism and eucharist are not valid apart from this understanding

(Ign. *Smy*. 8.1-2). So too, the unity and Christocentric orientation of the church are experienced through this structure, an ordering that ultimately provides a role and function for each member of the entire community with respect to the hierarchy. One may question whether the emphatic arguments of Ignatius do not in fact come close to divinizing the leaders of the church.[7]

The letter in which the concerns of Ignatius for freedom and bondage become most acute is his epistle to the community at Rome. It is to Rome that he journeys as a prisoner of the empire. He anticipates that it is in Rome that he will suffer the greatest hardships and eventually even death. But it is through this suffering that he hopes to become a "freedman of Jesus Christ" (Ign. *Rom*. 4.3), through whom he shall "rise free". He encourages his readers to permit the sufferings that he anticipates will soon be his, to be ground "as wheat" by wild beasts in the arena "as the bread of Christ" (Ign. *Rom*. 4.1), to be burned, crucified, cut, torn, mangled, crushed and otherwise cruelly tortured along the path to fulfillment in Jesus Christ (Ign. *Rom*. 5.3). Through such experiences he anticipates that he will receive "the pure light" and ultimately attain the model of humanity that God intends (Ign. *Rom*. 6.2).

As important and vibrant as such images of captivity and freedom are to Ignatius, especially in his letter to the Romans, their presence tends to mask the additional emphasis that is provided by the rhetorical structuring of the letter as a whole, especially as it relates to the issue of Christian freedom.[8] For example, the prologue of the epistle by Ignatius, as with the letter to Rome by Paul in the New Testament, appeals to the Romans as a community of "honor, worthy of blessing, praise, success and holiness", a community that is united in Jesus Christ through flesh and spirit without blemish. Such a level of praise and respect, which is unique among the writings of Ignatius, serves to prepare the community for the admonitions that are to follow. Ignatius' use of such extensive praise for the recipients of his letter, in lieu of the more commonly employed "thanksgiving section" (as exemplified by Paul), can be said to reflect a typical feature of the well-known "royal letter".[9] Indeed, his use of the "royal letter" genre here is not haphazard. As a bishop from the East he bears no specific authority. Presumably he must rely upon some means other than an appeal to personal acquaintance in order to negotiate his position.[10] Thus, it is through the formal structure of the "royal letter" that he can speak with the community at Rome as an official authority who is due a certain respect. And it is through the structure of an official correspondence that he offers an impassioned plea to be heard.

He is afraid that the love of the community, the authority that the church in Rome commands within the city itself,[11] not to mention the good intentions of the ecclesiastical leadership, will serve to hinder him in his progression toward torture and death. The essential substance of the letter to Rome is an attempt by Ignatius to dissuade the Romans from any temptation to act upon what would seem to be the will of God (i.e. to preserve a human life) in order to permit what in truth is the hidden will of God (i.e. to usher a human life toward salvation). In brief, Ignatius desires that a lesser good be withheld in order to propagate a greater good.

These symbols and the issues that they represent are expressed in a bold and clear manner. The history of research into the life and thought of Ignatius leaves no question that his devotion to God and his desire to suffer a passion that is worthy of Christ is sincere. Yet several elements remain in the appeal of Ignatius which subsequent Christian interpretation traditionally has failed to perceive or, at least, has chosen to ignore.

The first of these elements is the reality of the presence of a secondary motivation that undoubtedly lies behind the letter of Ignatius to Rome. While the question of freedom and bondage is directed almost exclusively toward the situation of the early church throughout the majority of the Ignatian letters, in the letter to Rome the argument is directed primarily toward the situation of Ignatius himself. No longer is captivity and suffering portrayed primarily as a means by which the congregations of Christ experience true discipleship. Instead, it now is the avenue upon which the very person of Ignatius treads toward his own freedom. With the letter to Rome, Ignatius' argument becomes self-oriented. Nowhere does he even suggest that the persecutions which he endures would be worthy goals for his Roman audience. They are his goals alone, goals that his readers should not mistakenly assume to be obstacles!

This shift from a community-centered view of Christian freedom toward a self-oriented understanding of suffering is a radical departure within the presentation of the theology of Ignatius. On the one hand, it is true that one does not detect any particular inconsistency within the framework of Ignatius' thought itself here. If suffering and struggle serve to increase the certitude and purity of the church, then it seems reasonable to assume that these same elements are binding and good for the leadership of the church. According to his own logic, since Ignatius is one of these very leaders, he too should assume the mantle of suffering that characterizes true discipleship—and "true discipleship" imitates the passion of Christ.

But on the other hand, the dramatic shift from community orientation to self-concern in the letter to the Romans suggests that Ignatius has more on his mind than is suggested by the glowing words that he proffers for his "ultimate freedom" in Jesus Christ. Behind these images is the essence of a certain appeal for some relief from his current predicament. He has crafted a letter with an unswerving conviction that through suffering and death comes freedom in Christ. He warns his audience (i.e. the members of the church at Rome), the one source of strength and authority within the empire that could have some influence over his future, that by no means are they to interfere with his future course. He describes his envisioned fate with terms and phrases that strike imagined horror into the average reader, both ancient and modern. He appeals to his situation as unworthy for consideration, yet casts his actions of faithful suffering within the very paths of those "worthies" who have preceded him to Rome, the apostles Peter and Paul. In every respect Ignatius offers the images of his convictions—vibrant and intensely-felt convictions. At the same time, though, it is the overwhelming way in which he leaves no room by which his sincerity may be questioned that one is led to consider a secondary motivation to his letter. If ever there was a faithful Christian, a worthy worker of the church, who *deserved* to be saved from the horrible torture and death that he portrays for the benefit of the community at Rome, it is Ignatius!

The letter to Rome, while an apparent denial of the need for help on the surface, is in fact a subtle plea for intercession that is disguised by the rhetoric of the epistle. Indeed, while the subsequent history of Christian tradition and interpretation has leapt quickly to classify Ignatius according to the very category of "worthy martyr" that previously was assigned to Stephen in the Acts of the Apostles, it seems reasonable to believe that such a role was not necessarily one that was desired by Ignatius himself—despite his claims to the contrary in his letter to the Romans. If one can assume that Ignatius already has suffered some affront to his self-esteem at Antioch—perhaps his arrest and related worries with respect to his worthiness as a bishop and disciple of Christ[12]—it would be natural for him to envision his subsequent bondage and journey to Rome as a test of discipleship, faith and theological certitude. In theory, such a test hopefully will lead to a restoration of the disciple to the master; in practice, this does not necessarily engender a desire for the destruction of the disciple's presence on earth as a consequence. While Ignatius harbors a passion against the power of the world that is represented by the will of the state and while he calls for a violent end to his travail under that power, he seems content to participate in the immediately hospitable environment of those churches who support him along his journey. For him, these oases represent his earthly home, a home for which he continues to provide both spiritual and ecclesiastical direction —a home that he does not necessarily seem eager to forsake, at least according to his scattered correspondence.[13]

The second of the elements that church historians often ignore is the issue of freedom as a category within Ignatius' theology. When one ponders the situation of Ignatius as bishop to the troubled city of Antioch, it is no wonder that he is careful to express his reliance upon some future freedom in Christ, a freedom whose future is assured by the course of events that ushers him toward persecution. He revels in the images of martyrdom that traditionally are used to characterize those who have been persecuted.[14]

The model that Ignatius seeks to imitate is that of a long tradition, the tradition of the death of a worthy individual for a worthy cause. It is this model that comes to demonstrate for the Christian heritage what might be considered as evidence of true faith in Christ. Ignatius certainly was in a position to understand and incorporate the elements of this concept into his own theology. The famous "martyr sequences" of 2 Maccabees 6-7 and 4 Maccabees were widely known among the Jews of the diaspora and, no doubt, this vision of righteous Jews who endured through the persecution of the Seleucid empire probably was well known by Ignatius in his role as a religious leader in Antioch. But more to the point, Ignatius seems to share with Paul the broader understanding of Greco-Roman thought about the "noble death", or the death of one individual for the benefit of all. Thus, while the death of Jesus is depicted as an event of salvation "for all who can believe", according to Ignatius, the bishop's own death is offered as a vehicle by which he himself may demonstrate the cross and resurrection of Jesus and may imitate the "passion of God" (Ign. *Rom*. 6.3).[15] And it is Ignatius, through his own capitulation to the powers of Rome, who serves as the early Christian figure through whom this model becomes solidified. He quickly becomes the funnel for the vision of "persecuted martyr" in early Christianity. The circumstances of his death are incorporated into the list of those paradigmatic persons who have died for their faithfulness.

Christian views of freedom thus have become interpreted through the lenses of martyrdom, based to a large extent upon the figure of Ignatius himself. He stands as a significant link between the first-century situation and modern theological considerations of freedom within the Christian mindset. The common argument continues: to suffer for Christ in the present ultimately must lead to some future reward of freedom in Christ in the future. How happy are those who suffer now, for theirs is the joy that comes with eternal freedom—in the future. This is the view that is supported by the letters of Ignatius.

Such a perception, as it is funneled to the modern church through the line of martyrs that influenced the thought of early Christian theology, however, is representative of only a portion of the early teaching of first-century Christianity. As is suggested throughout the New Testament, the freedom that comes through Christ has an existential relevance that is applicable to the believer in the world of one's daily existence.[16] But the proclamation of this reality within the early church soon falls victim to the urgency of eschatological concerns. This call for an existential perception is swallowed by the infestation of apocalyptic awareness that dominates the first-century vision of the world, a vision that is concerned more for the conclusion of creation than for its regeneration. And of course, it also becomes a proclamation that Ignatius sublimates in his letters as he writes to churches and bishops from his current situation of persecution.

While Ignatius offers himself to the Romans as a believer who is faithful to the passion of Christ, the subsequent early Christian image of Ignatius as martyr is oriented in large extent around the paradigmatic figure of Stephen in Acts 6:8-8:1. Whatever the circumstances of the death of Stephen, the Lukan vision of that occasion portrays Stephen as "a man who is full of faith and of the Holy Spirit" (Acts 6:5) and as one who indicts and attacks the high council of the Jews for their infidelity to God. But Stephen's speech against the council as it is preserved in the Acts is incomplete rhetorically, since his words should end with a return to the original charge against him, thereafter to conclude with a rejection of the authority of the council or with a general call for repentance, as in the speeches of Peter.[17] Instead, the episode is concluded with an epilogue in which Stephen abandons the claims of his earthly life and invokes the authority of the judgment of God (Acts 7:54-60). This is the dominant vision of first-century Christianity. And this is the very image into which the Christian tradition has cast the figure of Ignatius—accused, abused and abandoned to God's future mercy. The image has been abetted by the fact that specific references to the actual death of Ignatius are lacking in early Christian literature.[18] Thus it is that he can pass through the world as a prisoner, a faithful and pure disciple of Christ who is led through persecution to "his final reward". The tradition provides no room in which Ignatius can do otherwise.

The third element that the Christian tradition often has misunderstood relates to the complexity of Ignatius' own theological structure. While he struggles against docetism with its enthusiasm for esoteric spirituality (Ign. *Trall.* 9-10; *Smy.* 6.1) and its claims that Jesus did not in fact suffer the passion (Ign. *Trall.* 10.1; *Smy.* 2.1; 5.1-3), he often exhibits traces of gnostic thought within his own theology. Most noticeable here is his language concerning God[19] and his view "of the harmony of spiritual powers within the divine fullness".[20] Ignatius also shows much concern for the "stillness" (Ign. *Eph.* 19.1) and "silence" (Ign. *Mag.* 8.2) of God. Most significant as well is the distinct dualism that Ignatius envisions in his anticipation of martyrdom. The transcendence of "the divine" places God apart from "the world" in a most dramatic form. Of course, the use of such language and ideas can no more condemn Ignatius to the ranks of gnosticism than one might accuse Paul or the author of the Gospel of John of the same perspective. Early Christian speculation is replete with theological claims and counterclaims that often mystify the modern theologian. But one must be careful to recognize that Ignatius shows no evident association with the world as it surrounds him. His goal is for the future; his destiny is with the world beyond. And in this respect he leans toward the perception that the material world is a place for trial and testing, a temporary moment in a journey toward salvation. This view of creation and the role of Christ in that creation indeed borders on the edge of a defective view of freedom in Christ in the opinion of later church councils.[21]

Modern notions of freedom through Christ for the present life, as well as freedom in Christ for the current situation, certainly do not reflect the ancient perspective that is depicted in the letters of Ignatius. For him, service in the name of Christ is in fact bondage, a bondage that will become true freedom only after the successful completion of a tour of duty in the service of God. He makes no effort to define for his readers just exactly what this freedom is, nor can one assume that in the course of his bold exclamations about his desire to suffer and die that he does not in fact relish the possibility that such a path will be altered.

In the final analysis, Ignatius serves a pivotal role in early Christian thought by which the desire for a "future freedom" in Christ comes to outweigh the reality of a "present freedom" in Christ. No doubt, this is to some extent the product of Ignatius' own situation in captivity. He writes to the churches at Antioch, Philadelphia, Rome and elsewhere with a certain insistence upon the need for a valid separation of Christianity from its Jewish heritage, an established institutional hierarchy for the early church and an ethic whereby Christian leaders can learn to survive within the boundaries of secular authorities. These are features of a theology that indeed seeks a certain institutional freedom in the rise of Christianity. Yet all of this insight is offered in light of the realization that his own ability to influence the growth of a youthful faith soon may come to a conclusion. And in this process he sacrifices the reality of the image of individual freedom in Christ that comes to each and every believer in the course of daily existence.

One must wonder to what extent the concerns and approaches of Ignatius may have been altered if his future as bishop of Antioch in the early second century had not been threatened and finally terminated by his present circumstances. It is the threat of the state and the glory of his eschatological vision that lead Ignatius to defend his freedom in Christ as a future reality. It is this defense that has led subsequent Christian interpreters to define Ignatius as the paragon of martyrdom. It is this flawless image of Ignatius as a devoted disciple, "faithful unto death", that has been employed by subsequent generations of Christians as an endorsement for the argument of Ignatius on behalf of a "future freedom" in Christ.

One must question whether the letters of Ignatius in fact could have offered a different view of Christian freedom for the church if there had been no pressure from an impending martyrdom. To some extent the prominent image of martyr and theologian that Ignatius has left as a legacy has served to set an example for much Christian theology. At the same time, the modern image of Ignatius unfortunately has continued to shift the tide of common Christian perspective in a direction that much of New Testament Christianity may never have intended: toward the conviction that freedom in Christ only offers relief from human turmoil through some future life; away from the realization that freedom in Christ shapes the reality of daily living.

Notes

* A preliminary form of the following essay was read under the title "A Perception of Freedom in the Epistles of Ignatius" at the Eleventh International Conference on Patristic Studies in Oxford, England held 19-24 August 1991.

1 Cf. e.g. Ign. *Mag*. 10.1-3; *Phil*. 6.1-2.

2 Elias J. Bickerman, *The Jews in the Greek Age* (Cambridge, MA and London: Harvard University Press, 1988) 91-92.

3 Jos. *JW* 7.3.1-4. Cf. Wayne A. Meeks and Robert L. Wilken, *Jews and Christians in Antioch* (SBLSBS 13; Missoula, MT: Scholars Press, 1978) 1-6.

4 So Meier in Raymond E. Brown and John P. Meier, *Antioch and Rome* (New York and Ramsey, NJ: Paulist, 1983) 22-27.

5 E.g. the Didache may attest to the presence of this three-tiered hierarchy at Antioch prior to the influence of Ignatius; cf. my "Presbyters in the Community of the *Didache*," in *Studia Patristica* (ed. E.A. Livingstone; Leuven: Peeters, 1989) 21.122-128. See also William R. Schoedel, *Ignatius of Antioch* (Hermeneia; Philadelphia: Fortress, 1985) 22-23.

6 Cf. Rom 16:7; Phlm 1, 9; Acts 16:19-40; 21:27ff.

7 Schoedel, *Ignatius of Antioch* 22.

8 The letters of Ignatius suggest that he was "trained in the dramatic Asianic rhetoric of his time"; so Robert M. Grant, *Ignatius of Antioch* (AF 4; London: Thomas Nelson & Sons, 1964) 1.

9 Hermann Josef Sieben, "Die Ignatianen als Briefe: Einige formkritische Bermerkungen," *VC* 32 (1978) 16.

10 Cf. the list of personal greetings that are offered at the end of Paul's own letter in Romans 16.

11 To some extent this assumption that the early Roman church wields influence within the larger realm of the secular government may be a misunderstanding on the part of Ignatius or, more likely, may represent an element of rhetorical flattery. On the early Roman Christians,

see James S. Jeffers, *Conflict at Rome* (Minneapolis, MN: Fortress, 1991) 3-35.

12 Cf. Schoedel, *Ignatius of Antioch* 13-14.

13 While Ignatius commonly speaks poorly of "the world", it is interesting that the overwhelming majority of these statements appear in the letter to the Romans (Ign. *Mag.* 5.2 *bis*; *Rom.* 2.2; 3.2, 3; 4.2; 6.1, 2; 7.1); cf. Schoedel, *Ignatius of Antioch* 14-15.

14 W.H.C. Frend, *Martyrdom and Persecution in the Early Church* (London: Basil Blackwell, 1965) 197-201.

15 See the general discussions by S.K. Williams, *Jesus' Death as Saving Event* (HDR 2; Missoula, MT: Scholars Press, 1975); David Seeley, *The Noble Death* (JSNTSup 28; Sheffield, England: Sheffield Academic Press, 1990).

16 Thus, e.g., traces of sympathy for "the world" appear in John's prologue by means of the participation of the Word during the creation of the world (John 1:1-18; cf. 3:16-19); according to Mark, the message of Jesus is that God's reign is "at hand" (Mark 1:14-15); and, Paul argues that God's invisible nature is clearly perceived in the world itself (Rom 1:18-20); cf. Claus Westermann, *Creation* (Philadelphia: Fortress, 1974) 1-15.

17 George A. Kennedy, *New Testament Interpretation through Rhetorical Criticism* (Chapel Hill, NC and London: University of North Carolina Press, 1984) 121-122.

18 The so-called "Martyrdom of Ignatius" generally is considered to be spurious. Even Eusebius does not record the death of Ignatius in his history, but provides material that is available primarily through the Ignatian epistles (Eus. *HE* 3.36).

19 Schoedel refers to such words and phrases as "'sharing' God (*Eph.* 4.2), 'being entirely of God' (*Eph.* 8.1), being 'full' of God (*Mag.* 14), and 'having' God (Christ) in oneself (*Rom.* 6.3; cf. *Mag.* 12)" (*Ignatius of Antioch* 19).

20 Schoedel, *Ignatius of Antioch* 16.

21 Grant, *Ignatius of Antioch* 22-24. Cf. L.W. Barnard, *Studies in the Apostolic Fathers and their Background* (New York: Schocken Books, 1966) 19-30. A thorough presentation of the gnostic link to Ignatius has been argued by Henning Paulsen, *Studien zur Theologie des Ignatius von Antiochen* (FKD 29; Göttingen: Vandenhoeck & Ruprecht, 1978).

John Courtney Murray, SJ and Giovanni Cardinal Morone Connected

Simeon Daly, OSB

Seared into my psyche is the hurt that I felt as a young man when I learned that John Courtney Murray had been "silenced". As a theological student at the Catholic University of America, I had enjoyed a campus debate between Murray and Francis Connell on whether error enjoyed any rights. Connell taught a moral class in which I was enrolled, but I was more sympathetic to Murray and his arguments in that debate. I began to follow the career of Murray with interest. It is fair to say that I was hurt at the news in 1955 that he was no longer permitted to write on church-state issues without prior censorship. Correspondingly, I was delighted to learn later that he contributed substantially to Vatican II. I am not prepared to say how much these events shaped my thinking, but they left me with great empathy for those who seem to be crushed by institutions. I found that I nourished within myself the secret hope that eventually all would be well and that the suffering party would be able to forgive and forget. When the institution in which one believes deeply uses a heavy hand, the issues are more sensitive. When the institution is the church in which one believes with all one's heart, one is forced to make many distinctions, only in the end, perhaps, to bow in the face of mystery.

No longer young and less naive, I recognize that injustices do sometimes occur. Thus, the celebration is all the more satisfactory when an individual who is hurt by the system comes back in the pattern of the forgiving Christ to serve the church again. It is a mark of grace that is worthy of note. Church history is peppered with various stories of grace. I take the occasion of this essay to tell two such stories. Father Murray and Cardinal Morone are totally unrelated in time and circumstance. I bring them together because I have noted the pattern of repression and pain, followed by forgiveness and service. Also I find a correspondence of decades, centuries apart. Both men were burdened in the sixth decade of their respective centuries, only to return and to function positively at an ecumenical council in the subsequent decade.

I was prompted to consider Morone through the offhand remark of Albert Outler in his response to the Vatican II document on the church: "It calls to mind the spirit of those great Catholic reformers, Contarini, Sadoleto, Gropper, and Morone, of the 16th century whose efforts on behalf of unity were thwarted by both 'Papalists' and 'Protestants'."[1] He refers to Gasparo Contarini (1484-1542), Jacobo Sadoleto (1477-1547), Johannes Gropper (1503-1559) and Giovanni Morone (1509-1580), great men of the period, each of whom deserves serious study. Each has his own particular story, but it is Morone's story that leads to Murray and the issue of freedom that confronts the church today.

Giovanni Cardinal Morone

Although serious scholars of the period would be familiar with the name of Morone, a biographical sketch is desirable here. Giovanni Morone was born 25 January 1509 in Milan, Italy of Girolamo and Amalia (Fisaraga) Morone. Girolamo was the Grand Chancellor of Francis II Sforza, Duke of Milan, and was no stranger to the political struggles of the time, especially between the great rivals King Francis I of France and Emperor Charles V of Germany, struggles that kept all of western Europe in turmoil. After a military invasion of Milan by King Francis, the Morone family took refuge in the Italian city of Modena, where young Giovanni began his studies and was raised.[2]

In 1527 Rome was sacked and the Roman pontiff Clement VII was imprisoned in Castel Sant' Angelo for six months. As a reward for the efforts of Girolamo on behalf of the papal cause, the bishopric of Modena was given to Giovanni. Although Giovanni was already respected for his piety and wisdom, the appointment was symptomatic of a larger problem of the times, since he was a layman and only twenty years of age.

More than anything else, the appointment of seculars to bishoprics (men who frequently possessed no theological or pastoral formation, or even concern) and/or the acquisition of diocesan revenues while in residence outside the diocese contributed to the decline in moral leadership of the church at this time. The popes dispensed bishoprics to relatives and friends like financial chips. The Roman curia was particularly plagued with this problem, which contributed to the very secular lifestyle of the clergy that so scandalized the faithful and led to moral degradation, a target of Protestant church reformers of this era.

Morone's appointment as bishop on 7 April 1529 caused a controversy, not because he was so young and not ordained, but because Modena had been promised to the son of another official. This problem was not resolved until 1533 when the newly ordained young bishop took control in Modena. Money was involved in the resolution of the dispute.

In the meantime Morone served a term as nuncio to the King of France, Francis I. After this mission he returned to Italy and was ordained as priest and bishop in Bologna on 12 January 1533. He took possession of his diocese on 28 January. At the time Modena had twelve parishes, twelve male religious communities, fourteen convents and three hospitals.

In 1535 he served on a committee that investigated heresy in Milan. From this time he gained a reputation, not fully deserved, as a man who was "soft" on heresy. This suspicion was fed by his formulation of a profession of faith for some academics of Modena in 1542, a suspicion that was not resolved officially until all of the charges were declared to be false in 1572.

From 1536 to 1538 Morone was nuncio to Ferdinand I of Hungary and Bohemia, where he was very influential in his attempt to design plans for a proposed church council, a council (now known as the Council of Trent) that did not occur until 1545 after much political maneuvering. Ferdinand came to appreciate Morone's wisdom and dedication to the church. This helped tremendously in 1563 when they worked together to prepare for the last session of the council.[3]

In 1542 Morone was appointed as nuncio to Germany and took part in the second Diet of Spira, which concluded with a definitive call for an ecumenical council. On 31 May 1542 Morone was appointed as a cardinal in recognition of his pastoral and diplomatic service. Ceremonies to bestow the red hat followed in June. He was made Cardinal Protector of England, Hungary, the Archduchy of Austria, of the Order of St. Benedict, of the Cistercians and Dominicans. Also, he became Cardinal to the House of Loreto.[4] He contributed substantially to the House, and attributed to our Lady of Loreto a miraculous cure from an unspecified illness.[5]

In 1543 Morone was appointed as legate to the proposed Council of Trent. But for various reasons, particularly because he was sent as a legate to Bologna, he never arrived for the opening sessions.

Because of his numerous external duties, Morone resigned from the bishopric of Modena in 1550 (though he resumed it again in 1564). Here again was a major concern of the time: cardinals who were also bishops of dioceses were absent so much that they could not perform their episcopal duties, or were so busy in their dioceses that they could not perform the functions that were expected of them in the service of the pope and the church.

In 1522 Morone begged Ignatius of Loyola (1491-1556) to found a theological college for Germans in Rome in order to provide a place for German clerics to receive a proper theological formation and to counteract the errors of entrenched German Protestantism. His long association with the Germans made him sensitive to their needs. Later in life he established a Congregation of Cardinals for Germany and participated in the Imperial Diet at Regensburg (1576).[6]

Throughout this period each of the popes that Morone served—Clement VII (1523-1534), Paul III (1534-1549), Julius III (1550-1555), Marcellus II (1555)—held Morone in high regard. He frequently was employed to counter the effects of heresy that had spread into Italy. It also was during this period, however, that the Roman Inquisition officially had begun to consider the charges of heresy that were made against him.[7] Unfortunately for Morone, Gian Pietro Cardinal Caraffa became Pope Paul IV and immediately began a renewed effort to verify charges that Morone had held heretical positions. After almost two years of harassment, Morone was confined without warning in Castel Sant' Angelo, and a rigorous process of trial began in earnest.

Pope Paul IV was a driven man, full of zeal and thoroughly convinced that he served the church through the silencing of Morone. He was seventy-nine years of age when elected, and was determined to suppress those who in his opinion were "soft" on heretics. He also had targeted Cardinal Pole of England and Ignatius Loyola, but both of them died before the charges could be considered. Pole died a broken man after he was deprived of his office as papal legate to England and was summoned to Rome for trial. Pole could not fathom how he could be considered disloyal to the church that he had served for so long and so faithfully. Historians concur that no matter how zealous, how genuinely pious and blameless of life, Paul IV was a ruthless, unbending zealot. He was almost paranoid about the guilt of Morone in the face of overwhelming evidence to the contrary.[8] The names of Pole and Morone frequently were linked, even by the Inquisition. Pole escaped imprisonment only by his death in 1557.[9]

The Inquisition had considered accusations against Morone on several occasions, but each time these were proven to be false. No doubt because of the prejudice of Paul IV, new accusations arose and old ones were renewed. Even after Morone had been jailed and the process was enjoined against him, he was found to be innocent by the special panel that was appointed to review his case. He was offered the option of release from prison with a pardon from the pope. The implication was that he would admit to doctrinal errors and repent. Morone refused and said that he would rather die in jail than to leave the impression that he had ever besmirched his faith or the cause of the church. He remained in prison until the death of his accuser, a man who had remarked once that he would carry the wood to torch his own father if he were convinced that the latter were a heretic.[10]

Because Paul IV was so afraid that Morone might be elected as pope, he had an elaborate bull composed that renewed past anathemas against convicted heretics, thus to deprive them of all rights and privileges, all benefices and income from church-related responsibilities. He added to these penalties the loss of active and passive vote in any conclave that was called to elect a new pope. The first version of that document as presented to the cardinals for approval included the condition of "even those who have been accused of heresy by the Inquisition". The cardinals insisted that the document be softened to include only those who had been proven to be heretics, in the light of how easy it would be to manipulate conclaves by false accusations. Paul IV agreed and the bull was published.[11] Only a few days later, however, he issued a decree that restricted those who were accused from eligibility for election to the papacy.[12] The decree never became operative and Morone participated in subsequent conclaves with no restrictions. The memory of the accusations against him were there, though, and in subtle ways made him *non-papabile*, even though he enjoyed a strong and loyal following among the electors.

Almost immediately after the death of Paul IV, convinced of the innocence of Morone, the supreme senate of the church voted the release of the cardinal from prison and restored his rights.[13] The new pope, Pius IV (1559-1565), appointed a committee of four to review the proceedings against Morone. Their findings included the following: two days after his election, Paul IV had sent envoys throughout Italy to gather damning information and accusations of heresy against Morone in such a way so as to result in vague, false and inaccurate accusations that were all refutable. Morone was jailed unjustly without proper procedure and was held inhumanely—even deprived of his right to attend Mass. The whole series of proceedings were motivated by a vindicative and false zeal rather than by any valid interest in justice. In a consistory on 13 March 1560, a public statement of Morone's innocence was entered into the record.[14] Despite the memory in his own heart and the subtle influence that the whole episode had upon subsequent conclaves, Morone entered fully into the life of the church and exercised great leadership and wisdom in countless ways until his death in 1580.

Almost immediately after the election of Pius IV in 1559, Morone was offered a position in the curia. He declined at that time, but after the renewed sessions of the Council of Trent stalled and the entire project was threatened in the spring of 1563, he accepted the role of papal legate and president of the council. He is given much credit for the successful continuation and conclusion of the council, having exercised great diplomacy with governmental and ecclesiastical factions.

Although the council concluded on 4 December 1563 in a hurried frenzy for fear that the pope would die before its conclusion, Pius IV did in fact sign the decrees early in 1564. The actual date of promulgation for the ratification of the dogmatic decrees, the canons and the decrees of reform was not until 30 June 1564. A sacred congregation was established to continue the reforms that were commissioned by the council, which included the revision of the liturgical books and a new edition of the Vulgate.

After the death of Bishop Foscherari, who had been Morone's successor at Modena, Morone once again assumed responsibility for his diocese and was very active in the promotion of the decrees of the council and the reform of clergy, faithful and religious.

In 1571 Morone once more resigned his office as Bishop of Modena because of increased responsibilities on behalf of Pius V (1566-1572). At the time of the Turkish danger, eastern European problems occupied his mind. He was especially interested in Russian-Polish relations. The conclusion of the Lepanto League in the Roman Conference (1570-1571) was to a large extent a result of his efforts.[15] In his latter years he had assumed residence in Rome in the Palazzo di S. Maria Trastevere, where he died on 1 December 1580 "*tota urbe collacrimante*".[16]

One need not be an accomplished church historian to know that the late Middle Ages and the Renaissance periods were times when abuses were rampant in the church. Perhaps the great religious upheaval of the sixteenth century might never have occurred if the reforms in "head and members" that was demanded so stridently by councils and synods had actually come to pass. During its sessions in the early sixteenth century, the Fifth Lateran Council echoed the call for reform that already had been urged by the Fourth Lateran Council a century before.[17] The upheaval occurred, and the polarization that began then exists still in the numerous Christian denominations that continue to this day. This is not to say that new and improved insights have not arisen from the rich intellectual ferment that divisions introduced, but circumstances may have been different if proper reforms had occurred.[18]

The church was conscious of reform during the sixteenth century. There were fits and starts at reform and much "name calling". The struggle between papalists and conciliarists was at the heart of the program, though obviously there were many other legitimate concerns. So much energy was given to the protection of the rights of the popes in opposition to the councils and vice versa, that actual reforms were slow to come. Accusations of heresy or of favoritism toward individual groups created an atmosphere of tension and suspicion that eroded personal and public peace. There is no question that Giovanni Morone, who contributed so much to the reforms of the period, was an innocent victim of such suspicion.

John Courtney Murray, SJ

The story of John Courtney Murray[19] can be told more easily than that of Giovanni Cardinal Morone. Both were men who were well educated in the classics. Murray was more the technical theologian and perhaps less concerned with the larger direction of the church. He was silenced in the 1950s only to come to the fore a decade later during an ecumenical council, a pattern that compares to the career of Morone. Interesting parallels in the lives of the two men present themselves along the way.

Murray was born in New York City on 12 September 1904 of a Scottish Father and an Irish Mother into a staunch Catholic family of modest means. At the early age of sixteen he became affiliated with the Jesuits. He obtained a BA from Weston College in 1926 and an MA from Boston College in 1927. During his tertianship as a young Jesuit, he taught Latin and English literature at Ateneo de Manila in the Philippines.

After his assignment to the Philippines, Murray was summoned back to the United States, where he studied theology for four years at Woodstock College in Woodstock, Maryland. After his ordination in June 1933, Murray proceeded to Rome and studied at the Gregorian University, where he obtained a doctorate in theology (1937). He then returned to Woodstock as a professor of theology. His areas of specialty were "Grace" and the "Holy Trinity". He continued as a member of the Woodstock faculty until his death on 16 August 1967. Speculative theology was always his major interest.

Murray was keenly sensitive to the practical order of life. He long felt a concern for the role of religion in society in general, and the role of Roman Catholics in a pluralistic society in particular. How fully could a Catholic enter into the political system? Could a Roman Catholic conscientiously allow the freedom of religion that was proclaimed by the constitution of the United States, or was the freedom of religion only tolerated because of the minority position that Catholics had at the moment in the country? As Catholics began to enter the mainstream of American political life, these questions were asked and needed to be addressed.

Murray began a serious study of the American constitution, and his reflections began to appear in various publications. He became editor of *Theological Studies* in 1941 and was able to use that publication as a forum for his studies. In 1945 the first of a series of articles on the freedom of religion appeared.[20] Murray's church-state doctrine and his position on intercredal cooperation were not shared by all. Francis Connell (1888-1967) and Joseph Clifford Fenton (1906-1969), both noted theologians, took issue with him in various forums, especially the *American Ecclesiastical Review* which Fenton edited.[21] Both Connell and Fenton favored the position that "error has no rights", and therefore, freedom of religion is to be tolerated only as long as Catholics are in the minority. This doctrine fed the anxiety of Protestants in the US who feared that in some future time "Rome and Romanism" would prevail. This anxiety was fueled by the anti-catholic writings of Paul Blanshard, author of *American Freedom and Catholic Power* (1950), and the non-denominational group known as Protestants and Other Americans United for the Separation of Church and State (POAU).

While Blanshard sounded an alarm about Catholicism, Murray sounded his own alarm against the radical secularism that he detected both in Blanshard's work and in the general drift of society.[22] It was this larger concern about secularism and a desire to construct a positive theory of how religion should function in American society that consumed his energies and evoked some of the most creative writing on church-state relations of the century.

One should note that *Humani Generis*, the encyclical of Pope Pius XII, was published about this same time (12 August 1950). Because it named and rejected such new trends as historicism, the false theory of evolution, existentialism and a number of other trends of the time, it contributed to the atmosphere of tension among Catholic intellectuals and widened the breach between liberal and conservative theologians. Fenton was aggressive in his pursuit of Murray's ideas on the relationship of the church to the state. Waves which were made in the United States were felt in Rome where Cardinal Ottaviani, a powerful conservative figure in the Holy Office, made moves that effectively silenced Murray on this issue.

This silencing was not as radical nor as devastating as the imprisonment of Morone which was discussed above, but it was indicative of an attitude of mistrust and caution that can pervade those who are determined to preserve others from error. One would not equate the repression of the pontificate of Pius XII with that of Paul IV in his affairs with Cardinal Morone, but there is sufficient evidence of other such silences—Yves Congar and Henri de Lubac, both eminent French theologians who were silenced during this same period—to warrant the judgment that it was a dangerous time for theologians.

There was no one moment of collision for Murray. His speech at the Catholic University of America which interpreted Pius XII's discourse to Italian jurists (*Ci Riesce*, 6 December 1953) incensed Fenton and eventually Cardinal Ottaviani.[23] Murray was convinced that Pius XII had made a move toward greater tolerance of other religions. This position would be a reversal of the widely held position that, in such circumstances where Catholics were in the majority, the state was obligated to favor Catholicism and restrict other religions. Because of inside information, Murray felt confident that the pope would reject the position that was held by Ottaviani. The text was ambiguous enough, however, to be open to various interpretations. As a direct result of this talk, Murray was asked not to publish anything more on the church-state issue without prior approval by Rome. For all intents and purposes this requirement removed Murray from the scene. The final article in a four-part series that he had prepared on Leo XIII and public religion for *Theological Studies* was never published because of this censure.[24] There can be little doubt that Murray found his position hard to accept. Some of the bitterness is reflected in a letter that he wrote to his provincial:

> All the books on Church and State and on allied topics have been cleared from my room, in symbol of retirement, which I expect to be permanent. When Frank Sheed returns, I shall cancel the agreement I had with him to edit and revise the articles on Church and State for a book. Fortunately, my gloomy prescience impelled me to refuse an invitation to give the Walgreen Lectures at the U. of Chicago. And all other practical measure will be taken to close the door on the past ten years, leaving all their mistakenness to God. (At that, I do not believe that I was mistaken on the central issue—the need for a unitary theory.)[25]

To his credit, Murray did not simply "fold his tent". He continued to write and to lecture, as the full bibliography of his work in this period demonstrates. He turned his attention to the subject of public morality and particularly to the moral role of Catholicism in a pluralistic society. He served on the President's Atomic Energy Commission. He worked with Robert Hutchins's Fund for the Republic, Inc. on the whole relationship of religion to free society. He was active in the National Conference of Christians and Jews.[26]

With the death of Pius XII in October 1958, John XXIII was elected as pope. Already in January 1959 the new pope called for an ecumenical council in the course of which Murray would be summoned for his expertise in a most direct way. Ultimately his patience and perseverance in the face of opposition would be vindicated completely.

In 1960 Murray published *We Hold These Truths: Catholic Reflections on the American Proposition*, a book which was to be his "primer" of pluralism with special attention to the dilemmas that are posed to and by Catholics in a pluralistic society. The book received immediate and wide attention, especially since it appeared early in the presidential campaign of a Roman Catholic, John F. Kennedy. Catholics and Protestants alike sought him for advice on the Kennedy campaign, on American public policy and religious dialogue. His picture made the cover of *Time* magazine (12 December 1960). The story that accompanied the photograph was in effect a long discussion of Murray's book.[27]

Fenton was not pleased to see Murray back in the fray. He reviewed *We Hold These Truths* quite negatively.[28] Fenton had great hopes that all ambiguity on church-state relations would be put to rest by the council, presuming, of course, that his view would become the definitive position. He was invited as an expert by Ottaviani himself, and at the first session was conspicuous in that role. That Murray, on the other hand, had been "disinvited" was only a small footnote in the life of this scholar, a distinction that he shared with other such leading theologians as John L. McKenzie, Henri de Lubac, M.D. Chenu, J. Danielou, Victor Hugo and Karl Rahner. A number of these, including Murray, eventually had their say.[29] Murray's only recorded comment on his feelings at this time was that "a man doesn't live long and if something this big is going on, a man feels that he ought to be there."[30]

Get there he did. He served as a theological expert for the second, third and fourth sessions at the direct invitation of Francis Cardinal Spellman of New York, who respected Murray's ideas and trusted his judgment. In fact, most of the

American bishops relied upon his papers and instructions so completely that one foreign bishop was quoted to say, "The voices are the voices of the United States Bishops, but the thoughts are the thoughts of John Courtney Murray."[31] With all of the political maneuvering that occurred throughout these sessions, the final text from Murray's perspective was somewhat weakened by compromise.[32] The major aspects of his view were preserved, however, and the "Declaration on Religious Freedom" as a separate document of Vatican II owes much to the efforts of Murray on its behalf and much of its wording to his hand. A key paragraph of that document is worthy of note:

> This Vatican Synod declares that the human person has a right to religious freedom. This freedom means that all men are to be immune from coercion on the part of individuals or of social groups and of any human power, in such wise that in matters religious no one is to be forced to act in a manner contrary to his own beliefs. Nor is anyone to be restrained from acting in accordance with his own beliefs, whether privately or publicly, whether alone or in association with others, within due limits. The Synod further declares that the right to religious freedom has its foundation in the very dignity of the human person, as this dignity is known through the revealed word of God and by reason itself. This right of the human person to religious freedom is to be recognized in the constitutional law whereby society is governed. Thus it is to become a civil right.[33]

Murray's health was never particularly strong. He had frequent setbacks from exhaustion and heart problems. At the very end of the council, on 5 October 1964, he suffered a lung collapse and was hospitalized. His main work was done, however, and he did not feel that his forced absence in those closing days affected the outcome of the document.

While he was in Rome and still recovering from the October lung collapse, Murray was invited on 18 November to concelebrate mass with Paul VI and a number of other theologians at St. Peter's. It was a solace for all of the troubles that he had experienced at the hands of the church over the past ten years. He was quoted to say that it was one of the most wonderful Masses of his life. Like Morone before him, Murray had weathered the storm and was big enough to return to serve where he had been rejected by forces over which he had no control.

Murray died on 16 August 1967 of a heart attack in a taxi in Queens, New York. A eulogy by his longtime friend and fellow Jesuit, Walter Burghardt, provides a fitting tribute to his work and a conclusion to this short review of the second of our protagonists:

> Unborn millions will never know how much their freedom is tied to this man whose pen was a powerful protest, a dramatic march against injustice and inequality, whose research sparked and terminated in the ringing affirmation of an ecumenical council. "The right to religious freedom has its foundations" not in the church, not in society or state, not even in objective truth, but "in the dignity of the human person."[34]

Conclusion

I have provided numerous details to the stories of Morone and Murray because the events clearly demonstrate how men of great learning, dedication and zeal can have their rights restricted drastically in the name of religion. It seems evident too from the conduct of their lives that Morone and Murray did honor to religion by the principled way in which they faced their accusers, and the forgiving, non-vindictive way in which they continued to serve the church.

> For freedom Christ has set us free; stand fast therefore and do not submit again to the yoke of slavery. (Gal 5:1)

Paul's challenge to the Galatians clearly refers to the slavery of sin, but it is not a large leap to see in his words a challenge at all levels to keep watch over precious freedoms, whether from the tyranny of sin or of oppressors, whether secular or ecclesiastical. Human nature leaves humanity in constant threat of sin. The human condition also exposes humankind to domination by those who wield power. This essay has probed two moments in ecclesiastical history where freedoms were curtailed in the presumed interest of the common good. Power was overzealously used, freedoms were abused, but in the end the injustices were reversed to the benefit of the common good.

Notes

1 Albert C. Outler, "Response," in *The Documents of Vatican II* (ed. W.M. Abbott; Piscataway, NJ: American, 1966) 102-103.

2 Cf. Erio Eleuterio Gazzetti, *Il Cardinale Giovanni Morone: Patrizio Modenese* (Modena: Tipographia Immacolata Concezione, 1952). Apart from encyclopedia articles, this is the most recent biography. I have relied heavily upon it for the biographical details that are used in this study of Morone. Gazzetti's work is, in turn, totally dependent upon Nicola Bernabei, *Vita del Cardinale Morone* (Modena: Tipografica Rossi, 1885).

3 Robert Trisco, "Reforming the Roman Curia: Emperor Ferdinand I and the Council of Trent," in *Reform and Authority in the Medieval and Reformation Church* (ed. G.F. Lytle; Washington, DC: Catholic University of America Press, 1981) 257.

4 There is a pious belief of long-standing tradition that the House of Loreto is the house of Mary in Nazareth that was transported by angels (circuitously) to Loreto, Italy. A devotion to Mary continues to exist there, but there are serious doubts about the theory of how the house got to Loreto. The tradition was recorded in 1472, but the event is said to have occurred in the late thirteenth century. Cf. H.M. Gillett, "Loreto," *New Catholic Encyclopedia* 8 (1981) 993-994.

5 Gaetano Morone, "Morone, Giovanni," *Dizionario di Erudizione Storico-Ecclesiastica* 46 (1847) 300.

6 H. Lutz, "Morone, Giovanni," *New Catholic Encyclopedia* 9 (1981) 1150.

7 One of the accusations against Morone was that he had authorized the publication of Benedetto da Mantova's *Il Beneficio di Christo*, a very popular devotional work that eventually was shown to have heretical tendencies.

8 For an excellent, brief biographical assessment of Paul IV, see Ludwig Pastor, *The History of the Popes from the Close of the Middle Ages* (ed. F. Kerr; St. Louis: B. Herder, 1923-1953) 14.65-81, 418-424. Virtually the entire volume is dedicated to the pontificate of Paul IV. As harsh as Paul IV was on Morone, he could see no fault in Morone's nephew Carlo Carafa, whom he promoted to the cardinalate and then even to the office of Secretary of State. Carlo, in fact, was an unscrupulous, corrupt and conniving man, and a disgrace to the church. Paul IV

came to realize this fact only as he himself neared death. He suffered bitterly when he learned the truth (cf. 14.417).

9 Pastor, *History* 14.307-311.

10 Pastor, *History* 14.302.

11 Pastor, *History* 14.302-304. Cf. Giovanni Morone, *Il Processo Inquisitoriale del Cardinal Giovanni Morone* (ed. M. Firpo; Rome: Istituto Storico Italiano per L'Etat Moderna et Contemporanea, 1981) 1.138. The bull *Cum apostolatus officio*, 15 February 1559, is to be found in *Magnum Bullarium Romanum* (Luxemburg: A. Chevalier, 1727) 1.840-843.

12 Pastor, *History* 14.304.

13 Pastor, *History* 15.3.

14 Pastor, *History* 14.307.

15 Lutz, "Morone, Giovanni" 9.1150.

16 Pio Paschini, "Morone, Giovanni," *Enciclopedia Cattolica* 8 (1948) 1422.

17 Hubert Jedin, *The History of the Council of Trent* (trans. E. Graf; St. Louis: Herder Book, 1957-1981) 1.3. Jedin is one of the modern authorities on this period and has directed a number of doctoral theses in Europe on specific topics in sixteenth-century church history, including Morone, though I have not had access to any of them.

18 Cf. Richard M. Douglas, *Jacopo Sadoleto 1477-1547* (Cambridge, MA: Harvard University Press, 1959). This work covers the same period of Morone's life and work. Sadoleto's friendly letter to Melanchthon created a stir among his co-religionists. Sadoleto made it clear that the tone of his letter was intentionally cordial because he wanted to secure the confidence of a man who was worth saving. He bluntly added that those who proceed "more contentiously and spitefully" have little enough to show for their efforts, and reiterated his belief that the present bitterness and sedition would never exist if clemency and restraint had been followed from the start (cf. p. 122). Morone had given Sadoleto his private approval of the letter. He wrote to Sadoleto: "It is far better to treat these modern heretics with clemency than to try to antagonize them with insults! And if from the start such a manner had been observed, the reunion of the church might now be a simple matter."

19 Most of the biographical details of this study were taken from Donald E. Pelotte, *John Courtney Murray* (New York: Paulist, 1976). I have not tried to replicate here the extensive bibliography that is available in Pelotte and is extended in Robert W. McElroy, *The Search for an American Public Theology* (New York: Paulist, 1989). A wealth of resources is provided in these two volumes.

20 John Courtney Murray, "Freedom of Religion I: The Ethical Problem," *TS* 6 (June 1945) 229-286.

21 "As early as 1945, he engaged in extensive debate on the issue [of church and state] with two theologians at Catholic University, Joseph C. Fenton and Francis J. Connell." Cf. J.P. Whalen, "Murray, John Courtney (1904-1967)," *Encyclopedic Dictionary of Religion* 2 (1979) 2461-2462.

22 Cf. McElroy, *Search* 19-38.

23 Cf. Pelotte, *John Courtney Murray* 43-49.

24 Cf. McElroy, *Search* 188.

25 Murray to McCormick on 3 August 1955, as quoted in Pelotte, *John Courtney Murray* 53.

26 Pelotte, *John Courtney Murray* 55.

27 Douglas Auchincloss, "City of God and Man," *Time* 76 (12 December 1960) 64-70.

28 Joseph C. Fenton, "Doctrine and Tactic in Catholic Pronouncements on Church and State," *AER* 145 (October 1961) 274.

29 Xavier Rynne, *Vatican Council II* (New York: Farrar, Straus & Giroux, 1968) 33.

30 J. Cogley, "John Courtney Murray, S.J.," *America* 117 (September 1967) 221.

31 Robert E. Tracy, *American Bishop at the Vatican Council* (New York: McGraw-Hill, 1966) 172.

32 In a three-page introduction to the document on religious freedom as printed in *The Documents of Vatican II*, Murray himself gives a very succinct history of the development of the document through five corrected versions. He indicates in a rather interesting manner that the "notion of development, not the notion of religious freedom, was the real sticking-point for many of those who opposed the Declaration, even to the end" (see Walter M. Abbot, ed., *The Documents of Vatican II* [Piscataway, NJ: American, 1966] 673).

33 Abbott, *Documents of Vatican II* 678-679.

34 Walter Burghardt, "A Tribute to John Courtney Murray," *CM* 66 (June 1968) 31.

Vera Libertas: The Concept of Christian Freedom in the Euchology of the Roman Missal

Cassian Folsom, OSB

Introduction

One of the richest sources of theology and spirituality, close at hand but often overlooked, is the church's liturgy.[1] In this essay I propose to examine the Roman Catholic liturgical tradition for an understanding of Christian freedom. Since the field of liturgy is so vast, however, it is necessary to narrow the focus of inquiry: 1) To speak in general terms, liturgy can be described under the two headings of text and gesture. I will discuss texts only. 2) Liturgical texts may be biblical, patristic or euchological.[2] I will consider euchological texts only. 3) Euchological texts may be orations, prefaces, anaphoras, blessings or other poetic compositions. From the category of orations I will study one representative text only, namely, the collect for the fifth Sunday of Easter, taken from the *Missale Romanum* of Paul VI. This collect contains an explicit and very rich understanding of Christian freedom. The text reads as follows:

> *Deus, per quem nobis et redemptio venit et praestatur adoptio*
> *filios dilectionis tuae benignus intende,*
> *ut in Christo credentibus*
> *et vera tribuatur libertas et hereditas aeterna* (MR 303)

> O God, through whom redemption comes to us and adoption is given to us,
> graciously incline unto your beloved children,
> so that *true freedom* and an eternal inheritance
> might be granted to those who believe in Christ.

This study of true freedom (*vera libertas*) will be in two parts: an examination of the origin and history of the collect *Deus per quem*, followed by a liturgical and theological study of this oration.

Origin and History

The post-Vatican II revision of the Roman Missal had as one of its goals the expansion of the euchological section of the sacramentary to include a much greater variety of orations. The intent was not only to avoid frequent repetition of the same prayers but also to restore to public circulation many gems of the euchological tradition which, in the course of the centuries, had been lost.[3] The prayer *Deus per quem*, which originated in an early period of the western liturgical tradition, was retrieved as part of this effort.

The earliest collection in which this oration is found is the seventh-century Gelasian sacramentary,[4] where it has this form:

Deus, per quem nobis et redemptio venit et praestatur adoptio
respice in opera misericordiae tuae,
ut in Christo renatis
et aeternam [sic] tribuatur hereditas et <u>*vera libertas*</u> (Gel 522)

O God, through whom redemption comes to us and adoption is given to us,
look upon the works of your mercy,
so that an eternal inheritance and *true freedom*
might be granted to those reborn in Christ.

In the Gelasian sacramentary this oration is the seventh in a series of twenty-five prayers (Gel 516-540), a series which has the title *Incipiunt Orationes Paschales Vespertinales*. The oration then was used in the liturgical context of vespers during the Easter season, but no further specification is given.

The same prayer is found in the seventh-century Gregorian sacramentary (Greg 427),[5] where there is a precise indication as to the context in which this prayer was used. Here it is included among the euchological texts for Friday of Easter week. On this day the Mass was celebrated in the stational church of *Sancta Maria ad Martyres* (more commonly known today by its pre-Christian name, the Pantheon). For this Mass formulary, the Gregorian sacramentary gives the customary three orations, plus a special *hanc igitur* (a variable section of the Roman canon). Two other orations follow: the prayer *Deus per quem* of the present study accompanied by the rubric *Ad vesperos in hierusalem* (indicating that vespers was held in the stational church of the Holy Cross in Jerusalem) and a prayer to be said at the baptismal font at the end of vespers.[6]

A Frankish redaction of the Gelasian sacramentary, made in the time of King Pepin (r. 751-768), the father of Charlemagne, contains this prayer in two places. In this liturgical book (the manuscript that seems closest to the original Frankish redaction is known as the sacramentary of Gellone[7]) the redactor, although relying primarily upon the Gelasian sacramentary, drew freely upon the Gregorian sacramentary as well.[8] This double source is in evidence where the prayer *Deus per quem* is concerned. In Gellone 815 the oration is found among the general listing of orations for vespers in paschal time, thus to follow the schema of the Gelasian sacramentary. In Gellone 785 it is given as part of the expanded euchology of Easter Friday, following the Gregorian sacramentary's indications for the stational liturgies of that day.[9]

In the course of the long and complex history of Roman euchology from the earliest manuscripts to printed books, this particular prayer fell into desuetude.[10] It was not included in the first printed missal of 1474 nor in the missal that was promulgated by Pius V in 1570 as part of the post-Tridentine liturgical reforms. There are at least two reasons for the disappearance of this prayer. In the first instance, it was no longer possible to celebrate the stational liturgies of the basilicas of Rome when the pope and his curia, in the course of the thirteenth century, began their exilic wanderings from Rome, which culminated in the establishment of the papacy at Avignon. Secondly, the officials of the Roman curia took with them to Avignon the breviary of the Friars Minor, which retained none of the ancient office. It was this new arrangement of the liturgy of the hours that prevailed in the subsequent history of the Roman rite.[11] The recovery of the oration *Deus per quem* today is due to these factors: the scholarship of recent decades in the area of liturgical texts and the liturgical reforms which followed upon Vatican II.

With the completion of this brief historical survey I turn now to a liturgical and theological study of the oration *Deus per quem*. Since the prayer exists in two forms, however—the original version as it appears in the ancient sacramentaries (Gel 522 and Greg 427) and the adapted version as it appears in the sacramentary that actually is in use today[12] (MR 303)—both forms must be examined in order to understand what this liturgical text says about Christian freedom.

A Liturgical and Theological Study of Gel 522 and Greg 427

A Liturgical Study

The twenty-five orations of Gel 516-540, *Orationes Paschales Vespertinales*, form part of the ancient secular (i.e. non-monastic) office of Rome.[13] The evidence of the Gelasian sacramentary, however, is insufficient to tell us more precisely how these orations fit into the office of vespers during paschal time. Are they intended for the octave only? If so, why are there so many? Are they intended for the entire liturgical season from Easter to Ascension? If so, why are there so few? Other major feast days in the Gelasian have orations for lauds and vespers attached to them: six for Christmas (Gel 24-29), six for Pentecost (Gel 646-651), three for the Annunciation (Gel 851-853), eight for Sts. Peter and Paul (Gel 931-938) and three for St. Lawrence (Gel 979-981). It is easy enough to see that when there are six orations, they could be distributed evenly throughout the octave, and when there are three, they could be used for the feast itself and a two-day commemoration of the feast. But why eight? And why twenty-five? It could be that the multiplicity of orations simply made for a wider selection from which to choose upon any given occasion.[14] In any case, the evidence of the Gelasian is inconclusive, and one must turn to the Gregorian sacramentary for more detailed information.

In the Gregorian sacramentary the days of the octave of Easter are marked by daily vespers, celebrated for the most part at St. John Lateran. For solemn vespers from Easter Sunday to Easter Thursday, there were three successive orations, which in the text are given the rubrical headings *Ad vesperos, ad fontes* and *ad sanctum Andream.* From Easter Friday through Low Sunday, vespers was held at various stational churches: Friday *in hierusalem,* as we have seen; Saturday *in sancta maria* (Greg 433; this would be St. Mary Major) and on the octave itself *ad sanctos cosmas et damianum* in the Roman forum (Greg 438). In all of these cases where vespers is not at the Lateran, there are only two orations indicated: *ad vesperos* and *ad fontes.* For a description of the liturgical ceremonies behind these rubrical indications, one must turn to *Ordo Romanus XXVII,* an eighth-century ordo that contains the most ancient description extant of the special vespers of Easter week in Rome.[15]

Once the pope, his suburbicarian bishops, titular priests and deacons had assembled at the Lateran, vespers was sung in the basilica itself (OR 27:67-73). At the end of vespers, when the gospel canticle (the *Magnificant)* had been sung, the rubric gives this direction: *dicit sacerdos orationem* (the priest says the oration; OR 27:73). This was the first oration, corresponding to the indication *ad vesperos* in the Gregorian sacramentary (e.g. Greg 389). Then there was a procession to the baptistery where Psalm 112 was sung in Latin and Psalm 92 in Greek (OR 27:74), followed by an antiphon from one of the resurrection gospels, *deinde oratio* (and then, the oration; OR 27:75). This was the second oration, corresponding to the indication *ad fontes* in the Gregorian sacramentary (e.g. Greg 390). On two sides of the octagonal baptistery Pope Hilary (461-468) had chapels constructed, one called *S. Iohannes ad Vestem,* the other *S. Andreas ad Crucem.*[16] On Easter Sunday, after the station at the baptistery, a visit was made to each of these side chapels with psalmody, an Easter antiphon and an oration (OR 27:76-77). During the remainder of Easter week, indication is given for a procession to the Chapel of St. Andrew only. Thus the third oration that is given in the Gregorian sacramentary has the rubric *ad sanctum andream* (e.g. Greg 391).

Ordo XXVII adds an interesting description of three kinds of wine that were served to all the ministers after vespers (OR 27:78-79), following which the acolytes and presbyters went to their respective titular churches to celebrate vespers for the local congregation (OR 27:79). The ordo then states that the same arrangement for the celebration of vespers was observed throughout Easter week (OR 27:79). The prayer *Deus per quem* is part of Easter Friday vespers, which was held in Holy Cross, not in the Lateran church. Some elements of the service are unique, therefore, to this particular stational church. After vespers in the main body of the church, the first stop of the procession was the chapel of the Holy Cross,[17] in honor of the relics there. Only then did the procession continue into the streets, to make its way back to the Lateran baptistery for a final station there at the baptismal font.[18]

There are a number of elements in these liturgical arrangements which are of special importance for an understanding of the meaning of the oration *Deus per quem*. First, the prayer forms part of the celebration of Easter in which the mystery of the passion and resurrection of Christ is renewed in the heart of the believer. Secondly, the prayer is linked to baptism, not only because prayer during Easter week frequently refers to the sacrament of regeneration, but also because this prayer at the end of vespers is followed by a procession *ad fontes*. Thirdly, the prayer is related to the mystery of the cross, since it is said on Friday of Easter week, the octave of Good Friday, in the same stational church in which the passion was celebrated.[19] Thus the intrinsic connection between the cross of Christ, his resurrection and the baptism of the Christian is clearly in evidence. Christian freedom is rooted in the sacramental celebration of these saving realities. Fourthly, the prayer is part of the Liturgy of the Hours, not of the Eucharist. Solemn vespers during Easter week serves to prolong the paschal mystery in the lives of the baptized, especially since the evening sacrifice of praise has been understood from patristic times as commemorative of the passion of the Lord.[20] Finally, the prayer is part of the ancient practice of stational liturgies: public processions through city streets with all of the various characteristics of a parade, a mob and a pilgrimage. There is no separation here between liturgy and life, between sacred and secular. The mystery of Christ embraces all. These elements have a bearing upon Christian freedom as well.

A Theological Study

Having treated the liturgical context of the oration *Deus per quem* in the ancient sacramentaries, I now turn to a theological analysis of the prayer. This will be accomplished most readily by a reference to the structure of the collect itself. The prayer is written in the classical four-part Roman style: 1) the invocation of God, along with a description of God's attributes; 2) a relative clause that recalls the *magnalia Dei*, the wonderful works that God has done; 3) an imperative that states the request of the prayer; and, 4) a purpose clause in which the desired result of God's intervention is described.

1) *Deus*

In this prayer the invocation of God, in reflection of the Roman penchant, is as simple as possible: *Deus*. No adjectives or descriptive phrases are added, such as one sometimes finds in other prayers (e.g. "Almighty everlasting God" or "God creator and redeemer", etc.): simply *Deus*. The point to be made here is that it is God the Father who is invoked and that the prayer is offered through Jesus Christ. The classical Trinitarian construct of Christian prayer thus is clearly and succinctly established.

2) *per quem nobis et redemptio venit et praestatur adoptio*

The prepositional phrase *per quem* is the link between the first and second section of the prayer. It is through God the Father and the divine plan that God the Son comes into the world. That divine *missio* clearly is soteriological, that is, it is for "us" (*nobis*). According to this oration, the nature of salvation is twofold (notice the *et...et* [both...and] construction, for it will be repeated later in the same prayer): through God, both redemption and adoption are offered to humanity. This double action of God refers to the entire economy of salvation, embracing both its historical beginnings and its future fulfillment. Redemption is an accomplished fact in the passion, death and resurrection of Christ. But the work of redemption is not complete in humankind, since adoption as God's children is, for the present, offered in the manner of a "down payment", and will be realized fully only with the resurrection of the body.

3) *respice in opera misericordiae tuae*

The imperative *respice* ("look upon") and similar expressions that often are found in Roman euchology might be construed as descriptive of God's distance, of the fact that God looks upon the world from afar.[21] Is this not a contradiction of the Christian proclamation that "the Word became flesh and lived among us?" (John 1:14) In fact, the two affirmations are not exclusive. The petition *respice* affirms that God is independent of the world which has been created and redeemed and that salvation is offered from outside of humankind itself. The very closeness of the Word of God is by its very nature an objective reality that is revealed as something quite beyond the limits of human knowledge, experience or understanding. Therefore, the imperative *respice* expresses a fundamental reality of Christian faith: salvation is given to humanity, it comes from outside as grace.

The prayer asks God to look upon the works of divine mercy. A further specification of what *opera misericordiae tuae* means can be found in the first phrase of the final section of the prayer.

4) *ut in Christo renatis et aeterna tribuatur hereditas et vera libertas*

The prayer is offered for those who have been reborn in Christ. Since the newly baptized are the recipients of this great gift of salvation, they are the works of God's mercy. The baptismal context of this prayer is, thus, quite explicit. (This fact will be important later in the discussion of the contemporary adaptation of this prayer.) One has only to recall the liturgical setting in which this oration was prayed: the newly baptized and all the faithful gathered together for vespers on Easter Friday at Holy Cross in Jerusalem, the very stational church where the passion had been celebrated one week earlier on Good Friday.

What is the desired outcome of this prayer which the priest offers on behalf of the newly baptized? Corresponding with the double action of God in the second part of the prayer, there is a double result that is given in this final section. The passive verb *tribuatur* serves for both subjects: that both (note the *et...et* construction again) an eternal inheritance and true freedom might be granted. In the poetic composition of the prayer there seems to be a direct connection between the double *et* of Part II and the double *et* of Part IV. What this does is to form a chiastic structure as is depicted below.

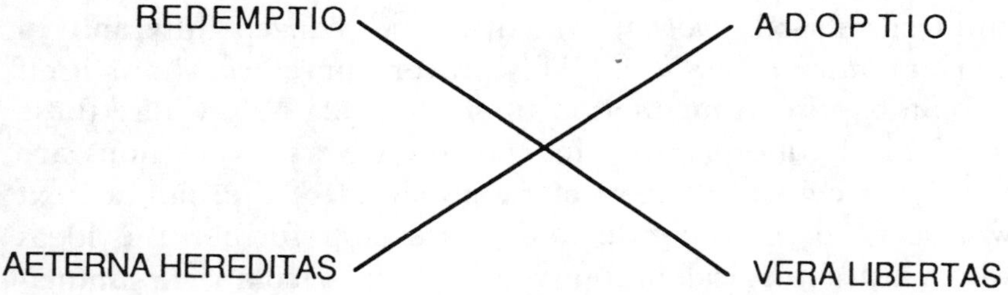

Redemptio is linked to *vera libertas*, and *adoptio* is linked to *aeterna hereditas*. This is to say that the desired effect of redemption is true freedom. If redemption is an accomplished fact, although imperfectly realized in the Christian who still is on pilgrimage (*homo viator*), then it should have some result in one's earthly life. In the scriptures, especially in the Old Testament, when someone is redeemed, that person is bought back and restored to freedom from a state of enslavement or captivity. This applies not only to persons, but to property as well.[22] The analogy of the Lord's redemption of Israel with outstretched arm (cf. Exod 6:6) is based upon these examples of redemption as taken from ordinary life. It is an easy step for Christian typology to interpret this Old Testament act of redemption as the liberation of the Christian from the bondage of sin. When the oration describes this *libertas* as "true" (*vera*) freedom, it makes a precise theological affirmation. While there are other kinds of freedom, the specific kind of freedom that is intended here is freedom from sin as is brought about by the redemption of Christ.[23]

If the desired effect of redemption is true freedom, then according to the same poetic structure the desired effect of adoption is an eternal inheritance. If adoption as children of God is but a pledge in this life, a hope, a "down payment", then the full realization of that filial relationship to God, as co-heirs with Christ, will be manifested only in the eschaton. The inheritance is yet to come, it is eternal. The oration thus embraces the whole sweep of the economy of salvation: the plan of God before all ages (*Deus per quem...*), the redeeming work of Christ (*redemptio*) which frees the baptized from sin (*vera libertas*), the liberty which is precisely the freedom of the children of God (*adoptio*), which will be realized fully only in eternity (*aeterna hereditas*). This prayer, therefore, shows itself to be a baptismal meditation upon Rom 8:12-25, where these theological concepts and, indeed, these very expressions are clearly in evidence. A brief examination of the biblical text will serve to corroborate and to develop further the ideas which this liturgical oration presents in a compact, summarized fashion.[24]

In the context of the dichotomy between flesh and spirit, Paul writes:

> For you did not receive the spirit of slavery (*spiritum servitutis*) to fall back into fear, but you have received the spirit of the adoption of children (*spiritum adoptionis filiorum*), by which we cry: Abba, Father (Rom 8:15)

Although the word *libertas* is not yet used, its opposite *servitudo* is. The spirit of slavery is life according to the flesh, whereas the spirit of adoption—true freedom—is life according to the Spirit. The apostle thereafter says:

> But if we are children, then also heirs (*heredes*), heirs of God, and coheirs (*coheredes*) of Christ—if, however, we suffer with him, that we might also be glorified with him. (Rom 8:17)

The promise of the inheritance, the future glory, is conditioned upon one's present participation in Christ's sufferings. True freedom, therefore, is not only freedom *from* sin, but also is freedom *for* this participation in the suffering and glory of

Christ. The specific nature of this in between time is demonstrated clearly by Paul:

> For creation itself shall be freed (*liberabitur*) from the slavery of corruption unto the freedom of the glory of the children of God (*in libertatem gloriae filiorum Dei*) (Rom 8:21)

Note the future tense—the fullness of Christian freedom is yet to come. Meanwhile:

> Not only creation, but we also, who have the first fruits of the Spirit (*primitias spiritus*), groan within ourselves, awaiting adoption as children of God (*adoptionem filiorum Dei*), the redemption of our body (*redemptionem corporis nostri*) (Rom 8:23)

The author of the oration *Deus per quem* has drawn very clearly from this text of the apostle the key concepts of *redemptio, adoptio, hereditas* and *libertas*, with meditation on their power and meaning in the context of Christian baptism into the Easter mystery of Jesus Christ. This is an outstanding example of a common method of prayer among the ancients: steady rumination upon the sacred text, which the heart then pours forth in the written word, with all the beauty that human art can muster.

When one connects the liturgical context and the theological content of this prayer, its richness and depth become evident. The Christian believer, newly baptized on Easter, goes to stational vespers at the church of the Holy Cross on Easter Friday, the octave of Good Friday, there to offer the evening sacrifice of praise. The prayer *Deus per quem* is the closing oration of vespers in which redemption by Christ is proclaimed boldly as resulting in the glorious freedom of the children of God. This freedom from sin is true freedom, although the children of God still groan in their suffering after the manner of Christ until the perfect inheritance is realized: the resurrection of the body and life everlasting.

A Liturgical and Theological Study of MR 303

A Liturgical Study

When the oration *Deus per quem* from Gel 522 was recovered from the treasury of the euchological tradition and proposed for inclusion in the 1970 Missal, it must have been received with great enthusiasm by the people involved,[25] for it appears no less than three times in the present sacramentary. It is the collect for the fifth Sunday of Easter (MR 303). Further, it appears as one of the weekday collects during the Easter season, the second Saturday (MR 322). Finally, it is given as the collect for the twenty-third Sunday *per annum* (MR 362).

Two observations can be made about the new liturgical context of this prayer. First, its primary locus is no longer vespers as in the ancient sacramentaries, but rather the Eucharistic celebration. When it does appear in the liturgy of the hours, it does so as a derivative from the Eucharist, for the post-Vatican II revision of the Divine Office takes much of its euchology from the Roman Missal.[26] The prayer, then, was recovered from its ancient context of vespers, placed in the new context of the Eucharist, and, because of the impact of the Roman Missal upon the liturgy of the hours, found its way back into the office again.

Secondly, this prayer is now used not only in its original context of Easter, but also on an ordinary Sunday as well. This can be interpreted both positively and negatively. Positively, it can be seen as an affirmation that every Sunday is stamped by the paschal character, since historically speaking, Sunday was the original celebration of the paschal mystery even before the annual feast of Easter was developed.[27] Negatively, it can be seen as a dilution of the specific paschal focus of the prayer. A closer look at the text itself will bring both of these possible interpretations into sharper relief.

A Theological Study

When the oration *Deus per quem* was reintroduced into current usage, it underwent certain modifications, which can be seen by the following comparison:

Gel 522	*MR 303*
Deus, per quem nobis et redemptio	*Deus, per quem nobis et redemptio*
venit et praestatur adoptio,	*venit et praestatur adoptio,* filios
respice in opera misericordiae tuae,	dilectionis tuae benignus intende,
ut in Christo renatis, et aeterna	*ut in Christo* credentibus, *et vera*
tribuatur hereditas et vera libertas.	*tribuatur libertas et hereditas aeterna.*[28]

I will examine three phrases: the imperative clause *intende*, the first half of the result clause *in Christo credentibus*, and the new arrangement of the two expressions *vera libertas* and *hereditas aeterna*.

The original phrase *respice in opera misericordiae tuae* was replaced with *filios dilectionis tuae benignus intende*. Presumably this was done because the meaning of the phrase *opera misericordiae tuae* was not immediately obvious. As I have suggested above, the expression "works of your mercy" seems to refer clearly to "those who have been reborn in Christ". Be that as it may, the new phrase has its own richness. There is the addition of the word *benignus*, an adjective that frequently is used in Roman euchology to describe God as gracious, as inclined to be favorable to the prayer which is being offered in humility. The phrase *filios dilectionis tuae* perhaps may be best rendered in English as "your beloved children". The immediate association is Christological. In Gen 22:2 the Lord says to Abraham: "Take your son, your only son Isaac, whom you love" (*Tolle filium tuum unigenitum, quem diligis*). The Easter Vigil interprets this reading in a typological sense: Isaac is a type of Christ, the beloved, only-begotten son of the Father. Jesus himself, at two of his greatest earthly epiphanies, is called "beloved son" by the voice of the Father. At his baptism the voice from heaven says, "This is my Son, the Beloved" (*hic est Filius meus dilectus*; Matt 3:17), and at his transfiguration one hears the same (Matt 17:5). While Jesus is "beloved son" by nature, the baptized are beloved children by adoption. The phrase *Filius dilectionis tuae*, which refers to Christ, appears several times in the 1970 Missal.[29] The phrase *filios dilectionis tuae*, which refers to Christians, appears only in the prayer *Deus per quem*. This turn of phrase, although unnecessary for the clarification of the meaning of Gel 522, does add a wealth of associations to the prayer and reaffirms the basic meditation on Romans 8.

At first glance the substitution *in Christo credentibus* for *in Christo renatis* seems to weaken the paschal significance of the prayer. This perhaps was necessary in order to use the prayer for other occasions besides Easter time. It is interesting to note, however, that the phrase *in Christo credentes* also is found in the Exultet:

> This is the night, which today restores to grace and joins to holiness all those throughout the entire world *who believe in Christ*, and who have been set apart from the vices of the present age and the darkness of sins.[30]

While it is true that the expression "those believing in Christ" is less explicit than "those who have been reborn in Christ", the baptismal and paschal connection still remains.

The final emendation is less felicitous, however. To end the oration with the words *et vera libertas*, as is found in Gel 522, is aesthetically pleasing, because it follows the artistic structure of the *cursus*, which is a Latin prose rhythm that is based upon word accent, gracefully bringing the end of a phrase or sentence to a measured conclusion.[31] In this case we have a *cursus planus*: the final word of three syllables, with the accent on the penultimate, and the second-to-last word (of an indeterminate number of syllables) also having its accent on the penultimate. The *cursus planus* may be diagrammed as below.

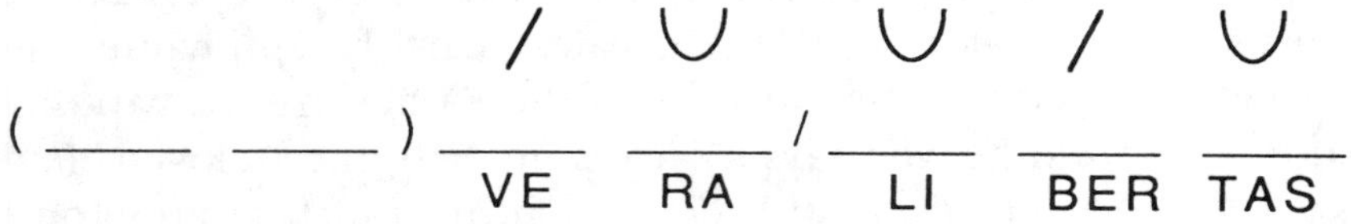

To end the oration with the words *hereditas aeterna*, however, does not correspond to any of the standard varieties of the *cursus*. Thus the prose rhythm, which was sedulously cultivated by the ancient masters of Roman euchology, is not maintained, and the beauty of the original (Gel 522) thus is somewhat diminished.

Aside from these differences, however, the prayer is carried into the 1970 Missal almost intact, and since the four key words *redemptio, adoptio, hereditas* and *libertas* are retained, the theological import of the prayer remains much the same. Christian freedom is deliverance from sin by the passion of Christ, which results in the glorious liberty of the children of God.

Related Texts in the 1970 Missal

The prayer *Deus per quem*, because of its internal coherence, provides a clearly focused meditation upon Christian freedom (*vera libertas*), admirable for its breadth and completeness. The 1970 Missal, however, uses the word *libertas* in a good number of other prayers as well. A brief excursus on these other usages will serve to complete what has been said above, not in order to add anything substantially new, but simply to offer some variations upon a theme.

While the 1970 missal occasionally uses the word *libertas* in the context of political or religious freedom,[32] the interior freedom of the heart[33] or the perpetual freedom of eternal life,[34] the majority of references to *libertas* may be brought together under two headings: 1) God as the author or source of Christian freedom, and 2) freedom as directly linked to adoption as children of God.

"God is the author of true freedom" (*Deus, verae libertatis auctor*) proclaims the collect for a Mass for peace and reconciliation (MR 824).[35] (The rubric indicates that this oration is especially suitable for use during the paschal season.) The argument of the prayer is that God wills to form the human race into a single people, which has been freed from servitude. The paschal context of the prayer leads one to interpret the servitude that is mentioned as a spiritual slavery to sin, from which God, the author of true freedom, liberates humanity. In another prayer, which also is for use during the Easter season, God is called *libertatis nostrae auctor et salutis*: "the author of our freedom and our salvation" (MR 321).[36] Here the prayer is offered for those whom the Father has redeemed through the outpouring of the Son's own blood. It is clear that freedom in this case is also to be understood in a soteriological sense and that the author of this economy of salvation is God the Father. A third text prays that those who are redeemed might be able to extend the freedom of Christ to all (*libertatem Christi ad omnes possimus extendere*; MR 824).[37] In this prayer Christ is described as humanity's peace and reconciliation: freedom comes from Christ because he has removed the sin of the world by his blood. In all of these instances, whether it is God the Father who is described as the author of Christian freedom or whether it is Christ himself, it is clear that the nature of this freedom is redemption from sin, achieved through the passion of Christ.

In the Missal of Paul VI several other orations besides *Deus per quem* use the word *libertas* in the context of divine adoption. In a post-communion prayer for confirmation the petition is made that the newly confirmed might always manifest before the world the freedom of God's adoption (*ut coram mundo tuae libertatem adoptionis iugiter manifestent*; cf. MR 741).[38] There is a clear Trinitarian dimension here, since the prayer is offered on behalf of those whom God the Father has filled with the gifts of the Spirit and has strengthened by the nourishment of the only-begotten Son. While the prayer itself does not develop the theme of Christian freedom any further, the connection between baptism and confirmation is clear, and according to Romans 8 (upon which the prayer *Deus per quem* is based), the first fruits of the Spirit are the pledge of the fullness of adoption yet to come. The Roman Missal also includes the renewal of baptismal promises at the Easter Vigil. One of the possible formulas is this: "Do you renounce sin, so as to live in the freedom of the children of God?" (*Abrenuntiatis peccato, ut in libertate filiorum Dei vivatis?* cf. MR 286). This is yet another confirmation of the intimate connection between Easter, baptism, redemption from sin and Christian freedom.

There are a few other usages of the word *libertas* in the Missal of Paul VI that should be interpreted in this soteriological sense. In the same prayer in which God is described as *verae libertatis auctor* (MR 824), there is an assertion that the church receives *incrementa libertatis*,[39] increases of freedom. Here one detects the important notion of progress in Christian liberty. If God is the author of the true freedom that is inaugurated by the redemption that is wrought by Christ, and if perfect or eternal freedom comes only with the final resurrection of the body, then what about the state of Christian freedom in between? This prayer indicates that the believer is to make progress in spiritual freedom, is to grow in Christian holiness from the moment of baptism to the consummation of this age. A final example recalls the great price of freedom, *nostrae libertatis pretium*.[40] The prayer is for captives, imploring their release. But while physical freedom is the object of this prayer, the more profound freedom of the Spirit is also considered: a freedom that was purchased at great price.

Conclusion

This study of the prayer *Deus per quem* can, in my estimation, contribute two things to an understanding of Christian freedom. First of all, from an investigation of the liturgical context of the prayer it is clear that true freedom is linked intimately to the cross, Easter and baptism. What baptism does for Christians is to plunge them into the saving mysteries of Christ's passion and resurrection: the paschal mystery is the source of all genuine freedom. The freeing grace of baptism is not limited to that one sacramental moment only, but is continued in the Eucharist, because, as the famous *super oblata* of the Holy Thursday Mass of the Lord's Supper says, "as often as the commemoration of this sacrifice is celebrated, the work of our redemption is carried out."[41] In the recovery of the prayer *Deus per quem* from the euchological treasury of the past, the Missal of Paul VI expands the original Easter context of this prayer to embrace other liturgical seasons as well. Each person encounters Christian freedom as often as the commemoration of this sacrifice is celebrated, whether it is in the Eucharist itself, in the liturgy of the hours or in the sacrifice of praise which is one's daily life.

Secondly, this oration adds to an understanding of Christian freedom by its definition of *libertas*—true freedom, that is (*vera libertas*)—in relation to redemption, adoption and the promised eternal inheritance. There cannot be true freedom apart from these things. The glorious liberty of the children of God consists precisely in redemption from the bondage of sin, which freedom was won for humanity by the blood of Christ. Through Christ, who is Son by nature, all become children by adoption, the full inheritance of which will only be realized in the resurrection of the body. In the meantime, human freedom is a limited, but real, participation in the divine nature.

Notes

1 Traditionally, when the liturgy is considered as a *locus theologicus*, the word "theological" is used in the specific sense of "doctrinal": cf. Cyprian Vagaggini, *Theological Dimensions of the Liturgy* (trans. L.J. Doyle and W.A. Jurgens; Collegeville, MN: Liturgical, 1976) 542-571. In this essay my emphasis is more on the liturgy as a source of spirituality than of doctrine, although it certainly is both.

2 For a discussion of the various kinds of liturgical texts, cf. Matias Augé, "Principi di interpretazione dei testi liturgici," in *Anàmnesis* (ed. S. Marsili; Casale Monferrato: Marietti, 1974) 1.159-179.

3 Cf. Annibale Bugnini, *The Reform of the Liturgy: 1948-1975* (trans. M.J. O'Connell; Collegeville, MN: Liturgical, 1990) 396-398.

4 There are two principal hypotheses with respect to the origin of the Gelasian sacramentary. The first, put forward by Antoine Chavasse, is that this is a presbyteral (as distinct from papal) sacramentary, composed in Rome for use in the titular churches of the city and later transcribed in Frankish territory. The second is that this was composed in Frankish territory from the beginning. The argument has these implications: if the first theory is correct, then the Gelasian sacramentary is the first Roman sacramentary, properly so-called; if the second theory is correct, that distinction goes to the Gregorian sacramentary. For a good summary of these arguments, cf. Adrian Nocent, "Storia dei libri liturgici romani," in *Anàmnesis* (ed. S. Marsili: Casale Monferrato: Marietti, 1978) 2.147-183.

5 The Gregorian sacramentary was a papal sacramentary for use in the stational churches of Rome. Since some of the feasts which are included in the sacramentary were introduced during the reign of Pope Honorius I (625-638), one can trace the date of the Gregorian with some precision. Some scholars also theorize that an earlier text existed, dating from the time of Pope Gregory himself (590-604). Cf. Nocent, "Storia dei libri" 152-154.

6 The text of the oration *Deus per quem* in the Gregorian sacramentary is identical to that in the Gelasian, with one minor grammatical correction. The nonsensical accusative case *aeternam* in Gel 522 is changed to the nominative *aeterna* in Greg 427.

7 Cf. Nocent, "Storia dei libri" 156.

8 The question of the sources of the Gellone sacramentary is discussed in detail by Antoine Chavasse, *Le sacramentaire dans le groupe dit "Gélasiens du VIIIe siècle"* (Brussels: St-Pietersabdij Steenbrugge, 1984).

9 The text of Gel 785 is exactly that of Greg 427, while the text of Gel 815 shows a slight re-working of the final phrase. Gel 815 reads thus: *ut in Christo renatis et aeterna tribuatur hereditas, vera et libertas* (I have standardized the spelling and written out the abbreviated words). Note that this emendation only detracts from the poetic style of the original. While Gel 522 ends with a *cursus planus* (*et vera libertas*), Gel 815 does not end with any of the classical *cursus* at all. For a description of the *cursus* in the Latin of late antiquity, cf. Henri Leclercq, "Cursus," *Dictionnaire d'archéologie chrétienne et de liturgie* 3.2 (1948) 3198.

10 In addition to the Gellone sacramentary, Bruylants indicates that this prayer also is found in the sacramentary of St. Gall (ninth century), in various fragments of the Salzburg sacramentary (eighth-ninth centuries) and in the Rossianum sacramentary (mid-eleventh century). Cf. Placide Bruylants, *Les oraisons du Missel Romain: texte et histoire* (Louvain: Abbaye du Mont César, 1952) 1.45-46.

11 For a more thorough treatment of these historical exigencies, cf. Pierre Jounel, "Les vêpres de Paques," *LMD* 49 (1957) 110.

12 When I speak of the liturgical book that is used by the priest for the celebration of the Mass, I use interchangeably the words "missal" and "sacramentary". Technically speaking, however, these are two different kinds of book. A sacramentary, properly so-called, contains only prayers (and sometimes rubrics) for the priest. The missal gathers together into a single volume the priest's book (the sacramentary) as well as the book of readings (lectionary). In the liturgical books of the present reform, the sacramentary and lectionary are in fact separate, but the sacramentary is still commonly called the *Missale Romanum*.

13 Cf. Chavasse, *Le sacramentaire gélasien* 455.

14 Chavasse, a noted authority on the Gelasian sacramentary, admits that he has tried from every angle to find an explanation for these variations, but without success. Cf. Chavasse, *Le sacramentaire gélasien* 454-455 and n. 70.

15 Brief descriptions of this ordo are given in John F. Baldovin, *The Urban Character of Christian Worship* (OCA 228; Rome: Pontificium Institutum Studiorum Orientalium, 1987) 137, and Chavasse, *"Gélasiens du VIIIe siècle"* 68. Andrieu explains that this ordo is in two parts: sections 1-66, which concern the last four days of Holy Week; sections 67-94, which concern vespers during Easter week (cf. Michel Andrieu, *Les Ordines Romani du haut moyen age* [Louvain: Spicilegium Sacrum Lovaniense, 1974] 3.339-343). There is a recent doctoral dissertation on this topic by John Brooks-Leonard, "Early Vespers in Early Medieval Rome: A Criti-

cal Edition and Study" (PhD dissertation, University of Notre Dame, 1988).

16 For more information about these chapels cf. Andrieu, *Les Ordines Romani* 3.364 n. 76.

17 OR 27:90 gives the indication *ad crucem, ad cubicellum Rigodem*. I have not been able to ascertain to whom or what the adjective "*Rigodem*" makes reference. A detailed description of the original construction and subsequent renovations of *Santa Croce* may be found in Richard Krautheimer, *Corpus Basilicarum Christianarum Romae* (Vatican City: Pontificio Instituto di Archeologia Cristiana, 1937) 1.165-195, with the accompanying plates 22-28. The Chapel of St. Helen is behind the apse on the right-hand side.

18 Although these are actually the directives for Thursday, Andrieu demonstrates, based upon a variant reading, that due to a scribal error the rubrics for Thursday and Friday have been switched. Cf. Andrieu, *Les Ordines Romani* 3.371 n. 92. For a description of Friday vespers at Holy Cross and Saturday vespers at St. Mary Major, each with a procession back to the Lateran baptistery, cf. Jounel, "Les vêpres de Paques" 98-99.

19 The rubric just before the Good Friday texts in the Gregorian sacramentary reads: *Orationes quae dicendae sunt VI feria maiore in Hierusalem* (Greg 338).

20 "That then is the 'evening sacrifice,' the Passion of the Lord, the Cross of the Lord, the offering of a salutary Victim, the whole burnt-offering acceptable to God. That 'evening sacrifice' produced, in his Resurrection, a morning offering." (Augustine, "Commentary on PS 140," in *Sancti Aurelii Augustini: Enarrationes in Psalmos CI-CL* [CCL 40; Turnholt: Typographi Brepols Editores Pontificii, 1956] 2029; English translation in *Saint Augustin: Expositions on the Book of Psalms* [NPNF 8; ed. P. Schaff; Grand Rapids, MI: Wm. B. Eerdmans, 1983] 645).

21 Cf. Ps 112:5 in the Vulgate: *Quis sicut Dominus Deus noster, qui in altis habitat, et humilia respicit in caelo et in terra?*

22 Cf. for example, the prescriptions in Lev 25:25-55 and Leviticus 27, as also Exod 13:11-16 and 34:19-20.

23 The ancient sacramentaries use the word *libertas* in a variety of ways. I have divided these usages into four general categories. 1) *Freedom from enemies*: enemies from outside the society, especially in time of war (cf. Ver 732, 736 and 1026; Gel 1477 and 1507; Gellone 2095); enemies from within the society, such as wicked judges (Gel 510) or false brethren within the church (Ver 530). 2) *Freedom vis-à-vis concupiscence*: freedom from concupiscence (Gel 790) or licence for concupiscence (Gel 788). 3) *Eternal freedom*, described as *perpetua libertas* (Gel 1124; Greg 1758). 4) *Freedom from sin*, especially in the context of Easter. This

is by far the most frequent usage, with such expressions as the following: *splendor libertatis* (Gel 426), *vox libertatis*, that is, the Our Father as the voice that proclaims the freedom of the children of God (Gel 320), *mysteria nostrae libertatis* (Gel 1133), *reparatus status libertatis* (Gel 1353), *praemia libertatis* (Gel 2012), *restituta libertas* (Gel 2010), and *perfecta libertas* (Greg 392). The examples in this last category clearly confirm my interpretation of *vera libertas* in Gel 522.

24 The scriptural text that underlies this euchological formula is that of the Latin Vulgate. The English translation of the Vulgate given here is my own.

25 This was Study Group 18b of *Concilium*, headed by Bruylants. Bugnini describes this as a group of "careful, sensitive specialists with a good knowledge of the Church's euchological sources, both Eastern and Western" (Bugnini, *The Reform of the Liturgy* 397).

26 The collect for the Eucharist on Sundays, as well as on important days and seasons of the ecclesial year, is used also for certain parts of the liturgy of the hours on those days. For example, on the fifth Sunday of Easter, *Deus per quem* is the collect for the Mass and also the collect for first and second vespers, for the office of readings and for lauds. On Saturday of the second week of Easter, the collect is used for the Mass, for the office of readings and for lauds. On the twenty-third Sunday of the year the collect is used for the Mass, for first and second vespers, for the office of readings and for lauds. This is the same pattern that was seen for the fifth Sunday of Easter, with this exception: during the *per annum* season the Sunday collect continues to be used for the office of readings throughout the entire week. Thus the oration *Deus per quem* appears each day of the twenty-third week in at least one of the hours, in addition to the Mass on Sunday.

27 For a discussion of this topic, see SC 106; cf. also Adolf Adam, *The Liturgical Year* (trans. M.J. O'Connell; New York: Pueblo, 1981) 35-56 (the chapter entitled "Sunday as the Original Celebration of the Paschal Mystery").

28 The translation of ICEL renders the prayer thus for the fifth Sunday of Easter and Saturday of the second week of Easter: "God our Father, look upon us with love. You redeem us and make us your children in Christ. Give us true freedom and bring us to the inheritance you promised." For the twenty-third Sunday of the year, there is a slight, but curious difference: "God our Father, you redeem us and make us your children in Christ. Look upon us, give us true freedom and bring us to the inheritance you promised."

29 Cf. MR 220, where the phrase *in regnum Filii dilectionis suae* is part of a communion antiphon, quoting from Col 1:13. The phrase *Filium dilectionis tuae* appears also in two prefaces: *Praefatio Communis III* (MR 435) and *Praefatio Communis VI* (MR 456), which is the same as the preface for Eucharistic Prayer II (MR 456).

30 *Haec nox est, quae hodie per universum mundum in Christo credentes, a vitiis saeculi et caligine peccatorum segregatos, reddit gratiae, sociat sanctitati* (MR 272).

31 See note 8 above.

32 Cf. MR 255, 256, 640, 788, 789, 819 and 837. Since the word *libertas* itself is subject to various interpretations, the context is crucial in order to understand a given instance of the word. For example, MR 255 uses the expression *vera libertas* in the context of freedom of religion, not the soteriological liberty of which I have been speaking.

33 Cf. MR 806 and 935.

34 Cf. MR 140, 294, 498 and 837. MR 140, in speaking of eternal freedom, uses the phrase *ut ad verae perveniamus praemium libertatis*.

35 MR 824: Collect, the Mass for fostering peace and justice, #22b: for reconciliation (during paschal time): *Deus, verae libertatis auctor, qui omnes homines unum vis efformare populum a servitute solutum (quique gratiae et benedictionis tempus nobis praebes,) concede quaesumus, ut, incrementa libertatis accipiens, universale salutis sacramentum in mundum Ecclesia tua vividius appareat atque in homines caritatis manifestet et operetur mysterium.*

36 MR 321: Collect, Friday of the fourth week of Easter: *Deus, qui et libertatis nostrae auctor es et salutis, exaudi supplicantium voces, et, quos sanguinis Filii tui effusione redemisti, fac, ut per te vivere, et perpetua in te valeant incolumitate gaudere.*

37 MR 824: Prayer over the gifts, the Mass for fostering peace and justice, #22b: for reconciliation (during paschal time): *Memorare, Domine, Filium tuum, qui est pax et reconciliatio nostra, mundi peccatum suo sanguine delevisse, et munera Ecclesiae tuae propitiatus aspiciens, da ut, (gratiam huius temporis cum laetitia celebrantes,) libertatem Christi ad omnes possimus extendere.*

38 MR 741: Post-communion, Set B, confirmation: *Quos tui Spiritus, Domine, cumulasti muneribus, tuique auxisti Unigeniti nutrimento,fac etiam in plenitudine legis instructos, ut coram mundo tuae libertatem adoptionis iugiter manifestent, et propheticum tui populi munus sua valeant sanctitate praebere.*

39 Cf. note 35 above.

40 MR 837, Post-communion, the Mass for those who are held captive: *Nostrae libertatis pretium recolentes, tuam, Domine, pro fratribus nostris imploramus clementiam, ut a vinculis solvantur, et servi fiant iustitiae tuae.*

41 *Concede nobis, quaesumus, Domine, haec digne frequentare mysteria, quia, quoties huius hostiae commemoratio celebratur, opus nostrae redemptionis exercetur* (MR 246).

Freedom and Slavery: The American Catholic Church Before the Civil War

Cyprian Davis, OSB

A topic such as Christian freedom demands a look at the absence of freedom in the context of Christian history. In modern times this regulated and legalized absence of freedom is most evident in the institution of slavery. This institutionalized "unfreedom", with its infrastructure of protective laws, police patrols, commercial ventures and insurance indemnity, built around the sale of human beings and the license to exploit this property as one saw fit, was a reality of American society from the beginning of the republic in 1776 until the passage of the thirteenth amendment to the constitution which prohibited slavery in 1865. For almost the first century of its existence the United States was a society that was dependent upon the labor of a subject race of peoples. Despite its dedication to the ideals that "all persons are created equal" and that all should enjoy equal protection under the law, this did not mean the descendants of Africans who were brought to this country.[1]

The Slavery Dilemma

From the beginning the various Christian churches were forced to confront the moral implications in the institution of slavery. Each church confronted the issue in a different way. For many Protestant churches the issue of slavery provoked a split in the membership. Oftentimes this split lasted through most of the twentieth century. In many instances idealistic Protestants, both clergy and laity, undertook direct action against the institution of slavery. They worked to sabotage the institution and to free the slaves out of a religious conviction that the institution basically was evil and unjust.[2]

The Roman Catholic bishops in the United States long avoided the issue of slavery. They practiced a form of denial and refused to concede that it was a moral issue. They were opposed to any effort to subvert the system. Many of them were convinced that freedom was not in the best interests of the African American. If the feeling of the bishops was cool to any talk of abolitionism, the sentiment of most Roman Catholic laity was openly favorable to the slaveholding system.[3]

Two things must be remembered, however. First, there were Catholics, both clerical and lay, who were opposed to the system. Secondly, the Roman Catholic Church as an institution profited from slavery and was oppressed by it. To say this another way, the church in the United States was as much an African institution as it was white, as much an enslaved community as it was slaveholding. Slavery and American Catholicism formed, however, a highly complex relationship. In this essay I propose to look at the geography of Catholic slaveholding, the involvement of the Catholic slaveholders and their viewpoint as expressed by the American bishops.

The Geography of Catholic Slaveholding

A look at Catholic slavery in the United States must look beyond the establishment of the country or even of the first English colonies. American Catholicism began with the arrival in 1565 of the Spanish settlers in what is now northern Florida. The Catholics who arrived were both slave and free, both white and black. The sacramental books, that is, registers of baptisms, marriages and burials, distinguished blacks from whites, mulattoes from mestizos, and always indicated those who were free. The sacramental books of St. Augustine are the oldest American ecclesiastical documents. They reveal a complex, multi-colored society.

From early in its history the Spanish colony at St. Augustine, which was a military outpost so situated as to afford a buffer zone between the Spanish possessions in the Caribbean and the English possessions in the newly established colonies of the Carolinas and Georgia, welcomed and encouraged English slaves to leave the colonies and to enter the Spanish settlement. Those who did so and who accepted baptism into the Catholic faith were freed.[4]

In 1738 a town was established north of St. Augustine in order to house the fugitive slaves. This town was known as the *palenque* of Gracia Real de Santa Teresa de Fort Mose. It was a totally black town, with the exception of the Franciscan priest who ministered to the inhabitants. This first black town in America was also the first black Catholic settlement in America. The inhabitants engaged in agriculture and other crafts. They also formed part of an armed militia for the defense of the colony. Unlike the English, the Spaniards depended in large part upon a military force that was black or mulatto. The military leader of Fort Mose was Francisco Menendez, a Mandingo warrior who had been one of the slaves who escaped from the Carolinas.[5] He had been a leader of black soldiers who fought against the English alongside of the Yamassee Indians.

During all of the time that Spain controlled Florida the soldiers who were garrisoned at St. Augustine were black. In 1683 there was a company of forty-two black and mulatto soldiers at the site.[6] The death registers for blacks indicate the presence of black soldiers in St. Augustine for the second Spanish period in Florida. From 1763 to 1784, the Spanish relinquished St. Augustine and the whole Florida territory following its defeat in the Seven Years War. Florida was exchanged for the city of Havana, Cuba. Only in 1784 did the Spanish return to Florida. From that period the sacramental books were divided between blacks and whites. The town of Fort Mose was not reestablished. Blacks lived in the towns of St. Augustine and Pensacola.

The baptism, marriage and death registers reveal the presence of a black Catholic community of slaves and free persons, all of whom had a complex system of relationships with the white community, ranging from concubinage, family relationships, relationship through baptismal sponsorship, etc. Many of the blacks in the sacramental registers still came from the English colonies, some from as far north as Maryland. Nevertheless, until the territory was ceded to the United States in 1821, the black population of St. Augustine and northern Florida, both slave and free, lived in an atmosphere of easy-going, mutually dependent relationships that would be unknown elsewhere in the country.[7]

Black Catholic communities before the Civil War were found in the Gulf region, in the French-speaking territory along the Mississippi, in central Kentucky and in Maryland. Black Catholics were to be found among the slaves in the area of Vincennes, Indiana and in Savannah, Georgia. By 1618 the French had settled in Louisiana. In this period many French males formed liaisons with black and Indian women. From these unions arose the Free People of Color. The baptismal registers in Mobile, Savannah and Baltimore indicate the presence of black Catholics. In places like northern Louisiana and Mobile, one finds settlements of blacks, French-speaking and Catholic, slave and free. In these communities, such as Isle Brevelle and Mon Luis Island as well as Baltimore, the baptismal registers indicate the fact that some black Catholics also were slave owners.[8]

The Catholic Understanding of Slavery

Mauro Cappellari, the Camaldolese monk who became Pope Gregory XVI in 1831, was perhaps one of the most reactionary and intransigent popes in modern times. This stance not only was theological but was also political. Deeply embroiled in the revolutionary movement that rocked Europe in the mid-nineteenth century, he seemed an unlikely candidate to serve as the first pope to take a strong and unequivocal stand against the slave trade, and by extension, against slavery. Yet this is what he did by the papal encyclical *In supremo apostolatus fastigio* in 1839.

The pope spoke about the "inhuman traffic" in slavery. He reviewed the diverse condemnations of slavery by his predecessors in the papacy. He condemned the fact that so many of the natives of Africa—Gregory specifically mentioned Africa—were doomed to a cruel and bestial toil. Finally,

Gregory forbade anyone to assist in, uphold or defend the traffic in slaves.[9] Unfortunately, Gregory's condemnation of the institution of slavery must still be deduced from the context. Later it would be argued that such a condemnation can be inferred from the outright condemnation of the slave trade itself. No doubt, this is true under the analogy that if one condemns the refining and trading in opium, one condemns the smoking of opium as well. One may ask why he did not say so from the beginning? It may be that Gregory XVI did not want to face the problem of how to liberate thousands of slaves both in the United States and in the Latin American countries.

A central problem was the meaning of Gregory's view of the "unjust" capture of individuals for slavery. Traditionally, the Catholic Church had faithfully followed the Roman law tradition which taught that slavery had a legitimate existence in law. In the tradition of Roman law it was considered that all persons are by nature free but by the "Law of Nations", the *Ius Gentium*, some persons are slaves. There are in that tradition six legitimate reasons why one can be enslaved or maintained in slavery. These reasons were: captives held through war; penalty for crimes committed; sale of the individual to pay off debts; sale of oneself because of poverty; sale of children by parents because of poverty; birth from a slave mother (*partus sequitur ventrem*).

Because of Roman law the individual had some recourse to freedom, some basis for rights and, in cases of doubt, some presumption for freedom. In other words, in those countries which were governed by a Roman law tradition, as well as in the Catholic Church, which based its legal reasoning upon the Roman law, slavery could be justified but slaves had certain rights. The Catholic Church in its legal traditions insisted that slaves had a right to practice the Catholic faith, and slave owners had a duty to see to the religious instruction of the slave and the exercise of his or her rights to marriage and a family life.[10]

None of this tradition existed in the United States. No doubt this was the result of the fact that slavery in the United States was combined with presumptions of racial inferiority.

The African was presumed to be a slave in American society.[11] The American slave had no recourse in law against his or her master or mistress.[12]

American Slavery in the Catholic Context

For all practical purposes, the Catholic Church in the United States had incorporated slavery into its structure. American bishops, beginning with John Carroll himself, owned or made use of slaves. It is not always clear from the documentation, however, which bishops were slaveowners. We know that Portier of Mobile, Flaget of Bardstown and du Bourg of Louisiana owned slaves.[13] We know that religious orders like the Jesuits, the Vincentians and the Capuchins owned slaves. The Sulpicians owned slaves who were employed in the first American seminaries. Religious women like the first contemplative nuns in the United States, the Carmelite nuns at Port Tobacco in Maryland, owned slaves.[14] The Ursuline nuns in New Orleans owned slaves. The Visitation nuns in Georgetown in the District of Columbia, the Dominican Sisters in Kentucky, the Sisters of Charity of Nazareth, the Sisters of Loretto in Kentucky, the Sisters of the Holy Cross in Louisiana and the Religious of the Sacred Heart, including St. Philippine Duchesne, owned slaves.[15]

In most instances these slaves were Catholics. They were often part of the household management and domestic staff, as was the case with the slave women who worked for the Vincentians in their seminary in Perryville, Missouri.[16] At other times they worked the land and provided revenue for the community, as was typical of the Jesuit slaves in Maryland and Missouri.[17] Others were part of the physical force in the construction activities, building trades, etc. The Vincentians often transferred their slaves from one Vincentian house to another as necessity demanded.[18] What is important to remember is that African American slaves provided the manpower that built the Catholic Church and maintained it in existence from a physical point of view throughout the South before the Civil War. It is one of the glaring omissions of American Church history that their role has been overlooked.

The moral conditions of the slave population was one of the items that troubled the American Church, as is seen from the *dubia* that were addressed to the Congregation of the Propaganda. These doubtful matters were raised especially with regard to the freedom of the slaves to marry. Bishop Flaget of Bardstown wrote to the Congregation of the Propaganda, which in turn posed the question to the Congregation of the Holy Office "for the decision of this question pending in the congregation for so many years concerning the marriage of Catholic slaves." The question was concerned with male slaves who had been forced to separate from the first wife and were obliged to marry another by the new slave owner while the former wife was still alive.[19] The bishop of Louisiana, William du Bourg, stated that since the civil laws forbade the marriage of slaves without the previous consent of the slaveowners and the slaveowners did not give their consent because they did not believe that it was in their interest, then the slaves were without any moral possibility of contracting marriage. He inquired whether they consequently were obliged to celibacy or to concubinage, and concluded that their marriage could not be contracted in the church.[20]

Bishop du Bourg asked again on another occasion whether missionaries should "disturb consciences over the possession of slaves and whether it is permitted to them to buy and to possess slaves for their service according to the norms of civil law since it is impossible to find others than slaves for domestic service."[21] In a further question, he asked "whether slaves must be permitted to forego manual labor on Sundays and feast days", because it was the only time that they had to take care of necessities for themselves in terms of food and clothing, even to gain some profit. Also the leisure of so many men of the lowest classes was a risk to "public tranquillity".

The *dubia* that were presented to the Congregation are very interesting. In the present state of research the response to these questions is not clear. The question with regard to the remarriage of slaves who had been forcibly separated and forcibly thrown together into a new quasi-marital union through the dominative power of the slave owner had to be referred to the Holy Office. Its response has not been found.

In the Propaganda archives there is a record of a response that was given to Joseph Rosati, CM, the bishop of St. Louis, on 25 October 1828. It concerned marriages between slaves without the knowledge or consent of the slave owner. Pope Leo XII (1823-1829) granted on 4 October that under the circumstances in which slaves were forced to contract marriages, the marriage that was entered in those circumstances was to be considered valid, despite the fact that the Council of Trent in its canons had decreed clandestine marriage invalid. Care was to be taken, however, that a record be kept of the marriage for future verification.[22]

Previously, America's first bishop, John Carroll, had shown pastoral concern with regard to the slaves in his letter to Rome wherein he expressed the hope that more of the vernacular could be used in the liturgy for the sake of the slaves who were illiterate.[23] On the other hand, William Henry Elder, the future archbishop of Cincinnati, had written about the slave population of Mississippi when he was still bishop of Natchez before the Civil War. His article for European consumption appeared in the little periodical that was published by the *Société de la Propagation de la Foi*, which was based in Lyons, France. Elder wished to explain to his European readers, who supported much of the apostolic work of the American bishops, some of the difficulties in the evangelization of the slave population. Elder spoke about the unwillingness of the slave-owners to allow their slaves to come to church. Slaves attached to one plantation were not to associate with slaves on another plantation. The slaves were so numerous that they alone would fill the church and thereby leave no room for the white parishioners. On the other hand, there were not enough priests to visit the various plantations and to minister to the slaves. He expressed the desire that there be a band of "traveling missionaries" who would make a circuit of the plantations.

Elder described the "slave character" as docile, dependent, weak in mind and will, fickle, "creatures of feeling", sensual and "animal in their inclinations". Despite this low assessment by Elder, who actually seemed to like blacks but who considered them inferior, he held much hope for evangelization efforts among them, because they were "creatures of feeling" and must be attained through that avenue. In fact, according to Elder, they would be recipients of much grace because of their humble condition.[24]

Looking at the *dubia* that were raised by the bishops in their inquiries of Rome, looking at the problems that were raised by the bishops from the pastoral point of view, one is struck by the bishops' reluctance to express any judgment upon the issue of slavery as such. Bishop du Bourg inquired as to whether slaveowners could possess their slaves with a tranquil conscience. He was silent, nevertheless, with regard to the justice that was owed to the slaves as humans or the justice of the original seizure of their foreparents who were taken from Africa and brought to this country. Bishop du Bourg, in fact, seemingly saw no possibility that the slaves could contract a valid marriage, leaving one with the perception of his lack of concern for their spiritual well-being. No bishop, it would seem, sought to question the justice of a socio-economic structure that was based upon slavery. No bishop raised any moral objections to the justification of a nation whose culture and laws upheld the system of slavery. In fact, the bishops as a body ignored the issue; certain individual bishops even defended the American form of slavery.

In Defense of American Slavery

John England, the first bishop of Charleston from 1820-1842, defended the American system of slavery in a series of eighteen public letters to John Forsyth (1780-1841), who at the time was Secretary of State in the cabinet of Martin Van Buren. Forsyth, a political leader from Georgia, had accused Pope Gregory XVI of the approval of the position of the abolitionists in his condemnation of the slave trade in 1829. England believed that it was his duty to prove that Gregory XVI could not be an abolitionist because slavery was not considered by the Catholic Church to be immoral.

England basically used a legal argument that was built upon historical precedent, which demonstrated the existence and thereby the acceptance of slavery through time. In every stage of human history beginning with the Old Testament, one finds the existence of slavery. In Christian revelation slavery is found. The New Testament pictured a society in which slavery existed. Christ lived in a world where slavery was a reality. Had slavery been wrong, then Christ would have condemned it. He did not do so, therefore slavery cannot be wrong. The same is true as one goes through each period of church history. England examined the canons of various ecclesiastical synods which concerned slaves. Laws were made with regard to slaves, but the practice was never condemned nor questioned. Had it been wrong, the church would have spoken. Hence, the church has never and will never join the ranks of those who work for the abolition of slavery.

England concluded that Gregory XVI, in his denunciation of the slave trade, was talking about that transoceanic traffic which was indulged in by the Spanish and Portuguese. He was not talking about that necessary buying and selling of slaves that normally took place between citizens within this country. England's arguments betrayed a great erudition. It was remarkable that he would have access to so many obscure medieval texts that enabled him to have the documentation to defend the cause of slavery. In the end, however, England's argumentation is flawed and his achievement reprehensible. His basic mistake was to treat each incident of slavery in the historical texts without any consideration of time, type or context. He never questioned the reason or background of canonical decrees. He never made any effort to analyze the forms of slavery—including the question of individual rights of slaves—that are found in history and how they compared to what existed in this country.

At the beginning of the Civil War, the French bishop Auguste Martin, who became the first bishop of Natchitoches in Louisiana in 1853, wrote a pastoral letter to the members of his diocese in 1861. The letter, written in French, was delated to the Congregation of the Propaganda. It was entitled "A Pastoral Letter of the Bishop of Natchitoches on the Occasion of the War of the South for its Independence".[25]

Martin wrote the letter to encourage his flock in their war effort, to show them the righteousness of the cause of the South, and finally, to prove the righteousness of slavery:

> In the admirable dispositions of his Providence, God, the Father of all, who loves the souls for whom he has given his only one and beloved Son, and who uses even the purely human interests for the profit of eternal interests has for centuries snatched from barbarism of savage customs thousands of children of the race of Canaan, on whom there continues to rest everywhere the curse of an outraged father. He entrusts them to the safekeeping of the privileged people of the great human family; and these latter in the providential view, must be for them shepherds and fathers more than masters.

The bishop continues to say that this slavery is God's will:

> The manifest will of God is that in exchange for a freedom of which they are incapable and which would kill them and for a lifetime of labor, we would give to these unfortunates not only the bread and the clothing necessary to their material life but also and especially their legitimate portion of the truth and the goods of grace, which will console them in their present misery by the hope of rest in the bosom of their Father, to whom they are called by the same title as us.[26]

The bishop indicates that contrary "to the egalitarian sophisms that are the legacy of the eighteenth century", their servitude is really "more than a material and moral improvement of a degraded class", and is instead "an eminently Christian work".[27] To put it succinctly, the bishop said that they had to remove from the Africans their freedom in order to save them. Nevertheless, the bishop suggested with some delicacy that there were for the most part those who had not achieved the noble mission of the use of the institution of slavery for the salvation of the slaves, but had used it for their own ends of exploitation, thus to make the slaves "the docile instruments of brutal passions". The bishop ended with a denunciation of the fact that in general the people of his diocese had not been very generous in the living of their Catholic faith.

Rome did not share the views of Bishop Martin on slavery and freedom. In fact, it was decided that the letter was to be condemned. The recommendation that it be condemned was based upon the fact that Martin attributed "to God what is an execrable violence of men", namely the slave trade. It was observed that in his condemnation of the slave trade, Gregory XVI had condemned the institution of slavery itself. The theologian who had been asked to judge the theological content of the pastoral letter of Bishop Martin, Vincenzo Gatti, OP, Consultor to the Congregation of the Index and Librarian of the Casanatense Library in Rome, observed that in his support of slavery, Martin

> favours the enemies of the Catholic Church who accuse her of approving slavery, which is the origin of the vile trade and of the brutal treatment of the Negroes from Africa. It makes the Church unjustly odious; it promotes the mistake of those who believe that the slave trade of the Negroes is lawful and who try to elude the condemnation of the Sovereign Pontiffs with every kind of cavil.... This mistake favours the preservation of slavery in the Southern States in opposition to the will of the Sovereign Pontiffs who...have condemned not only the slave trade but slavery itself.[28]

Gatti referred to the words of Pope Urban VIII of 1639 which were cited by Gregory XVI to support his condemnation of the slave trade. Urban VIII wrote in condemnation of those who "reduce to slavery the Indians...despoil them of their properties, conduct or transport them into other regions, deprive them of liberty in any way whatsoever, retain them in servitude...." But it is especially the words of Gregory XVI which are seen to condemn implicitly more than slavery itself:

> We warn and adjure earnestly in the Lord faithful Christians of every condition that no one in the future dare to vex anyone, despoil him of his possessions, reduce to servitude, or lend aid and favour to those who give themselves up to these practices, or exercise that inhuman traffic by which the Blacks, as if they were not men but rather animals, have been brought into servitude, in no matter what way, are, without any distinction, in contempt of the rights of justice and humanity, bought, sold and devoted sometimes to the hardest labour.[29]

Moreover, Gregory XVI forbade anyone, either ecclesiastic or lay, to defend or to teach in public or in private anything contrary to what was expressed in the papal letter. Martin's letter was condemned and the comments by Gatti were accepted by Pope Pius IX in 1864. In the end the defeat of the

South and the passage of the thirteenth amendment to the constitution made Martin's letter moot.[30] It is a pity that Martin was not forced somehow to make a public statement that would have expressed an opinion with regard to slavery and the dignity of African peoples in keeping with the papal teaching.

Augustin Verot was another American bishop who expressed a teaching on slavery in light of the Civil War. He preached a sermon at the Church of St. Augustine in St. Augustine, Florida on 4 January 1861. The day had been set aside by President James Buchanan as a day for fasting and prayer. He had as his text, "Justice exalteth a nation: but sin maketh nations miserable" (Prov 14:34). Verot's thesis was similar to that of England. Slavery was found in the scripture, was regulated by church councils and was recognized by the civil law; hence, slavery in the common estimation is not immoral.

> Let us now examine whether the Divine positive law condemns Slavery. If Slavery be immoral in itself, no Divine law can commend it or approve of it, because God cannot commend or authorize something immoral; if it be not immoral in itself still God could forbid it.... In this respect, however, we find that God in the Old Testament under the law of nature, and under the law of Moses, not only did not prohibit Slavery; but sanctioned it, regulated it, and specified the rights of master, and the duties of slaves.[31]

The same things hold for the New Testament:

> ...some might think that Our Lord Jesus Christ...has abolished Slavery, although it was allowed in times past. Indeed, this is what has taken place with regard to some points relative to marriage. Divorce and polygamy were allowed to them of old.... Our Lord has expressly, formally, and pointedly abolished divorce and polygamy...but he has not proscribed or forbidden Slavery.[32]

Verot proceeds to show how Jesus reacted on the occasion of slavery, as in the case with the centurion who begged Jesus to come to his home and to heal his slave. The centurion proceeded to talk about the men under him who did his bidding. On that occasion the centurion was praised and nothing was said about his slaveholding. When Paul returned Onesimus to Philemon with the request that Paul be allowed to have the services of Onesimus, "he would not detain his fugitive slave." Verot proceeds to contrast this with the abolitionists of the time. In fact, he blames the abolitionists for the difficulties of the period. It is true that many of the abolitionists were hostile to Catholicism. As a result many Catholics were doubly hostile to the abolitionists' fight against slavery:

> ...the pretensions of Abolitionists have no foundation whatever in nature, or morality, or the word of God either in the Old or New Testament, or in the enactments of law-givers of the religious or the political order. The fact is, that there has been, in the northern part of the country, an actual conspiracy against justice and truth...this conspiracy against justice and truth, is headed by fanatical preachers....[33]

With regard to the question of freedom, Verot remarks that all men and women are not necessarily born free and equal. Just as some are born wealthy and others poor, some are weak and others strong, some are of less intelligence and others "of quick and penetrating intellect", thus some are born free and others slave. For Verot, Christian slavery is totally independent of human slavery. For Verot, the statements in the New Testament that are relative to freedom refer only to spiritual freedom. In reference to slaves, the New Testament exhorts them to be obedient to their masters. As a result Verot felt that the South was justified in its fight on behalf of slavery. Slavery is part of the structure of civil law, and humanity is obliged to obey the laws of the state.

In the second part of his very lengthy sermon, however, Verot takes a different approach. He proceeds to show how the institution of slavery must be overhauled to make it just and humane, "...in this part...I may have to mention wrongs which the South ought to acknowledge and confess...." He continues to say that "a man, by being a slave, does not cease to be a man, retaining all the properties, qualities, attributes, duties, rights and responsibilities attached to human nature... and made to the image and likeness of God."

Among the issues which Verot saw as wrongs in the slavery system were: any talk of reviving the slave trade (it might be added that he meant by that the transoceanic slave trade); respect for the rights of free blacks; the sexual exploitation of black women, both slave and free; the observance and encouragement of marriage among slaves; the separation of husbands and wives and their families by slaveowners; the duty to provide sufficient food, clothing and shelter to all of the slaves; and finally, the duty to provide religious and moral instructions to the slaves. Verot called for the efforts of "the wise and virtuous" who would "divest Slavery of the features which... make it odious to God and man." Verot then called for the enactment of a slavery code by the Confederacy which would elucidate the rights and duties of both masters and slaves.

On the text of the condensed Italian version of the sermon in the Propaganda archives was written a remark that revealed a certain disagreement with the content. "Not everything can be affirmed" was the judgment. It could be added that the kind of slavery that Verot wanted was impossible. American slavery never recognized that African slaves had rights. The cruelty of the system was calculated to brutalize and dehumanize the slaves. The economic system demanded a "work machine". To be a machine was to destroy the slave's humanity. To prevent revolts, the slave had to be terrorized. Verot should have been aware of the clandestine traffic in slaves that continued to occur. He should have known that the South would have to reopen the slave trade if it were to expand its agrarian economy. In this respect, Verot's vision was an illusion and his exhortation was a deception. In the period after the Civil War, however, Verot's defense of and support for the blacks in his diocese would reveal a man of compassion, zeal and justice.[34]

In the spring of 1863, in the midst of the Civil War, Martin John Spalding, bishop of Louisville (the next year he would become the archbishop of Baltimore), wrote a "Dissertation on the American Civil War" for the curial officials in Rome.[35] The memorial later was published in the official newspaper of the Vatican, the *Osservatore Romano*, with the name and identity of the author concealed.[36] Spalding was a member of a prominent Catholic Kentucky family who owned slaves. Kentucky was a border state and during the Civil War did not secede from the Union. But Martin John Spalding, like many Kentuckians, was sympathetic to the Southern cause.

In this memorial to Rome Spalding makes the issue of slavery and the question of economic rivalry and competition between the North and the South to be the central reason for the Civil War. With regard to slavery, Spalding, unlike Martin and England, did not defend it. Rather, he blamed the British for slavery. He considered it "a great social evil left to us, as a sad heritage by Protestant England, more than two hundred years ago.... It is...generally admitted by all good and moderate men, even in the South where slavery exists, that slavery is a great social evil...." According to Spalding, however, slavery was an insoluble problem. He asked rhetorically how the South could relinquish slavery without bringing ruin upon the country and upon the slaves themselves. Although with no answer as to how the country would be ruined by the emancipation of the slaves, he had a very specific response with regard to the ruin that emancipation brought to the slaves themselves.

Spalding considered the free blacks to be generally depraved and unhappy:

> Our experience and observation shows us the evidence that those [the manumitted slaves] who are in such a way liberated ordinarily become miserable vagabonds, drunkards, and thieves; it would seem a curious thing, but nevertheless true, that such emancipated ones are lost in body and soul.[37]

Remarkably, Spalding considered religion as the reason for this situation of the freed slaves. He expressed the opinion that if the majority of the Southern states were Catholic, then "the Catholic religion, according to its spirit and its practice in time past, would first be able gradually to better their [the slaves'] condition, instructing them in their Christian duties and at the same time inclining the hearts of their masters to compassion...." Spalding indicated that in New Orleans, "where the dominant sentiment has always been more or less Catholic...almost half of the slaves had already been freed...."

Spalding noted that in the North, where slavery no longer existed, the situation of the blacks was terrible because of racial discrimination: "...the free Negroes form a class inferior and apart; they cannot stay in the same hotel with the whites, they cannot ordinarily travel in the same carriages...." He remarked that free blacks in the North were "a race despised and set apart, like the lepers of the gospel...." He concludes, however, that the ultimate question was "what to do with the freed Negroes?" Spalding had no solution. The conclusion of his dissertation, however, was that if the Catholic Church "keeps itself resolutely, as in the past, *apart from men*, and all for God, for peace, for fraternal love it will remain after the war in a favorable position in the eyes of all...." In Spalding's view the church "kept itself apart from men" by its silence on all the issues of the period, including the question of slavery.

Conclusion

In this essay only part of the Catholic Church's involvement with slavery has been examined. Although Catholics in the United States never joined the abolitionist movement, there were Catholics who were opposed to slavery. There was even more opposition in Europe. As has been indicated, Rome also was opposed to the institution.

The question remains as to how it was possible for Catholics, especially church leaders, to defend the Southern cause and ultimately to defend the cause of slavery? How was it possible not to see the injustices that were inherent in the slavery system? How was it possible to value freedom for oneself and for the church, yet to turn a blind eye to the absence of freedom in a large segment of the population?

Perhaps one answer is that white American Catholics shared the same sentiments and feelings of the white Protestant population among whom they lived. Their understanding of freedom was as narrow and circumscribed as was that of the general population in the region where they resided. Freedom for most of them was, and perhaps for some of us still is, security and safety with one's own.

Notes

1 See A. Leon Higginbotham, Jr., *In the Matter of Color. Race and the American Legal Process: The Colonial Period* (Oxford: Oxford University Press, 1980) 371-383.

2 See Albert J. Raboteau, "Black Christianity in North America," in *The Encyclopedia of the American Religious Experience* (eds. C. Lippy and P.W. Williams; New York: Charles Scribner's Sons, 1988) 1.635-648. See also Higginbotham, *In the Matter* 36.

3 Cf. notes 22-23 below; also Benjamin Blied, *Catholics and the Civil War* (Milwaukee, WI: 1945) 19-82. Not to be overlooked is Madeleine Hooke Rice, *American Catholic Opinion in the Slavery Controversy* (New York: Columbia University Press, 1944).

4 See Jane Landers, "Black Society in Spanish St. Augustine, 1784-1821" (PhD dissertation, University of Florida, 1988) 14-15.

5 Landers, "Black Society" 19-22. The Mandingo or Mande People are an African ethnic and linguistic group found in West Africa, especially in today's nation of Mali.

6 Landers, "Black Society" 12-14.

7 For an extensive look at the social situation of blacks in the Spanish colony of St. Augustine, see Landers, "Black Society" 66-145.

8 See Cyprian Davis, *The History of Black Catholics in the United States* (New York: Crossroad, 1990) 28-97.

9 For an English text of the encyclical, see Maria Caravaglios, "A Roman Critique of the Pro-Slavery Views of Bishop Martin of Natchitoches, Louisiana," *RACHSP* 83 (1972) 67-81 (encyclical = 72-75).

10 See John Maxwell, *Slavery and the Catholic Church* (Chichester, England: Barry Rose, 1975) 26-27, 44-80.

11 See Higginbotham, *In the Matter* 38-60.

12 Higginbotham, *In the Matter* 38-60.

13 See Davis, *History* 28-66. An example of an episcopal slaveholder is Cyrillo de Barcelona, who purchased an eleven-year old *Bozal* (African

born) in Florida while on a visitation of the Spanish mission at St. Augustine in 1788; see Davis, *History* 69.

14 Charles W. Currier, *Carmel In America, 1790-1890: A Centennial History of Discalced Carmelite Nuns in the United States* (Darien, IL: Carmelite Press, 1989) 83: "A portion of the property of the nuns, while they were at Mount Carmel [in Maryland], consisted of slaves. Many of the novices on entering the community, brought their slaves with them."

15 See Davis, *History* 28-39.

16 See Stafford Poole and Douglas Slawson, *Church and Slave in Perry County, Missouri, 1818-1865* (Lewiston, NY: Edwin Mellen, 1986) 148-158.

17 See Emmett Curran, "'Splendid Poverty': Jesuit Slaveholding in Maryland, 1805-1838," in *Catholics in the Old South: Essays on Church and Culture* (eds. R.M. Miller and J.L. Wakelyn; Macon, GA: Mercer University Press, 1983) 125-146.

18 Poole, *Church and Slave* 166-168.

19 *Lettere e Decreti della S. Congregazione e Biglietti di Mons. Segretario*, 1828, vol. 310, fols. 186v and 187r (UND Archives, microfilm). See Finbar Kenneally, *et al.*, eds., *United States Documents in the Propaganda Fide Archives: A Calendar* (Washington, DC: AAFH, 1966-1987) 3.340 no. 2141.

20 *Scritture Riferite nei Congressi*, vol. 9, fol. 339rv, undated, and *Decisioni cherichiede alla Sac. Congr' de Propaganda Fide: Il Vescovo d'alta Louisiana* (UND Archives, microfilm). See Kenneally, *Documents* 1.178 no. 1092.

21 *Scritture Riferite nei Congressi*, vol. 3, fol. 466 (UND Archives, microfilm). See Kenneally, *Documents* 1.36 no. 213.

22 *Lettere e Decreti della S. Congregazione e Biglietti di Mons. Segretario*, 1828, vol. 309, fol. 758r-758v (UND Archives, microfilm). See Kenneally, *Documents* 3.335 no. 2109.

23 John Carroll to Arthur O'Leary, Baltimore 1787, in John Carroll, *The John Carroll Papers* (ed. T. Hanley; Notre Dame, IN: University of Notre Dame Press, 1976) 1.225.

24 "Bishop Elder on the Apostolate to the Negro Slaves in Mississippi, 1858," in *Documents of American Catholic History* (ed. J.T. Ellis; Wilmington, DE: Michael Glazier, 1987) 1.325-328. During the Civil War Elder ministered to the sick and dying blacks who were in internment camps in Natchez. As the archbishop of Cincinnati, he gave aid and support to black Catholics in the establishment of the Black Catholic Lay Congresses.

25 *Scritture Riferite nei Congressi, America Centrale,* vol. 20, fol. 1207r-1213v (UND Archives, microfilm). See Kenneally, *Documents* 3.75 no. 473.

26 Kenneally, *Documents* 3.75 no. 473.

27 Kenneally, *Documents* 3.75 no. 473.

28 See Caravaglios, "A Roman Critique" 67-81 (citation = 80).

29 Caravaglios, "A Roman Critique" 74. Caravaglios gives the complete English translation of the bull of Gregory XVI.

30 Caravaglios, "A Roman Critique" 69-70, 80.

31 Augustin Verot, "A Tract for the Times," in *Scritture Riferite nei Congressi: America Centrale,* vol. 20, fols. 1262r-1268v (UND Archives, microfilm). See Kenneally, *Documents* 3.77 no. 489.

32 Verot, "A Tract for the Times".

33 Verot, "A Tract for the Times".

34 See Michael Gannon, *Rebel Bishop: The Life and Era of Augustin Verot* (Milwaukee, WI: Bruce, 1964).

35 David [Thomas] Spalding, "Martin John Spalding's 'Dissertation on the American Civil War.'" *CHR* 52 (1966-1967) 66-85.

36 Spalding, "Dissertation" 68.

37 Spalding, "Dissertation" 77.

American Catholics and the Civil Rights Movement

Isaac McDaniel, OSB

The black Baptist minister Samuel Williams, a professor at Morehouse College and mentor to Martin Luther King, Jr., once remarked: "The church has never been a leader in social change, always a follower, and we mustn't expect any more from the church except that it will, as it has in the past, sanctify that which has been accomplished by others."[1] Williams's bleak appraisal notwithstanding, Americans traditionally have regarded their churches and synagogues as tested and time-honored tribunes of the struggle to extend human rights to peoples of every race and color. For twentieth-century Americans, the civil rights movement of the 1950s and 1960s represented a high point of moral activism on behalf of equality for Americans of all races. How did Roman Catholics in the United States respond to this chapter in the quest for racial equality?

American Catholics entered the middle years of the twentieth century with a grim record with respect to their customary treatment of blacks. From the earliest colonial days until the eve of the Civil War, when more than a few Protestant denominations split geographically as a result of their quarrels over slavery, Catholics remained remarkably indifferent to the consuming moral questions that were raised by human bondage. Many Catholics themselves owned slaves.[2] A number of Catholic bishops trafficked in "black chattel", as did many priests and many, if not most, religious orders in the United States.[3]

More than a few prelates enthusiastically defended slavery, either privately or in public.[4] With a few exceptions—such as John Baptist Purcell, the archbishop of Cincinnati—Catholic bishops in the United States seemed either to embrace slavery or to ignore it altogether. Thus slavery never was mentioned in a single one of the seven provincial councils of Baltimore that were held between 1829 and 1849. Many prelates doubtless would have agreed with Louisville Bishop Martin J. Spalding (himself a slaveholder) when, midway through the Civil War, he confided in his journal: "While our brothers are thus slaughtered in hecatombs, Ab. Lincoln cooly [*sic*] issues his Emancipation Proclamation, letting loose from three to four millions of half-civilized Africans to murder their Masters and Mistresses.... Puritanism with its preachers and Common Schools has at last ruined the country...."[5]

Northern Catholics—many of them Irish and German newcomers to America, who struggled just to survive socially and economically in the New World—had little more use for blacks than did their fellow Catholics who were south of the Mason-Dixon Line. Irish immigrants in particular resented blacks as competitors in a crowded job market. They were glad to have at least one group of Americans who languished beneath them on the political, social and economic ladders. The black scholar W.E.B. DuBois remarked that when he grew up in Great Barrington, Massachusetts in the 1870s, "the racial angle was more clearly defined against the Irish than against me."[6] Throughout the Civil War most Northern Catholics remained hostile and condescending toward blacks.

Relations between American Catholics, nearly all of them white, and American blacks scarcely improved in the postwar years. For that matter, the American bishops showed little retrospective regret over the very existence of slavery. Shortly after Appomattox the prelates publicly registered their suspicion of Lincoln's Emancipation Proclamation: "We could have wished, that in accordance with the action of the Catholic Church in past ages, in regard to the serfs of Europe, a more gradual system of emancipation could have been adopted, so that they might have been in some measure prepared to make a better use of their freedom, than they are likely to do now."[7] If Catholics blew an uncertain trumpet with regard to the newfound freedom of blacks, they were not at all ambivalent about the alleged inferiority of blacks. Although occasional prelates such as St. Paul's Archbishop John Ireland vigorously denounced racism, the majority of bishops (like most Americans) still regarded blacks as innately backward by comparison with whites. Bishop William Gross of Savannah, Georgia summarized the feelings of many Catholics towards blacks when he remarked: "We know the history of this people. In their native country, Africa, they were sunken from time immemorial in barbarism; and their religion, Fetichism, was the most depraved that the world has ever known."[8] It is little wonder that at the Second Plenary Council of Baltimore in 1866 the bishops readily adopted a measure which accepted racial segregation in those areas of the United States where it already prevailed.[9]

Nor did American Catholics expend much effort to evangelize newly freed slaves in the postwar South. When Rome exhorted American Catholics to seek converts among their black compatriots, the American bishops firmly resisted. At the Second Plenary Council the bishops rejected a Vatican plan for the appointment of a national coordinator to preside over the evangelization of blacks in the United States.[10] Most bishops were not at all convinced that blacks represented an especially fallow field for the harvesting of souls. In 1875 Canon Peter Benoit, an Anglo-Belgian cleric, made a lengthy tour of the American South. Later Benoit ruefully recalled how the archbishop of Baltimore, James Roosevelt Bayley, had informed him "that he had but little hope for any substantial good being done among the negroes in America, that you had to cut the head off first of those whom you wished to instruct...."[11] Although a handful of religious communities—including the Josephites, the Society for African Missions and the Society of the Divine Word—ministered among blacks, most Catholic leaders in the United States remained blithely indifferent to the prospect of potential black converts.[12] Moreover, those priests and religious who labored among blacks often incited the ridicule both of Catholic and non-Catholic whites. Thus the Franciscan sisters who taught at St. Benedict the Moor School in Savannah were caustically labeled by local whites as the "nigger sisters".[13] Nearly a century later George Barry Ford, the progressive and outspoken

New York priest, recalled: "I once heard a widely known Catholic editor answer an inquiry as to why so few Negroes were Catholics by saying, 'Because in the past we didn't think they were worth missionary effort.'"[14]

Another reason for official Catholic neglect of American blacks may have been the nearly infinitesimal number of Afro-Americans who considered themselves to be Catholic in the years after Appomattox. When Lincoln issued his Emancipation Proclamation, only slightly more than one percent of the seven million blacks who lived in the United States were Roman Catholic, and the vast majority of these were clustered in Louisiana and Maryland.[15] As recently as 1920 there were scarcely more than 200,000 black Catholics in the United States.[16] They constituted less than two percent of the total black population in the country on the eve of the Great Depression.[17]

For that matter, the South included very few Catholics of either race. Catholics composed less than four percent of the population of the South at the end of the nineteenth century.[18] Because so few Catholics resided in the Old Confederacy, there were few priests to minister to the needs of black Catholics or to recruit new ones. The majority of Catholic clerics who lived and worked in the South were located in cities and thus had little contact with blacks, who were still primarily a rural people.[19] Black Catholics may well have envisioned themselves as a fragile subspecies within a larger endangered species known as Southern Catholics.

After emancipation many black Catholics abandoned Catholicism, in part because they realized that nineteenth-century, white Catholics accepted racial segregation and willingly shaped the institutional church to accommodate apartheid.[20] Accustomed to a view of religion as a prime vehicle for collective racial identity and self-expression, blacks were scarcely interested in a denomination that denied them even the most rudimentary forms of dignity or self-assertion. In Louisiana alone, several thousand blacks left Catholicism in the years immediately after the Civil War.[21]

Black Catholics rightly perceived that it was impossible for people of color to participate fully in the life of American

Catholicism. In many parts of the United States, black Catholics were forced to worship in non-white parishes.[22] Separate churches for blacks began to be formed immediately after the Civil War. They became more numerous around the time of World War I.[23] In 1928 fifty-four percent of the 204,000 black Catholics in the country were registered in all-black parishes.[24] "On the whole, the Roman Catholic Church prefers to have Negroes attend all-Negro churches, on the basis of residential segregation and of attempts to dissuade them from attending white churches," wrote Swedish economist Gunnar Myrdal in 1944 in his classic account of American race relations, *An American Dilemma*.[25]

Although some Southern parishes grudgingly allowed blacks to worship under the same roof as whites, even there blacks customarily were consigned to a side aisle or to a section in the back of the church or to the gallery.[26] In 1871 Father Herbert Vaughan, an Englishman, arrived in Baltimore and shortly thereafter began a tour of Southern cities. He noted crude benches reserved "for Negroes". First communion was administered on separate days for each race. Vaughan was shocked to discover that in one Catholic cathedral in the South a black soldier was refused communion by a white priest.[27]

Exclusion and racial segregation were not confined to the realm of liturgy. Black Catholics could not belong to most church fraternal organizations, such as the Knights of Columbus.[28] Catholic schools in the South excluded blacks, as did Catholic colleges and universities throughout the country. Most Catholic hospitals and charitable institutions refused to serve blacks, or they segregated clients and patients according to race.[29]

Despite papal exhortations to the contrary, it was next to impossible for a black to get ordained to the priesthood in the United States.[30] Only two blacks took holy orders during the whole of the nineteenth century.[31] In 1903 Joseph Anciaux, a Belgian-born Josephite, recalled that the vicar-general of New Orleans had solemnly informed him that "in America no black man should be ordained. Just as illegitimate sons are declared irregular by Canon Law...so blacks can be declared irregular because they are held in such contempt by whites."[32] In 1930

American Catholicism could boast of only three black priests.[33] Ten years later, only one male religious order and one diocesan seminary accepted black candidates, according to Rollins E. Lambert, the first black to be ordained as a priest in the Archdiocese of Chicago.[34]

In the early decades of this century American Catholicism was still a largely immigrant institution. Highly self-conscious in their struggle to fit into the mainstream of American life, Catholics in this country eagerly embraced the prejudices as well as the more enlightened precepts of their newly adopted land. Hence, Catholics generally responded to blacks according to the local climate within which they found themselves, rather than according to the loftiest teachings of their religious faith. In short, they were in the process of becoming as American as they were Catholic. In 1928 a bitter W.E.B. DuBois reflected on Al Smith's campaign for the presidency. "The Catholic Church, to which Smith belongs, knows no color line in all the world, except in the United States," he wrote. "But here it is 'Jim Crow' from top to bottom, in church attendance, in education, in philanthropy, in missionary endeavor...."[35]

As long as blacks remained largely confined to the Old South, American Catholics scarcely gave them a second thought. But the early decades of the twentieth century saw a massive exodus of black Americans from the South to cities and industrial centers that were north of the Mason-Dixon Line. In 1900 ninety percent of American blacks still lived in the South. Scarcely more than a quarter of American blacks lived in cities.[36] During World War I Southern blacks began to move northward in order to take higher-paying jobs in war factories. This growing diaspora continued between the world wars, largely in response to the mechanization of cotton farming in the South. By 1928 forty-five percent of all black Catholics lived outside of the South.[37] The migration gained further momentum during the years after the bombing of Pearl Harbor.[38] This vast resettlement was "one of the largest and most rapid mass internal movements of people in history—perhaps the greatest that was not caused by the immediate threat of execution or starvation," according to historian and journalist Nicholas Lemann. "In sheer numbers it outranks the migration of any other ethnic group—Italians or Irish or Jews or Poles—to this country."[39] Most restless blacks flocked to urban areas that were scattered throughout the North and West, nearly all of them Catholic strongholds.[40] In Chicago the influx of Southern blacks became such a phenomenon that Samuel Cardinal Stritch would go to the Illinois Central Station to watch the flood of immigrants pour into the waiting room.[41]

As blacks streamed into the North, the church at first tried to confine those few who were Catholic to segregated parishes. In many cities this policy had prevailed since the last decades of the previous century. It rarely was questioned. Where there were enough black Catholics to warrant it, the church began to set apart one parish in each city as reserved solely for blacks. These parishes generally were under the care of religious order priests. Although blacks would sometimes attend local white churches, they found that white clergy and laity tried hard to encourage them not to join such parishes. In Chicago blacks were not allowed to become full members of white parishes. As the trickle of blacks northward gathered momentum, more black Catholics began to attend white parishes. Whites deserted their neighborhood parishes in response. Parish populations (and revenues) often plummeted.[42]

Across the land white urban parishes became increasingly black as more black Americans moved into the cities and more white Catholics fled to the suburbs. Segregation became a function of economics as well as of episcopal fiat. A handful of suburban parishes made fleeting efforts to appeal to their inner-city counterparts. But increasingly, parishes flourished in the ring of suburban neighborhoods that encircled the older urban areas, while inner-city parishes languished financially and sometimes had to close for lack of funds.[43]

In reaction, some clergy left together with the local white laity and sought refuge elsewhere in all-white parishes. Other priests stayed and tried to stem the flood of black parishioners into urban parishes. Still others assumed a ministry among their new black parishioners and eventually began to agitate on their behalf. In nearly every Northern city at least one Catholic priest would emerge to minister to black newcomers and to champion their demands.[44] Dorothy Day's Catholic Worker Movement, begun in New York City in 1933, and Baroness Catherine de Hueck's interracial Friendship House in Harlem, launched in 1938, appealed to blacks in conspicuous and sometimes controversial ways.[45]

The massive influx of blacks into Northern cities also encouraged the beginning of scattered civil rights groups within American Catholicism. The Committee for the Advancement of Colored Catholics began in 1916.[46] In 1924 Thomas W. Turner, a professor at Howard University, founded the Federation of Colored Catholics to lobby for equal rights for blacks within the church.[47] That same year John LaFarge, SJ, Catholic journalist and later editor-in-chief of the Jesuit weekly *America*, gathered nearly two dozen black Catholics to consider ways in which the lot of blacks within the church might be improved. This group later became known as the Catholic Laymen's Union and worked steadily to advance the cause of racial equality.[48] In 1934 LaFarge helped to begin the first Catholic Interracial Council, which was organized to educate Catholics with regard to the need for racial justice within the church. Within a decade the Catholic Interracial Council had spawned a number of local organizations throughout the country and had become the preeminent organization within the American church to advance the cause of racial equality.[49]

As blacks moved northward, Catholic schools became a forum for the evangelization of blacks to Catholicism. Sisters, priests and laity also proselytized door-to-door with some success.[50] Meanwhile, the "GI Bill of Rights", which underwrote the tuition and living expenses of World War II veterans, enabled some blacks to apply to Catholic institutions for the first time. Among Catholic colleges, those that educated nonresident students opened their doors to blacks first. The rest slowly integrated, but only a few at a time.[51] In 1950, shortly after the Kentucky state legislature repealed legislation which had forbidden racial integration in public or private schools, Louisville's three Catholic colleges— Bellarmine, Nazareth and Ursuline—opened their programs to students of every race.[52]

In the years that followed World War II the momentum for racial integration began to accelerate on other fronts. For decades Catholic bishops in the United States had issued collective statements on the need for racial justice. Now, in the postwar years, a number of Catholic bishops began to integrate church facilities within their respective dioceses. Those prelates who began to mandate integration won widespread attention from Catholic and non-Catholic sectors of American society. One of the earliest and most conspicuous episcopal champions of civil rights was Archbishop (later Cardinal) Joseph E. Ritter. In 1947 Ritter called for the integration of parochial schools in St. Louis.[53]

Ritter's policy represented a sharp break with the past. When he arrived in St. Louis, schools, churches and most Catholic facilities were racially segregated.[54] Ritter's predecessor, John Cardinal Glennon, had resisted calls for diocesan racial integration, always with the insistance that the time was not yet ripe.[55] Glennon once imprudently informed a lay Catholic that he found blacks to be violent, ungrateful and irresponsible. He confided his fear that integration would one day lead to the horrors of miscegenation.[56]

Glennon's successor could hardly have chosen a more dramatic departure from the old "separate but equal" approach to Catholic race relations. In the spring of 1947, a few months after his installation as the archbishop of St. Louis, Ritter ordered the desegregation of Catholic schools throughout the city.

When Ritter instructed his pastors "to accept all children into parish schools without regard to race", his directive was met with quiet resentment from many pastors, especially among those whose parishes were nearest to the black ghetto.[57] Priests who worked in the black mission were widely known by colleagues as the "nigger priests".[58] Most pastors who objected to Ritter's directives, however, kept their dissent private.

Many parishioners were more overt in their resistance. Some Catholics organized themselves to thwart the official policy of integration through the courts. Parents from dozens of parishes created a group that was innocuously called the Catholic Parents' Association of St. Louis and St. Louis County. They requested a meeting with Ritter or one of his subordinates to explain their complaints. When Ritter ignored their request, the parents discussed whether they should go to court and ask for an injunction to prevent the integration of parochial schools. Ritter responded through a pastoral letter in September 1947 that threatened the excommunication of any Catholic who tried to thwart diocesan integration of parochial schools. The Parents' Association appealed to the apostolic delegate, Amleto Cicognani. The latter responded with a statement of complete support for Ritter's actions. The Parents' Association disbanded shortly thereafter. Its leader, a paint contractor and member of a local parish named John P. Barrett, remarked: "If it gets to the point where I have to sit beside the Negro to keep my religion I'll do it...."[59]

The difference in style and substance between Glennon and Ritter helps to explain why American Catholicism began to win for itself the reputation of a church that promoted civil rights for blacks. Like Glennon, church officials who resisted racial integration often did so quietly, sometimes even under the disingenuous guise of concern for racial harmony. Such priests and prelates drew little attention to themselves as opponents of integration. By contrast, prelates like Ritter who championed civil rights for blacks often did so in forthright and highly publicized ways. They drew attention to their support for racial justice. This reinforced the growing American impression of Catholicism as a faith that supported racial integration.

Other bishops began to mandate racial integration in the early postwar years. In 1949 Archbishop Joseph F. Rummel of New Orleans directed that signs which read "For Colored" be removed from churches throughout the archdiocese. Pastors were told to direct their ushers to allow blacks access to all Catholic churches.[60] Shortly thereafter, Rummel ordered the integration of the deanery and diocesan unions of the Holy Name Society, Sodality and the National Councils of Catholic Men and Women. In March 1953 he had a pastoral letter read from all pulpits which directed that "there be no further discrimination or segregation in the pews, at the Communion rail, at the confessional and in parish meetings.... Our colored Catholics...should not be harassed when they attend services in any parish church or mission, or when they apply for membership in parish organizations." Nine years later Rummel won national press coverage when he excommunicated three lay leaders in Plaquemines Parishes, one of them a prominent local political figure, for their outspoken resistance to racial integration.[61]

Not all Catholic bishops promoted racial justice. But many prelates from a variety of points on the religious and political spectrum, from progressive to conservative, supported civil rights. This gave the impression, not entirely erroneous, of a growing episcopal front for racial justice. Soon after his installation as the archbishop of New York in 1939, conservative Francis Spellman announced (at the dedication of a new school in Harlem): "This is a Catholic school – not a Negro school – which any Catholic child who is qualified is entitled to enter."[62] He added, "There are no schools for Negroes. There are no schools for whites. There are only schools for all children."[63] One of Spellman's first official acts as archbishop was to confirm black children.

In Washington, shortly after he became the archbishop of the nation's capital in 1948, Patrick O'Boyle rescinded the canonical regulation that pastors and ushers had used to prevent blacks from entering white churches.[64] O'Boyle gradually desegregated Catholic institutions in the northern part of the city between 1948 and 1952.[65] He began to desegregate Catholic schools throughout the city in September 1948. By 1952 all of them, elementary and secondary, were opened to blacks.[66] Archbishop O'Boyle helped religious leaders of other faiths to create an Interreligious Committee on Race Relations (ICR). The ICR labored to open new employment and housing opportunities for blacks in the nation's capital. It later worked for passage of the Civil Rights Act of 1964 and helped to organize the March for Jobs and Freedom (the famous civil rights march of August 1963) in Washington.[67]

In the years that followed World War II, the Chicago chancery was widely and accurately construed to be a friend of racial justice. Samuel Cardinal Stritch was acutely aware of the depth and breadth of racial animosity in Chicago, a city which by the postwar years was forty percent Roman Catholic.[68] Stritch, a close personal friend and principal public ally of Saul Alinsky (labor organizer and head of the Industrial Areas Foundation[69]), directed the archdiocese to help fund Alinsky's controversial work on behalf of racial integration in Chicago neighborhoods, to the abiding dismay of Mayor Richard Daley. The mayor despised Alinsky, whom he regarded as a political intruder and troublemaker. For years Daley was forced to sustain political relations with Alinsky, in large part because the archdiocese remained Alinsky's principal patron. Daley tried mightily but unsuccessfully to sever archdiocesan links to Alinsky. The mayor once cornered John Egan, head of the archdiocesan office of urban affairs, and told him: "Father, I think you should be careful of your association with some of these people in community organizing. They're not your kind of people."[70]

After Stritch died in 1958, episcopal support for Chicago racial justice continued. When Martin Luther King, Jr. took his movement to Chicago in 1966, Archbishop John P. Cody joined him in a much-publicized press conference at which the movement's agenda was announced and priests and nuns were invited to participate in the Southern Christian Leadership Conference (SCLC) campaign in Chicago. Cody's presence at the conference was an auspicious sign for King, since the archbishop had successfully cultivated strong ties with Mayor Daley, the police force and the city's business leaders.[71] In early July of that year Cody issued a forceful statement that supported King's Chicago civil rights campaign and listed the public and private agencies which had neglected the rights of Chicago blacks. The *New York Times* described it as the strongest statement on behalf of racial justice that was ever issued by a Catholic archbishop.[72] Cody paid a price for his imprimatur to King's Chicago campaign. In the summer of 1966 the archbishop found himself besieged with irate phone calls and letters from white Catholics. When the SCLC began to march through all-white neighborhoods, Cody appeared on the scene in time to witness white violence against the marchers. Some priests informed the archbishop that Chicago Catholics carried placards such as "Archbishop Cody and his commie coons".

Cody defended the marchers by writing, "They have not been guilty of violence and lawlessness, others have."[73] Yet eventually he began to waver in his support of the SCLC campaign. The archbishop asked King's movement to rethink its strategy, and warned that otherwise "the result will very likely be serious injury to many persons and perhaps even the loss of lives." Finally, he supported Mayor Daley's call for an end to the civil rights marches, a decision which struck many Chicagoans as more sympathetic to the mayor's objectives of peace and order than to King's strategy for the promotion of racial justice.[74]

The FBI tried to exploit Cody's ambivalence towards King and his branch of the civil rights movement. In 1966 an FBI agent was dispatched to present negative "evidence" with regard to King to the archbishop in the hope that Cody might be dissuaded from further association with the movement. The agent reported in return that the archbishop was "not impressed" with King, thought he had "a glib tongue" and "will do everything possible to neutralize King's effect in this area."[75] Yet, despite Cody's ambivalence with regard to local civil rights marches, Chicago Catholicism had come a long way since the early days of the century when George Cardinal Mundelein tried to herd all "coloreds" into a single parish (staffed by a religious order) which languished safely on the South Side.[76]

Cody's circumspection towards Martin Luther King, Jr. exemplified a strain of episcopal caution that occasionally tried to exert a restraining influence upon the civil rights movement. Some bishops seemed at times to believe that racial integration could be achieved solely by efforts within established channels. Such prelates wanted to help effect a seismic change in the established order, while at the same time to avoid any upset to the establishment. Thus many of them shied away from individuals and movements that seemed more inclined to agitation than to cooperation. During the famous march on Washington in late August 1963, Archbishop O'Boyle agreed to appear on the platform with civil rights leaders and to deliver the invocation. Days before the march, the archbishop received an advance copy of a strident speech to be delivered by the chairman of the Student Non-violent Coordinating Committee (SNCC), John Lewis, in which Lewis compared the civil rights movement to Sherman's march through Georgia and threatened to inflict a "scorched earth" policy on those parts of the South that resisted racial integration. Encouraged by the Kennedy administration, O'Boyle threatened not to deliver the invocation unless the more incendiary passages in the text were scrapped. In the end Lewis relented and delivered a considerably toned-down text.[77]

Although he was a genuine friend of racial justice, New York's Cardinal Spellman suspected that the civil rights movement might be communist-inspired. Uncomfortable with public challenges to authority of any sort, Spellman thought of sit-ins and freedom marches as close to subversive.[78] In 1965 Apostolic Delegate Egidio Vagnozzi inquired as to Spellman's reaction to priests and religious who participated in protest marches. Spellman replied: "My personal opinion is not in favor of these demonstrations."[79] The year before, Spellman had promised FBI director J. Edgar Hoover that he would try to persuade the Vatican not to schedule Martin Luther King, Jr. for an audience with Pope Paul VI. When Spellman proved unable to sabotage the meeting, Hoover wrote: "Astounding.... I am amazed that the Pope gave an audience to such a degenerate."[80]

A few bishops were unmitigated in their contempt for the civil rights movement. In Los Angeles, James Cardinal McIntyre described civil rights demonstrations as the conspiratorial work of mischief-makers. McIntyre gave the distinct impression that he believed that blacks actually preferred segregation. As late as 1966 he forbade priests in his archdiocese to preach on racial topics.[81] Los Angeles clerics privately implored the cardinal not to make derogatory racial remarks.[82] In the winter of 1967 New York's Senator Robert

F. Kennedy complained to Paul VI about problems of poverty and race in America. He lamented that when it came to race relations, the church in Los Angeles "was a reactionary force...." The pope reminded Kennedy, "You cannot judge the Church by its representatives in Los Angeles."[83]

In retrospect, Kennedy's complaint seems to have been a suggestive one. Indeed, the Kennedy name had helped to forge a link (however improbable) in the public imagination between Catholicism and racial justice. In the early 1960s the image of a Catholic president who supported civil rights legislation implied to many Americans that Catholics were at least potential friends of racial justice. The impression antedated the Kennedy administration, and it sometimes worked against Catholics. When John Kennedy ran for president in 1960, his religion became an even greater source of suspicion in the South, because so many Southerners identified Roman Catholicism with vanguard efforts to encourage compliance with the Supreme Court's desegregation decisions.[84] When Kennedy asked Lyndon Johnson to run on the ticket with him, some Southerners around the Texas senator argued that "for Johnson to run on such a ticket of civil rights and Catholicism would be treason to the Old South."[85] (Southern whites were not alone in their suspicion of a Catholic candidate. Harris Wofford, one of Kennedy's principal advisors on civil rights, later wrote of "the anti-Catholic mood of many deeply Protestant Negro clergymen."[86] Martin Luther King, Sr., himself a Baptist minister, had signed a newspaper endorsement of Richard Nixon, because of King's religious prejudices against the prospect of a Catholic president.[87])

Although John Kennedy's support for civil rights may have strengthened the American perception that Catholics were inclined to promote racial justice, there is no evidence that Kennedy's Catholicism informed his views on racial matters in any significant way. However much Kennedy may have been appalled and even angered by segregation and racial oppression, he does not seem to have approached civil rights from a particularly religious perspective. Arthur Schlesinger, Jr. was doubtless right when he wrote of John Kennedy: "One can find little organic intellectual connection between his faith and his politics."[88] Despite his Roman Catholic roots, Kennedy was decidedly secular in his approach to politics. Wofford recalls: "Unlike...President [Kennedy's] relations with Whitney Young and Roy Wilkins, which were easy and sophisticated, there was always a strain in his dealing with [Martin Luther] King, [Jr.], who came on with a moral tone that was not Kennedy's style and made him uncomfortable."[89] Kennedy envisioned himself as tough and practical. Equally uncomfortable with the labels "Catholic" and "liberal", he took few if any of his political cues from any particular strain of American Catholic thought. Sergeant Shriver, Kennedy's brother-in-law (who had helped to create the National Catholic Interracial Movement, and led its Chicago branch), found himself excluded from the Kennedy inner circle because he was regarded as too liberal, too impractical, too aligned "with the intellectual wing of the Catholic Church."[90] Still, the perception endured, at least in some sectors of American society, that Kennedy supported civil rights because he was Catholic.

John Kennedy's views on civil rights may not have been informed by his Catholicism, but he was prepared to use Catholic as well as Protestant religious leaders to pursue his civil rights agenda. In May 1963 Kennedy invited a variety of religious leaders to the White House, where he asked them to lobby Congress on behalf of the bill which eventually became the Civil Rights Act of 1964. Father John Cronin, who represented the National Catholic Welfare Conference at the White House meeting, organized an ecumenical gathering at Georgetown University to guarantee effective lobbying as the bill moved towards a final vote. These same clergymen later lobbied President Johnson to propose a voting rights bill.[91] Georgia's Senator Richard Russell was moved to complain that the Civil Rights Act of 1964 passed because "those damned preachers got the idea it was a moral issue."[92]

During the 1960s the civil rights movement became increasingly identified in the public imagination with "those damned preachers". In 1960 sixty Catholic Interracial Councils had joined with similar groups to found a national organization, the National Catholic Conference for Interracial Justice (NCCIJ). The merger was made to professionalize and unite efforts on behalf of racial integration.[93] Three years later this organization helped to form the National Conference on Religion and Race, the first interfaith organization to commit itself to the civil rights movement. When the group first met in January 1963, seven hundred religious leaders attended and urged the creation of local interfaith groups in ten cities across the United States to bring Protestants, Catholics and Jews together to work for racial equality. The NCCIJ organized Catholic participation in the August 1963 March on Washington. Two years later the NCCIJ was largely responsible for the orchestration of Catholic participation in the march from Selma to Montgomery, and for the procurement of ecclesiastical approval for the participation of priests and religious in the march.[94]

In the minds of much of the American public, Catholic clergy and religious became more solidly identified with the civil rights movement because of their widespread participation in the march from Selma to Montgomery in March 1965. Martin Luther King, Jr. publicly invited the nation's clergy to take part in this pilgrimage of protest.[95] Although Archbishop Thomas Toolen of the Diocese of Mobile-Birmingham denounced the participation of clergy and religious at Selma, insisting that they "should be home doing God's work",[96] more than four hundred Catholic priests and religious, along with a large number of Catholic laity from over fifty dioceses, helped to fill the ranks of marchers, joining with Protestant ministers and rabbis (including Rabbi Abraham Joshua Heschel).[97] Most of the sisters were still in full habit and, thus more readily identifiable, helped to gain much publicity for Catholic participation in the protest.[98] When news came over the radio that the Alabama state legislature had accused the participants of engaging in free love, fornication and constant orgies, several nuns among the marchers joked about their shattered reputations.[99] "Among Black youths," writes historian Cyprian Davis, "few can appreciate the euphoria of Blacks at seeing so many whites ready to sacrifice themselves for the cause of racial justice."[100]

Archbishop Toolen was not the only Catholic who resented the growing participation of Catholic clergy and religious in protest marches for racial integration. Catholic resistance to the civil rights movement appeared throughout the country. In Chicago some priests supported "improvement associations" that were created to keep blacks out of previously all-white neighborhoods.[101] Shortly before Bishop Richard Gerow of Natchez-Jackson, Mississippi ordered desegregation of Catholic schools throughout his diocese, one monsignor remarked: "Now you know segregation is not sinful. If it is, how come we've had it in the Church for so long?"[102] In the autumn of 1966 the Louisville *Record* supported passage of a local open-housing ordinance by the Louisville Board of Aldermen. Yet the archdiocesan paper admitted that many pastors chose not to take a lead in the promotion of such legislation. More than a few pastors readily conceded that "they are not leading the way" on the issue of open housing, according to the archdiocesan weekly. "Most of them, in fact, don't really want to."[103] New York's Father George Barry Ford later wrote:

> I remember a dinner at which the denial of rights to our fellow citizens was discussed. One of those present suggested that if every member of the clergy of all faiths spent five minutes every Sunday proclaiming the iniquity of segregation and discrimination, the consequences would be incalculable. I agreed, but pointed out that it would be necessary first to convince every member of the clergy that this was the right thing to do—and how many clergymen would agree?[104]

David Kirk, a radical priest in New York who had spent some time with Dorothy Day's Catholic Worker Movement and who founded Emmaus House, a New York locus of radical Catholic activity in the 1960s, once recounted how he had converted to Melkite Catholicism during his studies at the University of Alabama. He recalled: "What made me uneasy was the reactionary character of the Roman Catholic Church. In my part of Alabama, the Church was the Irish Catholicism associated with racial and political conservatism."[105] Supreme Court Justice Clarence Thomas remembers the pervasive racism which he encountered while in attendance at the previously all-white St. John Vianney Minor Seminary in Savannah, Georgia during the early 1960s. Thomas recalls that while he was hurt and dismayed by the discrimination which he endured at the hands of fellow classmates, he was shocked that the faculty and staff seemed to accept such prejudice as though it were entirely natural.[106]

Still, those priests who resisted integration usually did so quietly, rather than risk the wrath of the local ordinary. Like their scattered episcopal counterparts who dragged their feet with regard to racial integration, such clerics received relatively little press attention, even when they were effective in momentarily stymieing efforts towards racial justice. Thus, such priests did not often create the impression that Catholics as a whole were opposed to racial justice.

Many Catholic laity also responded with hostility to the church's growing support of racial integration. In 1953, when Bishop Vincent Waters of Raleigh, North Carolina mandated the racial integration of churches within his diocese, reaction ranged from reluctant compliance to violent defiance. Waters faced a mob as he presided at the first racially integrated service of one North Carolina church.[107] When Catholic desegregation began in southern Maryland in 1956, one mission church closed after parishioners refused to offer further financial support.[108] When Martin Luther King, Jr.'s marches made forays into neighborhoods on the southwest side of Chicago in the summer of 1966, many of the white teenagers who demonstrated against the marchers wore scapulars around their necks and shirts that bore the names of Catholic schools.[109]

Occasionally those laity who openly defied their local ordinary were excommunicated. On 17 April 1962 New Orleans' Archbishop Rummel excommunicated three Louisiana Catholics for their open resistance to church efforts towards racial integration.[110] Leander Perez, one of those excommunicated, asked: "How come we could have slaves, separate schools and churches for these Negroes for ages and ages and now all of a sudden it's a sin? Seems to me like some Communist got some kinda spell over that man [Rummel]."[111] Unlike Perez, most Catholics who resisted integration did so quietly and thus avoided the impression that they did so as Catholics. Although many were singularly unmoved by the local bishop's call to integration, they did not often defy him openly. Their resistance to integration appeared more frequently in public opinion polls than in front-page headlines. A 1966 survey of Louisville Catholic laity reported that sixty percent believed that open housing was not a moral issue. Seventy-two percent said that priests and religious should avoid any part in open-housing demonstrations.[112] White American Catholics responded to race questions much as did their Protestant counterparts. Catholics took virtually no part in the Congress of Racial Equality (CORE) or the NAACP during the 1950s. Young Catholics took little part in the early sit-ins and freedom rides. Yet the public perception of the church was one of active support for civil rights for blacks.[113]

If white Catholics often reacted to the church's promotion of civil rights with hostility, black Catholics often responded with suspicion. In mid-April 1968 the Catholic Clergy Conference on the Interracial Apostolate met in Detroit. On 16 April, hours before the opening session of the conference, more than sixty black priests met and issued a startling manifesto to the church in America. The statement began: "The Catholic Church in the United States, primarily a white racist institution, has addressed itself primarily to white society and is definitely a part of that society.... And unless the church, by an immediate, effective and totally reversing of its present practices, rejects and denounces *all* forms of racism within its ranks and institutions and in the society of which she is a part, she will become unacceptable in the Black community."[114] The black clergy urged greater control by blacks of Catholic institutions in the black community and warned that the church "is rapidly dying in the black community.... In many areas there is a serious defection...on the part of black Catholic youth.... The black community no longer looks to the Catholic church with hope."[115]

The black priests had a point. Even church leaders who were the most sympathetic to racial justice found it considerably easier to embrace civil rights, both for society as a whole and within their respective dioceses, as long as it remained primarily a question of racial integration. When racial justice became a question of how to incorporate black culture into the larger Catholic community, the challenge became more problematic and Catholics proved to be more reluctant to change.

Integration was fine only so long as it connoted a melting pot, with blacks presumably melting into the larger cauldron of white Catholicism (in much the same way that Catholic immigrants once had blended into the mainstream of American culture).

Although recent public opinion polls suggest that American Catholics today are considerably more tolerant on racial questions than are their Protestant counterparts,[116] black Catholics still experience pervasive forms of more subtle racism. For that matter, they often find themselves regarded as all but invisible within the larger Catholic community. In many cities, churches that were built by immigrant communities now find that former immigrants and their children have retreated to the suburbs, while black families from the central cities have moved into the downtown parishes.[117] Often black parishes find that middle-class blacks move out and the parishes fail financially, thus tempting church officials to merge black parishes, an option which seems more satisfactory to ecclesial bureaucrats than it does to local black parishioners.[118] Bishop Joseph A. Francis, auxiliary bishop of Newark and chairman of the bishops' committee that in 1979 drafted the American bishops' pastoral document on race relations in the United States, entitled "Brothers and Sisters to Us", has noted: "There are still parishes, especially in the Northeast, where blacks are not being welcomed or where, if they are allowed to come in, it is with a great deal of reluctance." Francis adds that discrimination often takes forms of which whites are scarcely aware, including the failure to invite blacks to participate in readings at Eucharist, not offering them a say in liturgical planning, music and other forms of religious expression.[119]

In the two decades since the heyday of the civil rights movement, American Catholicism has groped for new ways to remedy such omissions and to meet the needs of black Catholics, as well as occasionally to incorporate the riches of black culture into the larger American Catholic experience. By 1970, when the National Office of Black Catholics was created, virtually all seminaries in the United States accepted blacks, although some were still reputed not to encourage black vocations to the priesthood.[120] In 1984 ten black bishops issued a pastoral letter on evangelization and black Catholics entitled "What We Have Seen and Heard". The first black Catholic congress of this century was held in Washington in 1987, the same year that the Black Secretariat was created to serve the National Council of Catholic Bishops. The following year Eugene Marino became the first black archbishop in United States history.[121] In November 1989 the American bishops voted unanimously to support the National Black Catholic Pastoral Plan in the creation and implementation of a blueprint for evangelization within the black community.[122] Most dioceses with a large black community now include a diocesan agency that is devoted to ministry among black Catholics.[123]

Today black Catholics often admit that the church has become more responsive to their needs, including the need for liturgies that are adapted to their unique cultural experience. In a growing number of parishes within the United States the church allows black parishioners to make the liturgy resemble services that many remember from their experience in the rural South, including gospel choirs and vibrant music with room for spontaneous responses to the rites, African vestments for the celebrant and baptism by immersion for adults. Yet many black Catholics understandably complain that the liturgy remains too European and too white to resonate with the experience of black American Catholics.[124] In 1989 fewer than three hundred of the 54,000 Catholic priests in the United States were black. About one thousand of the 20,000 Catholic parishes in the United States had mainly black congregations, but most of these were presided over by white pastors.[125]

Sidney Hook once insisted that "in any crucial situation the behavior of the Catholic Church may be more reliably predicted by reference to its concrete interests as a political organization than by reference to its timeless dogmas."[126] Catholicism in America has brought its share of complacency, contradiction and cynicism to the struggle for racial justice. Yet, sometime during the middle years of this century, decisive elements within American Catholicism began to realize that the church's self-interest and the interests of racial justice were ultimately one and the same. Someone once quipped that "the church always arrives fifty years late and out of breath." American Catholics came late to the struggle for racial justice. In many ways they remain far behind the cutting edge of what is required to insure equality for Americans of every race. Yet, however halting and desultory their progress, however slow and out-of-breath their gait, American Catholics seem at least (and at last) to be moving in the right direction.

Notes

1 Howard Zinn, *The Southern Mystique* (New York: Alfred A. Knopf, 1964) 127.

2 Cyprian Davis, *The History of Black Catholics in the United States* (New York: Crossroad, 1990) 58; Clyde F. Crews, *An American Holy Land: A History of the Archdiocese of Louisville* (Wilmington, DE: Michael Glazier, 1987) 92-94.

3 Davis, *Black Catholics* 36-38; Albert J. Raboteau, *Slave Religion: The "Invisible Institution" in the Antebellum South* (New York: Oxford University Press, 1978) 112.

4 Davis, *Black Catholics* 47-48, 65, 116.

5 Davis, *Black Catholics* 40, 51-52, 65, 89, 117; Crews, *Holy Land* 92-94, 149-151.

6 Arthur M. Schlesinger, Jr., *The Disuniting of America* (New York: Whittle Direct Books, 1991) 9.

7 Davis, *Black Catholics* 121.

8 Davis, *Black Catholics* 33-34, 181.

9 Richard A. Lamanna and Jay J. Coakley, "The Catholic Church and the Negro," in *Contemporary Catholicism in the United States* (ed. P. Gleason; Notre Dame, IN: University of Notre Dame Press, 1969) 151.

10 Davis, *Black Catholics* 120, 132.

11 Davis, *Black Catholics* 127.

12 Davis, *Black Catholics* 200.

13 David Margolick, "Judge Portrayed as a Product of Ideals Clashing with Life," *New York Times* 3 July 1991, 1.

14 George Barry Ford, *A Degree of Difference* (New York: Farrar, Straus & Giroux, 1969) 143.

15 William A. Osborne, *The Segregated Covenant: Race Relations and American Catholics* (New York: Herder & Herder, 1967) 20; Raboteau, *Slave Religion* 271-272.

16 Davis, *Black Catholics* 231.

17 Jay P. Dolan, *The American Catholic Experience* (Garden City, NY: Doubleday, 1985) 359.

18 Lamanna and Coakley, "Catholic Church" 149.

19 Lamanna and Coakley, "Catholic Church" 149.

20 Lamanna and Coakley, "Catholic Church" 149.

21 Davis, *Black Catholics* 200.

22 Osborne, *Segregated Covenant* 29.

23 Osborne, *Segregated Covenant* 29.

24 Lamanna and Coakley, "Catholic Church" 153-154.

25 Gunnar Myrdal, *An American Dilemma: The Negro Problem and American Democracy* (New York: Harper, 1944) 1.870.

26 Davis, *Black Catholics* 200; Dolan, *Catholic Experience* 365.

27 Osborne, *Segregated Covenant* 23.

28 Davis, *Black Catholics* 219.

29 Davis, *Black Catholics* 219; Osborne, *Segregated Covenant* 99.

30 Davis, *Black Catholics* 219.

31 Dolan, *Catholic Experience* 360.

32 Davis, *Black Catholics* 197.

33 Dolan, *Catholic Experience* 360.

34 Lamanna and Coakley, "Catholic Church" 170, 172; Rollins E. Lambert, "The Negro and the Catholic Church," in *Roman Catholicism and the American Way of Life* (ed. T.T. McAvoy; Notre Dame, IN: University of Notre Dame Press, 1960) 162.

35 Osborne, *Segregated Covenant* 124.

36 James Hennesey, *American Catholics: A History of the Roman Catholic Community in the United States* (New York: Oxford University Press, 1981) 305.

37 Lamanna and Coakley, "Catholic Church" 153-154.

38 Nicholas Lemann, *The Promised Land: The Great Black Migration and How It Changed America* (New York: Alfred A. Knopf, 1991) 6.

39 Lemann, *Promised Land* 6.

40 Lamanna and Coakley, "Catholic Church" 159.

41 Lemann, *Promised Land* 70.

42 Dolan, *Catholic Experience* 365-366.

43 Dolan, *Catholic Experience* 447-448.

44 Dolan, *Catholic Experience* 367-368.

45 Lamanna and Coakley, "Catholic Church" 158.

46 Davis, *Black Catholics* 218.

47 Dolan, *Catholic Experience* 368.

48 Dolan, *Catholic Experience* 369; Daniel G. Reid, ed., *Dictionary of Christianity in America* (Downers Grove, IL: Intervarsity Press, 1990) 627.

49 Dolan, *Catholic Experience* 369.

50 Hennesey, *American Catholics* 305.

51 Osborne, *Segregated Covenant* 35.

52 Crews, *Holy Land* 303.

53 Dolan, *Catholic Experience* 368.

54 Donald J. Kemper, "Catholic Integration in St. Louis, 1935-1947," *MHR* 73.1 (October 1978) 9.

55 Dolan, *Catholic Experience* 368.

56 Kemper, "Catholic Integration" 13.

57 Kemper, "Catholic Integration" 2.

58 Kemper, "Catholic Integration" 8.

59 Kemper, "Catholic Integration" 3-5; Osborne, *Segregated Covenant* 112-113.

60 Osborne, *Segregated Covenant* 74. When Rummel, by this time aged and nearly blind, arrived at St. Peter's to attend the first session of Vatican II, the assembled bishops gave him an enthusiastic ovation because of his courageous support of racial integration (Robert E. Tracy, *American Bishop at the Vatican Council* [New York: McGraw-Hill, 1966] 22-23).

61 Hennesey, *American Catholics* 306; Osborne, *Segregated Covenant* 75-76.

62 Osborne, *Segregated Covenant* 130.

63 Hennesey, *American Catholics* 305.

64 Hennesey, *American Catholics* 95.

65 Hennesey, *American Catholics* 305-306.

66 Osborne, *Segregated Covenant* 95.

67 Osborne, *Segregated Covenant* 111.

68 Lemann, *Promised Land* 70, 123.

69 Lemann, *Promised Land* 97.

70 Lemann, *Promised Land* 100.

71 Harris Wofford, *Of Kennedys and Kings: Making Sense of the Sixties* (New York: Farrar, Straus & Giroux, 1980) 212.

72 Kathleen Connolly, "The Chicago Open-Housing Conference," in *Chicago 1966: Open-Housing Marches, Summit Negotiations, and Operation Breadbasket* (ed. D.J. Garrow; Brooklyn, NY: Carlson, 1989) 69-70.

73 Connolly, "Open-Housing Conference" 69-70.

74 Connolly, "Open-Housing Conference" 69-70.

75 Wofford, *Kennedys and Kings* 212; Stephen B. Oates, *Let the Trumpet Sound: The Life of Martin Luther King, Jr.* (New York: Harper & Row, 1982) 391.

76 Edward R. Kantowicz, *Corporation Sole: Cardinal Mundelein and Chicago Catholicism* (Notre Dame, IN: University of Notre Dame Press, 1983) 212-214.

77 David J. Garrow, *Bearing the Cross: Martin Luther King, Jr. and the Southern Christian Leadership Conference* (New York: Random House, 1988) 282-283, 677.

78 John Cooney, *The American Pope: The Life and Times of Francis Cardinal Spellman* (New York: Times Books, 1984) 283-284.

79 Cooney, *American Pope* 283-284.

80 Wofford, *Kennedys and Kings* 208-209; David J. Garrow, *The F.B.I. and Martin Luther King, Jr.: From "Solo" to Memphis* (New York: W.W. Norton, 1981) 121. Hoover, one of King's most industrious and influential detractors, dispatched one FBI agent to dissuade Marquette University from awarding King an honorary degree. When the agent

succeeded, Hoover rewarded him with a special commendation and financial reward (Wofford, *Kennedys and Kings* 208).

81 Osborne, *Segregated Covenant* 226-227.

82 Cooney, *American Pope* 283.

83 Arthur M. Schlesinger, Jr., *Robert Kennedy and His Times* (Boston: Houghton Mifflin, 1978) 781.

84 Herbert S. Parmet, *Jack: The Struggles of John F. Kennedy* (New York: Dial, 1980) 502.

85 Wofford, *Kennedys and Kings* 56-57.

86 Wofford, *Kennedys and Kings* 56-57.

87 Wofford, *Kennedys and Kings* 12-13.

88 Arthur M. Schlesinger, Jr., *A Thousand Days: John F. Kennedy in the White House* (New York: Crown, 1965) 108.

89 Wofford, *Kennedys and Kings* 128.

90 Wofford, *Kennedys and Kings* 45; Lemann, *Promised Land* 114.

91 Garry Wills, *Bare Ruined Choirs: Doubt, Prophecy, and Radical Religion* (Garden City, NY: Doubleday, 1972) 146-148.

92 Garry Wills, *Bare Ruined Choirs* 146.

93 Lamanna and Coakley, "Catholic Church" 163.

94 Lamanna and Coakley, "Catholic Church" 164-165.

95 Davis, *Black Catholics* 256.

96 Osborne, *Segregated Covenant* 15.

97 Osborne, *Segregated Covenant* 15; Dolan, *Catholic Experience* 447; Wofford, *Kennedys and Kings* 181, 188.

98 Cyprian Davis, "Four Days in Selma," *Suggested Readings* (February 1989).

99 Wofford, *Kennedys and Kings* 194.

100 Davis, "Four Days".

101 Osborne, *Segregated Covenant* 207.

102 Osborne, *Segregated Covenant* 92.

103 Crews, *Holy Land* 326.

104 Ford, *A Degree of Difference* 116.

105 Cooney, *American Pope* 285-286.

106 Margolick, "Judge Portrayed" 1, 9; Neil A. Lewis, "From Poverty to the Bench, Clarence Thomas," *New York Times* 2 July 1991, 11. In 1967 Thomas entered Immaculate Conception Seminary in northwestern Missouri to begin studies for the priesthood. Friends recall that on the day that Martin Luther King, Jr. was assassinated, Thomas was watching television coverage of the tragedy with fellow students. Thomas heard one white student remark, "That's what they should do to all the niggers." Thomas later told friends that he thought, "We're supposed to be people of God. If people have that view here, then this is not a place for me to be." Shortly thereafter he left the seminary (Margolick, "Judge Portrayed" 9).

107 Osborne, *Segregated Covenant* 46.

108 Hennesey, *American Catholics* 306.

109 Osborne, *Segregated Covenant* 203; Dolan, *Catholic Experience* 447.

110 Osborne, *Segregated Covenant* 85.

111 Osborne, *Segregated Covenant* 78.

112 Crews, *Holy Land* 326.

113 Osborne, *Segregated Covenant* 14.

114 Lamanna and Coakley, "Catholic Church" 168-169.

115 Davis, *Black Catholics* 257-258; Lamanna and Coakley, "Catholic Church" 168-169.

116 George Gallup, Jr. and James Castelli, *The American Catholic People: Their Beliefs, Practices, and Values* (Garden City, NY: Doubleday, 1987) 59.

117 Anthony DePalma, "Catholicism is Embracing More Blacks," *New York Times* 24 January 1989, 7.

118 DePalma, "Catholicism" 7.

119 DePalma, "Catholicism" 7.

120 Lamanna and Coakley, "Catholic Church" 170, 172; Dolan, *Catholic Experience* 447.

121 Davis, *Black Catholics* 260.

122 Cyprian Davis, "Brothers and Sisters to Us: The Never-Ending Story," *America* 162 (March 1990) 320-321.

123 Davis, "Brothers and Sisters" 321; DePalma, "Catholicism" 7.

124 DePalma, "Catholicism" 7.

125 DePalma, "Catholicism" 7.

126 David J. O'Brien, *Renewal of American Catholicism* (New York: Oxford University Press, 1972) 202.

Social Sin and Fundamental Option*

Mark O'Keefe, OSB

The renewal of the Catholic theology of sin has progressed significantly since the period immediately prior to Vatican II. Personal sin is understood more in personalist and relational terms rather than exclusively in terms of individual acts and laws. Furthermore, many have come to view sin not primarily in terms of discrete actions, but in terms of a fundamental option at the core of the person. At the same time it has come to be more clearly recognized that sin is a social, as well as a personal, reality. This has resulted in a distinct theology of social sin. Despite the renewal of the theologies of personal sin and social sin, however, it must be noted that these developments have occurred largely in isolation from one another. This separation, while understandable in light of the tasks that are involved in the renewal of each, has resulted in the neglect of the *interrelationship* of personal sin (as fundamental option) and social sin.

How is the fundamental disposition of the individual person to be understood in relation to the social world in which s/he lives? In his 1976 book *Liberating Grace*, Leonardo Boff proposes that a strong interrelation exists between the "fundamental project" of persons and the cultural projects of the societies to which they belong.[1] Because humans are socially constituted, in part by their multiple relationships with the culture in which they find themselves, cultural directions and relationships will exercise a strong influence upon the most basic project of each individual. Although each person possesses an irreducible core that can resist or rise above the cultural norms, such resistance will always be difficult because of the enormous pressures of the cultural project. In proposing a relationship between cultural and individual projects, Boff's work suggests that the relationship between social sin and personal sin be understood as fundamental option. It will be the purpose of the present essay to further the examination of the interrelation between social sin and fundamental option, with a particular focus upon the social nature of freedom, knowledge and value.

Fundamental Option

The most basic tenet of a theology of personal sin as fundamental option is that sin cannot be understood primarily in terms of individual acts but only in terms of the person's basic "life direction" or orientation. The fundamental option, positive or negative, represents the person's response to the innate human longing for God and to God's gracious self-offering in Christ. At his or her deepest core, the person either says a fundamental "yes" or "no" to God, and this orientation is expressed in the dynamism of daily choices and in developed habits (virtues and vices).

Beyond its most basic lines, fundamental option theory has been developed in a number of different ways—none of them mutually exclusive. Bernard Häring, for example, who draws especially from scripture and from contemporary psychology, identifies the fundamental option with the biblical image of the "heart" as the deepest core of the person where conversion and authentic relationship with God develop.[2] Joseph Fuchs focuses upon the Thomistic understanding that the human is ordered to God as the ultimate end, which serves as the foundation for a fundamental option theory.[3] Perhaps the most influential starting point, however, has been the distinction that Karl Rahner has made between the transcendental and categorical levels of freedom.[4]

For Rahner, human freedom is not, in the first instance, the ability to choose between two objects. It is, rather, the capacity to decide about oneself, to dispose oneself and ultimately to say "yes" or "no" to God. This capacity or freedom to accept the divine self-offer is the constitutive core of a person. It is the most fundamental purpose of freedom at this transcendental level to "choose" God—that is, to make a fundamental option for God. The transcendental exercise of freedom becomes the ground for all conscious, categorical choices. The fundamental option itself cannot, however, be fully available to one's consciousness, because one can never grasp oneself totally as an object of knowledge. Sin, most basically, is the negative fundamental option, a life turned away from God, a basic "no" to God's self-offering.

What usually is called "freedom of choice", or what Rahner calls "categorical freedom", is the freedom to choose between different objects. The person consciously deliberates between and among various objects of possible choice. It is at this level of free choice that the transcendental orientation of the person is actualized. Because the transcendent God is experienced in mediated ways, one's transcendental orientation to God is realized in and through individual choices. Although the fundamental option is incarnated in such choices and is unavoidably affected by them, it can never be reduced to these choices. Thus, true personal sin is always mediated in discrete actions but cannot be irreducibly identified with such actions.

The distinction between levels of freedom can be further clarified as one notes the distinction between the value(s) toward which each type of freedom is directed. Categorical freedom is directed at individual, discrete values that are present in particular situations and that serve human flourishing. Transcendental freedom, on the other hand, is directed at the transcendent ground of value itself, which is God and in which all other values participate and have their end. In the choice of particular values in particular situations, the person implicitly chooses God in whom these values participate. Thus, the authentic exercise of categorical freedom is aimed implicitly at God. On the other hand, the fundamental orientation of one's life toward God includes an implicit orientation to particular values. Thus, transcendental freedom seeks to be realized, actualized, in individual choices. In fact, the dynamism of the transcendental "choice" for God seeks to integrate all of one's individual categorical choices into this most basic orientation. Again one sees that the transcendental and categorical levels of freedom are distinct but intimately interrelated.

Sin, understood as the negative fundamental option, is the most basic orientation of one's life *away from* God. The transcendental "no" to God will be realized and actualized in individual choices. The person who is directed away from the source of value cannot hope reliably to choose discrete values in particular situations. Sin will become realized in *sins*—in sinful actions. On the other hand, the positive fundamental option for God cannot be sustained in the face of persistent individual choices that are contrary to the authentic values that are present in a situation. To act consistently and seriously against discrete values is to undermine one's most basic commitment to the ground of all value.

While the perception of sin as fundamental option *does* overcome an older overemphasis upon actions, it continues to focus upon the inner orientation and freedom of the individual. In fact, taken alone, a fundamental option theory of sin might seem as susceptible to claims of individualism as did earlier understandings of sin. This is not the case, however, when freedom, knowledge and value are understood in their appropriate social context.

Knowing and Choosing Value in a Social Context

The freedom of the individual person never exists in a vacuum. While utterly personal, it is not isolated nor completely private. Rather, freedom is always exercised and indeed formed within the limits of physical and biological boundaries but also within the cultural, social, economic and religious environment in which the person develops. Thus, while freedom is not completely determined by social factors (and thus ultimately denied), it is necessarily limited, structured and, even to a degree, constituted by the social world in which the person lives. In his early work on "the sin of the world", Piet Schoonenberg referred to freedom as "situated".[5] Freedom, then, is never totally personal nor totally sovereign. Freedom is itself social,[6] and this is particularly true at the categorical level in which the person chooses between discrete values.

The social nature of freedom is intimately interrelated with the fact that the values which are the objects of free choice exist only within a social matrix. Values are learned precisely from the social world, beginning with the family and extending throughout one's life. In the process of entering into social interaction—socialization—the young person learns what is important and what is not. As the person takes on a role in society (e.g. as a parent, as a working person, or within a profession), s/he learns the implicit priorities and values of that role. Knowledge of values, then, like freedom, is a social reality.

Constituted in part by his or her social relationships, the person generally will appropriate uncritically the prevailing values of a culture—even though from an objective standpoint an outsider may see quite readily that the prevailing hierarchy of values is seriously disordered. Pope John Paul II has criticized western culture, for example, for the overemphasis that it places upon material goods and success, implicitly arguing that the prevailing cultural hierarchy of values is disordered. Similarly, a person will be largely blind to those values that are not embodied in their culture and its institutions. This is clearly exemplified in situations of sexism and racism, where the value of women and persons of color as well as the distinct values that are held by marginalized groups either are ignored or are relegated to a secondary place.

One sees that knowledge and freedom are intimately interrelated—to serve or to hamper the development of one is to serve or to hamper the development of the other. Freedom is directed inherently to value and ultimately to God in whom all values participate. If freedom were unencumbered by sin, a clear perception of value would lead naturally to the choice of the value. Knowledge and freedom would work harmoniously. The presence of personal and social sin, however, makes both the perception of value and the free response to it more difficult. When the knowledge of value is obscured, the development and action of freedom is hindered; and, on the other hand, when freedom is encumbered, the knowledge of value cannot be pursued.

The social embodiment of value and the social nature of freedom do not deny the ability of persons to transcend, criticize and even reject the prevailing values of their own culture. To claim that freedom and knowledge are "situated" is not to claim a form of determinism. At the same time, however, the embodiment of authentic value in society becomes crucial for the authentic development of persons. When society and its institutions manifest values and an authentic hierarchy of values, authentic human development is served. On the other hand, when authentic values are not manifest or their priority is skewed, the authentic development of persons will be more difficult—and this social situation will be difficult to overcome.

The social nature of knowledge and of freedom is clearly operative at the categorical level, where the person recognizes value and chooses to act for values. This has obvious implications for fundamental option itself, since the exercise of transcendental freedom cannot be isolated from the social interrelationships in which the person finds himself or herself. When the person is ignorant or acts against values at the categorical level, his or her fundamental option inevitably will be affected. The ability of the person to make, maintain and integrate a fundamental option for God will be influenced by that person's ability to recognize and to act upon authentic values in the social world. To understand how this is so, I will now turn to an examination of social sin itself.

Social Sin

While the social world in which one finds oneself is value-laden, it may also hide values, fail to embody certain important values or skew an authentic prioritizing of values. In this sense, social sin creates what Häring refers to as "value-blindness", [7] an inability to recognize and act for certain types of values or for particular values precisely because these values are absent in the social world. The blinding of persons to authentic values through their absence within structural relationships is an important aspect of social sin.

Gregory Baum's identification of four levels of social sin can serve to demonstrate how social sin blinds persons to value.[8]

The first level of social sin involves the injustices and dehumanizing trends that are built into the various societal institutions which embody people's collective lives. The injustices and dehumanizing trends within these structural relationships indicate that the inherent value of certain persons and some of the values that are essential to authentic human development have been hidden, masked or skewed in society.

The second level of social sin involves the cultural and religious symbols, which are operative in the imagination and fostered by society, that legitimate, reinforce and intensify the injustice and dehumanizing trends within the society. Symbols are the vessels in which values are enshrined and the avenue by which values enter the human imagination, self-understanding and worldview. When cultural and religious symbols mask or hide values, they support the structural relationships that perpetuate injustice and that hinder authentic human development.

The third level of social sin, according to Baum, involves the "false consciousness" that convinces persons that those actions which are based upon the ordinary structures of society and its prevailing symbols are right. At this level one sees that an entire worldview has been created in which even people of good conscience base their decisions upon an inauthentic ordering of values.

The fourth level of social sin is the level of collective decisions that are generated by this false consciousness, which further increase the injustices and dehumanizing trends that already are present. The blindness to value and the hierarchy of values is perpetuated by the ongoing interactions of persons who make decisions based upon their false consciousness.

Bernard Lonergan's notion of "bias" further highlights the power of social sin to blind a person to value.[9] "Bias" can be understood as the tendency to eliminate from consideration select data upon which to base understanding, judgment and decision because such data is perceived as a threat to the person's well-being. Bias is thus a threat to the authentic development of persons that requires the ability to challenge and transcend accustomed modes by which the self and the world are viewed. The harm to authentic personal development cannot but harm the authentic development of society.[10]

According to Lonergan, bias functions at both the individual level and the social level. Particularly relevant to the concept of social sin is what Lonergan calls "group bias", the tendency of a group to eliminate from all consideration that data which threatens the self-understanding, status and power of the dominant group. Bias therefore serves to eliminate certain particular values or types of value from consideration, because to accept the value would threaten the group. One can see here the "false consciousness" that is grounded in the group's symbols, that prevents its members from recognizing and acting on authentic values.

The interrelationship, then, of the categorical exercise of freedom and social sin can be readily seen. Human choice, the exercise of categorical freedom, exists within the context of the person's social interrelationships—including structural, institutional relationships. The individual choices of each person thus exist within the context of the values that are embodied or hidden within each society and within the context of the social development of personal freedom. When values are hidden by bias or their priority is skewed, the person will have greater difficulty in the choice of authentic values versus those which prevail in society. Likewise, when the person has not developed or witnessed a consistent ability to choose values in preference to mere satisfactions or in the face of obstacles and societal pressure, it will be more difficult to choose in a way that is contrary to this ordering—either in individual situations or in the sustained and habitual development of virtue.

Social sin, therefore, constructs a strong tendency to choose lesser values or to act against authentic values, a tendency that already is present *within* the person because of original sin. The disordered sense of value from outside meets the internal tendency to choose the lesser value in situations of choice or to act for mere satisfaction rather than for value. Social sin, like concupiscence, then, is an inducement to personal sin. But, since sin resides primarily at the transcendental level, according to fundamental option theory, such categorical actions against authentic value cannot immediately be identified as sin, properly speaking. Such disordered actions are sinful actions to the degree in which they manifest a negative fundamental option, signal its reversal or weaken the vitality of the positive fundamental option.

Although social sin represents a powerful tendency toward disordered actions, the identification of social sin and personal sin—even at the categorical level—is not a simple matter. Someone, for example, who uncritically accepts the materialistic bias of his or her culture cannot immediately be said to be guilty of personal sin. According to the traditional criteria for the determination of the true sinfulness of an action, mortal sin requires full knowledge, full freedom and grave matter. But social sin operates precisely to create a form of ignorance about value and a weakened ability to choose values freely. When people are truly ignorant of value, they cannot be guilty of true personal sin. In the same way, when the development of their freedom has been seriously hindered by societal pressures, people cannot be guilty of personal sin. Such pressures operate very subtly. We may think, for example, of the manner in which prevailing materialism affects the person's ability to grasp authentic values (and thus to choose these values) and their ability to choose contrary to prevailing patterns.

Further, the type of knowledge that is at stake in questions of sin is not an abstract, theoretical acceptance of values (conceptual or speculative knowledge) but a true, experiential and personal grasping of values (evaluative knowledge).[11] It is an evaluative recognition of value, grounded in personal and communal experience, which moves one to action—not an intellectual acceptance of value. Social sin, therefore, can influence persons very deeply even at those points when they are taught quite clearly by moral authorities about the nature of authentic values. At times, wider society can exercise such a powerful and even dominant influence that people find it extremely difficult to attain a true evaluative knowledge of authentic value. They are unable truly to grasp the value as worthy of choice, or are unable to muster sufficient moral effort to attain it in the face of obstacles.

Just as social sin and personal sin at the categorical level cannot be identified in a simple manner, neither can it be argued that social sin *causes* personal sin. People have the power to rise above prevailing societal values and disvalues, although it must be added immediately that such resistance may be extremely difficult to initiate or sustain in the face of societal pressures. Thus, while one can deny a strict determinism, human experience requires one to deny as well any understanding of freedom as unaffected by the environment. People have the (situated) freedom to act contrary to the influence of social sin. In fact, they have a responsibility to do so. The fact of powerful societal influences on human freedom and knowledge cannot be used to exonerate a person of the responsibility to overturn social sin. One may recall here the traditional notion of "culpable ignorance": a blindness to value for which a person is responsible. Häring talks as well about a "culpable loss of freedom".[12] Ignorance or impotence against the force of social sin should not be an easy excuse to perpetuate injustices and dehumanizing trends in society. This is especially true for Christians who belong to a community where an authentic knowledge of values is taught (though not always experientially grasped) and models of authentic exercises of freedom are enshrined (e.g. saints). The teaching and witness of Jesus, the perfect human, is certainly the most authentic illustration of value and of freedom.

Social Sin and Fundamental Option

As a powerful influence upon the categorical level of freedom, social sin exercises a subtle and indirect but nonetheless strong influence upon the fundamental option, the level at which sin, properly speaking, resides. As an exercise of transcendental freedom, fundamental option cannot be identified simply with choices that concern those individual values that are embodied or hidden by a particular society. At the same time, however, transcendental freedom is the ground of categorical choices and inevitably is affected by them. The relationship, then, between fundamental option and social sin is rooted in the relationship between the transcendental and categorical levels of freedom. Just as categorical choices influence and affect the fundamental option without being identified with it, so too social sin influences and affects the fundamental option without determining it.

All authentic human values mediate and participate in God as the creator and ground of value. To choose values and to act on their behalf is an implicit, though not direct, choice for God as their transcendent ground. This clearly is true where persons have a positive fundamental option, a life that is directed toward God. When such persons choose to act on behalf of a value, they are implicitly choosing God, and their categorical choice is a mediation of their transcendent orientation toward God. Right action then reinforces and strengthens the commitment of the person to the ground of value. To act against a value, on the other hand, contradicts the positive fundamental option—influencing it, weakening its commitment, though not necessarily reversing it entirely.

When the social world hides or skews values and fails to aid the development of authentic freedom (at the categorical level), the fundamental option is necessarily affected. Social sin affects the ability of the person to know and choose value. Thus it hinders the person's ability to know and choose the creator and the transcendent ground of value. The face of God is obscured further by blindness to values that are a manifestation of the divine goodness. When, for example, people are born into a world with subtle but powerful forces of racism, sexism and materialism, they will largely be blind to a whole realm of important values that can point them toward the creator and sustainer of these values. This is most especially true when people do not fully grasp the value of other persons who are the very image of God.

Social sin cannot, therefore, "cause" a reversal of a positive fundamental option anymore than it can determine freedom of choice. And yet, within the context of social sin in its various manifestations, the person's ability to strengthen his or her positive fundamental option through right choices will be lessened. The fundamental disposition of oneself at the transcendental level seeks not only to manifest itself in categorical choices but to integrate further all such choices into one's transcendental orientation. When social sin urges categorical choices that are contrary to this orientation, the ability to strengthen the fundamental option is made more difficult. Social sin hinders the integration that strengthens the fundamental option and makes a tragic reversal possible.

Social sin, therefore, does not "cause" either wrong choices or the reversal of a positive fundamental option, but it does exercise an influence upon both levels of freedom. Social sin creates an environment in which it becomes more difficult to make good choices and in which the positive fundamental option becomes more difficult to integrate and strengthen. In fact, social sin heightens the tendency that is present because of original sin to turn away from God, that is, to sin personally and mortally.

Conclusion

The fundamental option is the fundamental disposition of the self to God at the deepest core of the human. It therefore is utterly personal and irreducible. And yet, the transcendental "yes" of the person to God exists in the context of the "yes" of the entire body of Christ, extended in space and time, and is united to the "yes" of the head of the body, Christ himself. The positive fundamental option is incarnated in a world that is permeated with grace, mediated through persons and events, challenging the person to an ever-deeper response to God. But it is incarnate too in a world that is burdened by sin, which threatens the dynamic growth of the person's self-disposition to God. In the same way, the transcendental "no" of sin exists in the context of the history of human sin, the "sin of the world", dragging the sinner more deeply into the mire of sin. Even more, however, the negative fundamental option finds itself in a world of grace that calls the sinner to conversion.

The proper response to sin—in oneself and in the world—is conversion. For the person with a negative fundamental option, conversion is the turning back at his or her deepest core to God. For the person with a positive fundamental option, conversion is the daily, continual effort to integrate all of one's choices into this fundamental option for God. The response to *social* sin involves this individual conversion, but it demands no less the conversion of the societal structures that mask values and hinder the authentic development of human freedom.

The two conversions – personal and social – are inseparable. It is precisely those persons who have embraced values and their transcendent ground through the positive fundamental option who will work to embody such values in social relationships. On the other hand, the ultimate durability of any personal conversion and the ability of others to convert will require that authentic values be recognized and chosen within their social context. The positive fundamental option thus aims to overcome the blindness and constraints that are caused by social sin, even as the strengthening of the positive fundamental option is aided by the transformation of society so that authentic values are enshrined more perfectly in societal relationships and structures.

Notes

* An earlier version of this article appeared under the same title in *Irish Theological Quarterly* 58 (1992) 85-94.

1 Leonardo Boff, *Liberating Grace* (trans. J. Drury; Maryknoll, NY: Orbis, 1979) 141-147.

2 Bernard Häring, *Free and Faithful in Christ* (New York: Seabury, 1978) 1.164-222.

3 Joseph Fuchs, *Human Values and Christian Morality* (Dublin: Gill & Macmillan, 1970) 92-111.

4 Karl Rahner, *Theological Investigations* (New York: Crossroad, 1982) 6.178-196; *Foundations of Christian Faith* (New York: Crossroad, 1982) 90-115.

5 Piet Schoonenberg, *The Sin of the World: A Theological View* (trans. J. Donceel; Notre Dame, IN: University of Notre Dame Press, 1965) 104-106, 111-118.

6 Peter Hodgson, *A New Birth of Freedom: A Theology of Bondage and Liberation* (Philadelphia: Fortress, 1976).

7 Häring, *Free and Faithful* 1.183-184.

8 Gregory Baum, *Religion and Alienation: A Theological Reading of Sociology* (New York: Paulist, 1975) 200-203.

9 Bernard Lonergan, *Insight: A Study of Human Understanding* (reprint ed.; New York: Harper & Row, 1978) 218-242. The relationship of bias and social sin is discussed more explicitly and is furthered by Patrick Kerans, *Sinful Social Structures* (New York: Paulist, 1974) 77-78; Matthew Lamb, *Solidarity with Victims: Toward A Theology of Social Transformation* (New York: Crossroad, 1985) 2-12; Nancy Ring, "Sin and Transformation from a Systematic Perspective," *CS* 23 (November 1984) 303-319.

10 Lonergan refers to "societal decline" as the long-term social effect of bias (*Insight* 218-242).

11 Richard M. Gula, *Reason Informed by Faith: Foundations of Catholic Morality* (New York: Paulist, 1989) 83-87; Timothy O'Connell, *Principles for a Catholic Morality* (San Francisco: Harper & Row, 1990) 58-64.

12 Bernard Häring, *Sin in the Secular Age* (Garden City, NY: Doubleday, 1974) 135-136, 165-168; and, *Free and Faithful* 1.262-263.

Addiction: A Promise Betrayed

Bridget Clare McKeever, SSL

"Hi, I'm Gerry and I am an alcoholic. I started drinking when my husband died. The alcohol helped me to cope; it was like a miracle, at first!" "Hi, I'm Judy and I'm a pill addict. My doctor put me on Valium when I was going through my divorce. It helped me through. Ten years later I was still on Valium and hooked." "Hi, I'm Cliff and I am a compulsive gambler. I started gambling as an escape from an unhappy marriage and a boring job. It was great for a while. Two bankruptcies later I was still gambling. It wasn't so great any more but I couldn't quit."

In each of these twelve-step meeting introductions there is a common theme: the substance and the behavior were experienced initially as a salvation from a painful situation.[1] Not all addicted persons would describe the beginnings of their addiction as a dramatic experience of liberation in an overwhelming situation. Nevertheless, the expression "I felt no pain" is a recognizable description of "being high" on something, whether a drug or a process. There is an experience of rising above, escaping from, getting beyond a state of anxiety, fear, pain or simply discomfort.

Addiction creates the illusion of freedom while it breeds dependency. The thesis of this essay is that freedom and dependency are fundamental elements in the human condition, and that addiction creates a destructive facsimile of a radical and creative dynamic. This thesis will be elaborated through a brief exposition of some aspects of Karl Rahner's theological anthropology and a discussion of the structure and dynamics of addiction, both individual and systemic. Finally, the essay will discuss how freedom and dependency operate in the recovery process.

Freedom as Transcendence

In his book *Nature and Grace*, Rahner discusses the traditional view of nature as "what we experience of ourselves without revelation"; and grace as a "super-structure above man's [*sic*] conscious spiritual and moral life".[2] He then questions the adequacy of this notion of nature and grace, and ends with the argument that grace penetrates not only our essence but also our existence. For Rahner, one's entire spiritual existence is permeated by grace, which places a person in an order of being that transcends what is given in nature. Whereas, it is possible to have "primitive nature" (untouched by grace), in fact, human nature is always "nature in a supernatural order...." The substructure of graced nature, however, is the human condition of "openness to infinite being".[3] According to Rahner, the human experience of "openness to the infinite" takes the form of "infinite longing, radical options, discontent which cannot find rest, anguish at the insufficiency of material things, protest against death, the experience of being the object of love whose absoluteness and whose silence our mortality cannot bear, the experience of fundamental guilt, with hope nevertheless remaining."[4]

Rahner's transcendental anthropology implies that the very meaning of human existence is not exhausted by the psychological, sociological or biological dimensions of personhood. These modes of being are, however, ways in which God's presence is mediated and in which God is known as the fulfillment of all existence.

Richard McBrien summarizes Rahner's anthropology as follows: "...the human person is capable of transcending himself or herself in the knowledge of God to whom his or her own life is oriented because God is already present in the person as the transcendent force or condition which makes such knowledge possible."[5] It is this capability, this openness to transcendence that makes women and men at once human and both responsible and free. Responsibility and freedom at this level are not a datum of empirical investigation. They are, as Rahner conceives of them, subjective experience, that is, that which is known when a person experiences herself or himself, but not when one is the object of scientific reflection.

> When the subject experiences himself [sic] as subject and hence as the existent which, through its transcendence, has an original and indissoluble unity and self-presence before being, and when this subject experiences his [sic] action as subjective action although it cannot be made reflective in the same way, then responsibility and freedom in an original sense are experienced in the depth of one's own existence.[6]

This transcendental freedom is not only experienced at the depth of one's being, however, it also is mediated by concrete reality. This mediated form of freedom, in the action in which it is incarnated, is always ambivalent. Whether an action upon the part of an individual can be interpreted as the product of original freedom in any particular instance is a question that cannot be determined theologically. The incarnation of transcendental freedom eludes unambiguous reflection.[7]

In summary, Rahner places radical freedom in one's natural orientation towards the infinite and in the power to make choices that tend towards that infinite. The former is given with nature, the latter is given as grace. Freedom, however, has an essential concomitant—dependency. We are radically dependent upon God. In the first instance, people are dependent because God is the source and object of human longing and, without God, this yearning would remain forever unsatisfied. Secondly, people are dependent because the power to choose God above all is not innate but a gift from God.

Existential Transcendence as a Source of Anxiety

The fact that humans are open to the eternal and yet are themselves finite gives rise to anxiety. They must live in a tension in which they make responsible choices without the absolute assurance that these choices will lead to the ultimate fulfillment of their destiny. Their primitive nature also is oriented towards self-preservation. This orientation renders them divided in desire. On the one hand, they clutch whatever may promise temporary survival; on the other, they long for the eternal, the attainment of which means to risk and even to lose the temporal. And finally, although they know with certainty that they must die, they still must live, without empirical certainty, the hope of eternal life. Each of these human conditions gives rise to pain regardless of whether one's choices lean towards one's ultimate destiny or towards the deviation from that destiny by "eating, drinking and being merry".

Radical dependency also generates anxiety. One is dependent upon what one cannot control, upon God and upon God's free gift of self. Because freedom and dependency are fundamental to human existence, there is no escape from the anxiety that they generate. One either must live one's anxiety authentically or evade it and seek to substitute an illusion of omnipotence. As we shall see later, the cost for the maintenance of this illusion is an enslaving dependency to something other than God.

Psychoanalytic Theory and Addiction

Freudian psychoanalytic theory, if it is freed from Freud's biological reductionism, throws light upon transcendence and its facsimile, addiction. Here one needs to recall that nature, even in its most primitive form, already is an openness to whatever transcends the finite self. Moreover, nature is always graced nature, and therefore is capable of the transcendence of the encapsulated self in an on-going movement towards the infinite. With this Rahnerian insight in mind, I now will examine and expand Freud's understanding of the structure and development of the human personality.[8]

In Freud's theory, the newborn's first experience of the environment is discomfort. In this experience one might say that the first primitive movement towards transcendence is generated by the need to overcome discomfort, a need that finds expression in a cry. The cry typically will bring a nurturing response from the mother, which thus engenders comfort. The primary process of experienced pain and its replacement by pleasure is set in motion. In the course of maturation and psychic growth the primary process develops into a secondary process with its corresponding principle of reality. Gradually the person becomes able to satisfy the need to survive through a real object, food. The pleasure principle never disappears, however. Ideally it merges with the reality principle and becomes attached to real activities that enhance the person and, at least, do not interfere unduly with the fulfillment of need by others.[9] In the healthy person a further stage in transcendence is reached in the ability to sublimate, that is, in the ability to redirect some of that instinctual energy from personal pleasure and need fulfillment to activities that are more acceptable socially and that contribute to the well-being of others.[10] In this movement from the "needy self" to the mother and, further, to other sources of comfort, one sees the primitive matrix of transcendence. The human infant is not a being unto itself. Its freedom to survive depends upon others.

Contrary to what Freud believed, however, transcendence does not end there. Survival is not an end in itself, but an openness to further transcendence. Had Freud not been so convinced of his biological determinism, he might have seen a further and fuller transcendence in sublimation. Here, rather than simply being seen as a being that disposes of surplus instinctual energy in a socially acceptable way, the person can be seen as an entity that possibly can transcend mere self-interest in order to contribute to the well-being of others and to express (as in works of art and religious endeavors) the common human desire for the eternal.

For all of its limitations, Freudian theory does, however, throw light upon the dynamics of addiction. His focus upon the biological roots of human behavior has merit, because it indicates a possible relationship between addiction and a fixation at or regression to the level of the "pleasure principle".

Addiction as Primary Process

Fundamental to addiction is the discovery that a substance or process is able to give pleasure or alleviate pain. Not everyone who makes this discovery and avails of it, however, becomes an addict. It seems that for some, the pain which is alleviated and the pleasure which is experienced are not simply biological. The position of absoluteness that the substance or process holds in the person's life indicates that what is at stake is alleviation of the pain which attends the fact of being human. That existential angst may be enfleshed in some temporary experience of illness, deficiency or loss which may be identified as the cause of the addiction. In the case of true addiction, however, the removal of the apparent empirical cause does not terminate the addiction. It seems to have attained a life and purpose of its own. This phenomenon can be explained in Freudian terms. The person turns to "primary process" (using the pleasure principle), in order to confront an experience of anxiety that calls for sublimation.

Persons who work therapeutically with addicted persons soon are impressed and eventually are appalled by the power that the addiction has over its victim. The addict is like one possessed. S/he sometimes will employ any means in order to satisfy the addiction: steal, lie, rape or murder. Friends, spouses, family personal health often are sacrificed in favor of the addiction, whether it be to drugs, gambling, sex, money, possessions or work. The power of the addiction is understandable, however, when one realizes that it claims the displaced energy of a desire for the infinite. Survival at the most profound level is at stake. The addictive substance or process stands in the place of God. It proves not to be the God of compassion, however, but a Moloch of destruction.

The Anatomy of Betrayal

In her description of alcoholism as a paradigm of addiction, Vernelle Fox says:

> The principles of addiction are quite simple. Pain + relief = dependency. This is a basic phenomenon common to all of us. No problem so long as it is simple physical hunger that is being fed....
>
> For the disorder under discussion the pain is either physical, or psychological, or cultural, but more often than not an intermix of these factors. The relief is a learned experience of self-medication with a

> given, usually increasing amount of the ethyl alcohol with or without sedative chemicals.[11]

I would add that the pain which comes from physical, psychological or cultural sources is the empirical form of the existential pain that was mentioned above. There are, therefore, two reasons that the object of an addiction betrays its user. The object can alleviate pain only at the empirical level. Because it does so, however, it creates the illusion that the underlying existential pain also is alleviated. But it is suppressed, not alleviated. In order to maintain the alleviation of first-order pain and the suppression of second-order pain, it is necessary to take repeated doses of the substance or to indulge in the behavior repeatedly.[12] With the passage of time the substance or the behavior becomes less effective (due to habituation), so that dosages must be increased and/or the behavior is indulged more frequently.

The progress of the addiction creates its own pain. It affects the physical and psychological health of the person and disrupts interpersonal relationships. A new pain and a new guilt is added to the original ones, necessitating an even more intense involvement in the addiction. The person is caught in a vortex in which the addiction becomes both the affliction and the only perceived remedy. The original freedom from pain and the experience of pleasure is replaced by a desperate attempt to halt, or at least to slow, the spiral descent. The object of the addiction is seen as the only way by which to evade despair. The natural life-energy that motivates and enables a person to grow and to become more than s/he has been is radically diminished, and thus the remaining energy is diverted merely to survival. Sometimes the person's freedom to transcend is destroyed so thoroughly that suicide seems to be the only way to escape pain. The last gasp of an almost extinguished hope of escape from pain is a cry for death. The graced freedom to reach for the infinite and the radical dependence upon God that this freedom implies is replaced by an enslavement to and dependency upon the object of one's addiction.

Summary

In the foregoing sections of this essay, I have sought to connect Rahner's theological anthropology with Freud's personality theory. The following is a summary of the movement of that exposition. The human orientation towards transcendence and its concomitant freedom coupled with dependency generates fundamental anxiety. Freud's schema for human development provides us with a cognitive formulation which illuminates the way that this orientation and its associated attributes are developed in the human personality. In the context of human personality development, addiction can be understood as a way to alleviate anxiety temporarily. The addict's solution is understood in Freudian terms as a fixation at the level of primary process (an alleviation of pain or discomfort which creates the illusion of freedom). The outcome of addiction is that the person substitutes a temporary illusion of freedom and an enslaving dependency upon a substance or process in the place of true freedom itself, which comes through grace and radical dependency upon God.

Social Context of Addiction

Openness to the transcendent is not just the fundamental, distinguishing characteristic of persons, it also is the mark of an authentic human society. This urge to overcome limitations, to break through boundaries, has led to spectacular scientific developments, to the conquest of hostile environments and to the improvement in the lot of many. The horizons of finitude have been expanded and continue to widen. As yet, however, the majority of humankind do not benefit from these achievements. Many still remain below the level of subsistence. Others, while they benefit from the affluence that comes from modern technology, do so at the cost of their freedom to be fully themselves. Anne Wilson Schaef, in *When Society Becomes the Addict*, labels western culture as "The Addictive System". Schaef believes that this system is composed of two co-constituting systems: "The White Male System" and "The Reactive Female System". She describes the former as follows:

> I call the system in which we live the White Male System because the power and influence in it are held by white males and perpetuated by white males—with the help of all of us. As the prevailing system within our culture, it runs our government, our courts, our churches, our schools, our economy, and our society. I want to emphasize that I am not talking about individuals. I am talking about a system that all of us have learned and in which all participate. There are as many White-Male-System women as there are men operating in our culture today. I am talking about a system, a world view.[13]

In order to survive in the White Male System women must adjust the way in which they view the world. They must adopt the language, values and thought of the dominant system. To gain acceptance they must deny their own reality and surrender personal power. They are trapped in an externally defined system that tells them what they should think, feel and do. This is the Reactive Female System that is related symbiotically to and supports the White Male System and its myths.[14]

These two systems co-constitute one another and together form "the Addictive Society". As Schaef says:

> ...the White Male System and the Reactive Female System are not two separate systems; instead they are aspects of the same system. They cannot exist without each other. They support and perpetuate each other and are part of an inextricable dualism.... If there were no White Male System there would be no need for a Reactive Female System. If women stopped living in the Reactive Female System, the White Male System would collapse.[15]

The Addictive Society exhibits its addictive nature in several ways. In the first instance, the relationship between its two components is addictively co-dependent. Each is enslaved in the most radical sense; each requires the other for its very existence and identity. Secondary to this basic, addictive mode is the addiction to power and to subservience. The White Male System must have power in order to maintain itself. This power is exercised for the enhancement of the system. It is power over humans, animal life, plant life and inanimate nature. The Reactive Female System must be subservient in order to be accepted and to survive. This subservience is a by-product of the impotence to do anything other than to support or subvert the system. Subversion, however, is not an option so long as one believes that one needs the system in order to survive.

While it may seem that the half of the system that has power is free, this is not the case. The power of the White Male System is contingent upon the subjection and support of the Female Reactive System. Its freedom is an illusion. True freedom leads to a fuller life. The illusionary freedom of coercive power leads to a half-life just as truly as does the impotence of the Female Reactive System. Like the individual, the Addictive Society denies its condition. It has bouts of self-congratulatory grandiosity when it has indulged in an action that has brought euphoria. The cost of that action (as for instance, in war) is carefully concealed when possible. It covers its guilt with self-righteous condemnation of the very addicts that it breeds, deploring their addictions while it profits from them.

The Addictive Society coincides with the Affluent Society because it supports its addiction to power with its addiction to wealth. As with every addict, the more it gets the more it needs. It believes in salvation through accumulation. Here again, as with the individual addict, it seeks transcendence on the horizontal level, warding off pain and seeking to increase pleasure regardless of the consequences to itself as a whole and to its members.

Individual and Social Addiction

At first sight it would seem that individual and social addiction are not related, that they run upon parallel tracks. There are several points where these two forms of addiction touch, however. They have common characteristics. Each is fueled by the need to control. The Addictive Society maintains its identity and position through the control of material resources, of government, of law, of the arts, of weapons of war, even through the control of the belief systems and moral lives of people by means of religious institutions. Its omnipotence is invulnerable because it can discredit and punish anyone who dares to offer critique or to indicate its deficiencies. Similarly, the individual addict seeks to control either through violence or manipulation. S/he even claims to be able to control the addiction itself with the assertion that "I can quit any time I want." In the case of both forms of addiction this control is illusory, because ultimately their practitioners cannot control the consequences. They can only deny them. In the case of both, recovery is possible only when the pain that is attached to the maintenance of the addiction becomes greater than that which is experienced in the relinquishment of it.

Systemic addiction and individual addiction not only are alike, they also are interrelated. As in a dysfunctional family, the addiction of the individual is symptomatic of the addiction within the system. The disorder in the body appears within its members. Moreover, individual addiction is a way to escape the pain of life within the Addictive Society. Finally, as Schaef indicates, the individual addiction renders the members of the Addictive Society unable to challenge the tenets of that society.[16]

There is one way in which the Addictive Society differs from the addicted person. The systemic addiction is not a manifestation of a primary process that is substituted for sublimation. It seems to be, rather, a substitution of a secondary process for sublimation. It is a system that supplies a way to satisfy the need for power, pleasure and possession. In this sense it is a collective inflated ego rather than a wish-fulfilling infant. It is focused upon itself, existing for the benefit of those who create and sustain it. Ironically, both those who profit from this system and those who are its victims often turn to individual addictions in order to alleviate their pain. Alcoholics, drug addicts, compulsive gamblers, etc. are found equally in the slums of our cities and in the affluent suburbs. Apparently, the effort to transcend solely through an accumulation of material things is as unfulfilling as is the lack of the basic means of survival.

Recovery in the Individual: Up from Slavery

As persons recover from addictive disorders, they often describe the reversal in their affliction as "bottoming out".

They had reached the bottom of the spiral and, faced with the radical choice of life or death, they chose life. Sometimes that choice to live is made at the basic level of physical life. For others the choice is to live psychologically or spiritually. At the beginning of recovery the addict finds the extent to which her or his freedom is limited. The urge to indulge in the next drink, the next fix, the next compulsive activity is overwhelming. Those who recover describe their freedom as initially sufficient merely for one day, one hour, even one minute. With the help of grace in the form of the loving support of persons who understand their plight, the duration of that moment of freedom is extended "one day at a time" until the person's energy is freed from the constant need to resist temptation and is made available for more life-giving activities. As is said in recovery circles, the person is freed from the obsession with the object of their addiction.

In the recovery process it is imperative to resist a reflexive response to the need to experience pleasure and avoid pain. This is no easy task for a person who may never have learned to defer gratification or who may have long since forgotten how. The call to transcend at this stage of recovery takes the form of a desire to be able to "be normal", to be able to take reasonable charge of one's life. This desire, when it is strong enough, enables the person to endure the pain that is necessary in order to cope with life without the aid of their "drug". The goal of "being normal", however, is not sufficient for a continued recovery. The person must seek the eternal that is the goal of all human desire and strife, otherwise even the minimal ground of normalcy inevitably will be lost.

Even in the early stages of recovery many people experience a need for the transcendent, a need for "a higher power" that will enable them to maintain sobriety. This movement toward the transcendent can be distinguished from an esoteric interest in religious or theological matters that often is a grandiose way by which to deflect attention from the onerous task of recovery. In recovery it is necessary to experience and embrace one's finitude, to know the void within and without. This experience is the ground of that openness of which Rahner speaks:

> ...infinite longing, radical options, discontent which cannot find rest, anguish at the insufficiency of material things...the experience of fundamental guilt, with hope, nevertheless remaining.[17]

It is a desire to be fully human, and yet to know that one cannot accomplish the task, one cannot even take a step in its direction, without grace. Existential freedom is not the power to accomplish but the willingness to receive and respond to grace. Because this freedom takes the form of receipt and response, it is a continual process that is accompanied by humility. For this reason, one speaks of always "being in recovery", not of being "cured" of one's addiction.

In the recovery process the experience of freedom is radically linked with dependence upon a higher power. Many persons speak of their recovery as a conversion, because it involves not just a change in behavior, but also a radical change in attitude and perception. This change is not merely at the level of actions but at the level of existence. Recovery is not an achievement but a gift.

In this journey toward the transcendent, one still must confront the Addictive Society with its seduction, its coercion, its oppression. Recovery involves the process by which one makes a stand toward one's enmeshment in the Addictive Society. Central to this stand is the recognition of the omnipresence of the Addictive Society. It has infiltrated every institution that impinges upon daily life: the churches, the state, the economic system, the education system, the recreational system—the list is endless. To be immersed naively in any of these systems is to be addicted. No system is God and all people need to pause frequently in order to examine the tenets of all forms of the Addictive Society[18] in light of what each person, in the depth of their being, knows to be true. In some circles this attitude is called discernment; in others, freedom of conscience. It begins with a rigorous honesty within each person, a respect for one's own experiences and perceptions, a test of these perceptions against those of others who likewise take a stand towards the Addictive Society. This stand means a refusal to protect this society from the consequences of its behavior: its stress, its decline in credibility, its boredom, its ludicrousness, its masked dishonesty. It means, if a person is one of its beneficiaries, to throw one's lot with those who suffer most from its oppression. It means to unmask its pretensions, insisting constantly that "the emperor has no clothes".

Addictive societies do not recover spontaneously. They sometimes are overthrown through violence in the name of freedom. In this case they are replaced by equally addictive and oppressive societies. Sometimes they collapse when a sufficient number of their members recover and withdraw their support. Under these circumstances there is greater hope that they will be replaced by systems which nurture and support all life. In such systems freedom would mean the power to transcend the empirical self. In them dependency upon the finite would give way to the interdependency of mutuality that takes its strength from an ultimate trust in God's steadfast fidelity to all. This scenario is surely utopian. Just as the individual in recovery is never "cured", however, so too the system that seeks to recover is never to be equated with the realm of God. It too is constantly "on the way" and is equally dependent upon its higher power, if it is to persevere.

Conclusion

In this essay I have described addiction as a perversion of the fundamental need to transcend and a functional deification of something finite as a means by which to transcend. This perversion turns radical dependency and freedom into enslavement. It traps many people, both individually and collectively, onto a treadmill. In *The Poverty of Affluence* Paul Wachtel describes this treadmill in terms of an "adaptation level theory". Put simply, this theory implies that experiences offer rewards or disappointments, not according to their objective nature but according to one's expectations and assumptions. What once was satisfactory, because it was novel and beyond one's expectations, inevitably becomes a disappointment, because it ceases to surpass our expectations as it is repeated. At best it can only match one's expectations and even may fall short. As Wachtel says:

> Some pleasure may be afforded by our background level of material comfort, but unless we look elsewhere than the accumulation of material goods for the main source of pleasure and excitement in our lives, we are bound to be on a treadmill....
>
> The way off this treadmill, I will argue, lies in focusing more of our aspirations on experiences less subject to the adaptation level effect. Cultivation of the senses and of aesthetic experience can point us towards domains where "more and less" thinking while not completely absent is not so dominant....[19]

Wachtel believes that these dimensions of human aspirations have always been a part of the American experience and even now may be on the rise. He concedes, however, that the reason that is given by the director of a New York museum for involving it in large-scale commercial development ("The fact is that shopping is the chief cultural activity in the United States") contains considerable accuracy.[20] If this is so, then the addictive mentality may characterize more people than might be diagnosed as those who suffer the malady.

Notes

1 Alcoholics Anonymous has devised a process of recovery from alcoholism that consists of a twelve-step spiritual program. The "AA" program has bred many other twelve-step programs for persons who suffer from many kinds of addiction: drug, gambling, over-eating, etc.

2 Karl Rahner, *Nature and Grace* (New York: Sheed & Ward, 1963) 116.

3 Rahner, *Nature and Grace* 133.

4 Rahner, *Nature and Grace* 138.

5 Richard McBrien, *Catholicism* (Minneapolis, MN: Winston, 1980) 1.130.

6 Karl Rahner, *Foundations of Christian Faith* (New York: Seabury, 1976) 37-38.

7 Rahner, *Foundations* 37.

8 See also Don Browning, *Religious Thought and Modern Psychologies* (Philadelphia: Fortress, 1987) 57.

9 Freud uses the term "pleasure principle" to designate the primitive process by which the infant instinctually seeks to alleviate pain or discomfort and receive pleasure. With physical and mental maturation, the pleasure principle is augmented by the "reality principle", which connects the alleviation of pain and achievement of pleasure with real objects in the external world. The reality principle also refers to the growing ability to associate other functions with objects which satisfy the pleasure principle (such as nutrition with respect to food). The pleasure principle corresponds to the "primary process"; the reality principle to the "secondary process".

10 Calvin S. Hall, *A Primer of Freudian Psychology* (New York: The New American Library, 1954) 82, 83.

11 Vernelle Fox, "Substance Abuse: Mechanics and Management," paper presented to the World Congress of Rehabilitation Medicine, Mexico City, Mexico, October 1974.

12 "First-order pain" refers to that pain which arises from a proximate anxiety, for example, anxiety before a job interview that is generated by a fear of failure. "Second-order pain" refers to that which arises from

existential anxiety—the tension between the desire for the infinite and the experience of being finite. My perception is that first-order anxiety is the immediate concrete form which existential anxiety takes in a given instance. To alleviate the first does not resolve the second.

13 Anne Wilson Schaef, *When Society Becomes an Addict* (San Francisco: Harper & Row, 1987) 7.

14 Schaef, *Society* 8.

15 Schaef, *Society* 10.

16 Schaef, *Society* 16-17.

17 Rahner, *Nature and Grace* 138.

18 Schaef, *Society* 17.

19 Paul L. Wachtel, *The Poverty of Affluence* (Philadelphia: New Society, 1989) 23.

20 Wachtel, *Poverty* 23.

With Dignity and Freedom: Quality Religious Education in a Catholic Context

Thomas P. Walters

Religious education concerns itself with the formal search for truth. It is to be conducted in a manner that is proper to the dignity of the individual person and his or her social context. The inquiry, while under the guidance of a teacher or instructor, is to be a free exchange which at all times respects the fact that "faith is the free response to God revealing".[1] This is done by the promotion of "conditions favorable to the exercise of genuine human freedom"[2]—conditions which take into account the age and maturity of the learner[3] as well as contemporary cultural and religious factors.[4]

The following reflections upon the current state of Catholic religious education in the United States are offered not only in the hope of providing some insight into present-day religious education practice, but also with the intent of offering some practical strategies for the implementation of religious education programs that maintain this free exchange in a Catholic Church that is presently a maelstrom of ideologies, theologies and religious practices.

I have chosen to focus upon three areas of agitation: (1) the Catholic community itself; (2) a growing institutional emphasis upon "Getting-Back-to-the-Basics"; and, (3) the overwhelming influence of the ubiquitous television. In the first part of the paper I provide my reflections upon each of these by the identification of three clichés and through a demonstration that each cliché has its own special twist for anyone who is concerned to achieve a quality religious education in today's Catholic Church. The second part of the essay provides some practical strategies for the design and implementation of quality parish religious education programs that respect the freedom and dignity of the participants. My strategies flow from three biases with regard to present-day parish religious education efforts. I state each bias and describe my corresponding strategy.

PART I

Cliché One – We live in a changed and changing church. Trite but true. We currently live in a church where the fond and humorous memories that are captured in books like *Growing Up Catholic* and *More Growing Up Catholic*, and the nostalgia that is paraded on stage in *Do Black Patent Leather Shoes Really Reflect Up?* and *Nunsense*, and the old stereotypical pastor and young assistant who flash on the silver screen in *Mass Appeal*, and even the beloved Father Dowling are precisely that – fond memories, nostalgia and stereotypes of another era. They are not a reflection of present-day Catholicism. They do not portray the reality of the social context of the parishes and schools in which most adult Catholics live their lives and in which today's children are growing up Catholic.

Research on the lifestyles of those who were raised in this fondly remembered church of the 1940s and 1950s provides, at best, a rather complex picture of today's Catholic community. It appears that adult Catholics are more alike in their nostalgia on how they grew up Catholic than they are in their current religious beliefs and practices. Current research shows that there is little, if any, agreement upon what a "good Catholic" looks like or should look like in today's world.

Unlike the 1940s and 1950s, the term Catholic lacks behavioral referents. Even the pollsters find it difficult to identify the Catholic vote. Catholic has become a generic, self-selected term. It embodies a simmering pot of culturally influenced and very diverse religious understandings, attitudes and behaviors. Catholics are as likely to be on one side of an issue as they are to be on the other. Catholic leaders represent a wide diversity of opinion upon political and ecclesiastical issues.

The following is from a recent article in the *New York Times NATIONAL*, under the by-line "5 of 7 on New York Board Support Condom Distribution in Schools":

> "I'm a Catholic," Mr. Fernandez [Schools Chancellor] said. "But I have to give the best recommendations to board members who are faced with the fact that we have been preaching safe sex and no sex, and 80 percent of the kids are sexually active. Then we have to do something else."[5]

A recent *National Catholic Reporter (NCR)*/Gallup Poll of one thousand Catholics found that seventy percent of the respondents indicate that a person can be a good Catholic without going to church every Sunday. Sixty-eight percent believe that one can be a good Catholic without obeying the church's official teaching with regard to birth control. Forty percent do not think that it is necessary to donate time or money to help the poor in order to be considered a good Catholic. And fifty-four percent think that it is not necessary to obey the church's teaching with regard to divorce and remarriage in order to define oneself as Catholic.[6] A report from the *Notre Dame Study of Catholic Parish Life*, "Who is a True Catholic? Social Boundaries on the Church", states that "parishes that express a stronger sense of community are likely to have parishioners who draw boundaries less strict on premarital cohabitation, marriage outside the Church, abortion, homosexuality, and regular mass attendance.... People in parishes where a weaker sense of community is prevalent are more judgmental."[7] In other words, there is no agreement among the members of the Catholic community with respect to who or what a Catholic Christian is or should be. Ironically, the more effectively that parishes build a sense of community, the more likely they are to promote diversity.

The information that we have on the effectiveness of religious education endeavors over the past twenty years is not conclusive. But what is available gives pause for thought. It appears that the majority of today's youth border on illiteracy with regard to church history, theology and knowledge of scripture. In addition, the diversity of religious opinion and religious behavior that is modeled within the Catholic adult community is reflected in the youth. In a study of Catholic undergraduate college students who responded to a question which asked

> whether the Church "should approve of individual variations in doctrinal beliefs among its members" or should "insist on strict standards of doctrinal beliefs," [more] than half of all the students preferred tolerance for variations, the strongest preference being that of campus ministry leaders at Catholic colleges (seventy-one percent).[8]

On the other hand, according to Frank Kelly, the former Executive Director of the Department of Religious Education at the National Catholic Educational Association (NCEA), who agrees that actual intellectual knowledge of today's youth appears "shallow and superficial":[9] "Catholic students have caught quite well the essential kerygmatic message of Christianity: God's unconditional love for all persons, and his [sic] personal care for each individual, as well as the redemption and salvation brought by Jesus, God's Son."[10]

What is not clear in this portrait of today's Catholic community is how much of what currently exists is attributable directly to the endeavors of religious educators and is not simply the result of a cultural context which promotes diversity and the right of every person to determine his or her own self-identity. This hastily drawn portrait of the Catholic community illustrates our first cliché—we live in a changed and changing church. So what is the twist? The twist is that this changed and changing church is not a cliché to today's child. As such, the portrait that I have just painted is neither changed nor changing. It has no history for today's youngsters. It is the present. It *is* the church.

If students are to feel a part of and are to engage themselves as active members in this church, they need to acquire the information and develop the attitudes that will allow them to be part of such a diverse community. They need to learn the skills that are necessary to live their religious lives in what is, from our perspective, a changed and changing church, and from their perspective, simply *the* church.

Cliché Two—We need to get back to the basics.
Even if the 1940s and 1950s were as simple as some seem to remember, they are not returning, so there is no going back. A "quality" religious education will take this fact into consideration. Ironically, the adult Catholic population that is profiled above, which grew up in the 1940s and 1950s and to some extent in the 1960s, were raised in a church that thought it knew what the basics were. It was a unified church where there was an almost one-to-one correspondence between the beliefs that were taught in the religion classrooms of the parochial schools and the Confraternity of Christian Doctrine (CCD) programs and the beliefs and behaviors that were proclaimed and practiced by Catholics in the parish community. There has never been and probably never will be a time like this again. Being Catholic was an agreed-upon lifestyle (Sunday Mass, fish on Friday, weekly confession, May crownings) and a prescribed set of memorized beliefs. Many who grew up during this period still can recite answers to a good number of the questions in the Baltimore Catechism. They learned their catechism and they learned it well. They behaved as they were taught to behave. Why then did they grow up to be the "do-it-yourself" Catholics whose portrait I have just sketched?

It cannot be argued that there was a failure to teach the basics nor a failure to provide a supportive Catholic environment. Parents did their part. Children got the basics in both theory and practice. And here is the twist—our recent past provides no reliable educational "basics" to which to return in sharing the light of faith. It seems foolish to me that anyone would try to argue convincingly that a return to a catechismal approach to religious education will somehow turn things around.

To learn to be religious and to learn what it means to be a Catholic Christian is far more than the mastering of a specific set of beliefs. The Baltimore Catechism approach, which the majority of adult Catholics over forty experienced, did not produce more informed beliefs or more consistent religious behavior. It could not, not in this day and age. Religious educators in a pluralistic society, whether they serve as superintendent of schools, diocesan director of religious education, pastor, director of religious education (DRE), principal or teacher, need a broader vision than a "back-to-basics" uniform teaching of doctrine if they want to promote quality religious education that nourishes a living, active and conscious "faith life" in participants.

Also, to seek uniformity of religious practice appears to be a dead end. Does the true Catholic columnist take positions more in line with Pat Buchanan or Father Robert Drinan? Does the caring Catholic act more like Mother Theresa or Joseph A. Fernandez, New York Schools Chancellor? Does a Catholic prelate minister more like Cardinal Law or Archbishop Hunthausen? Does a Catholic peacemaker behave more like Alexander Haig or Father Daniel Berrigan? Does a Catholic theologian think more like Cardinal Ratzinger or Father Richard McBrien? Does a Catholic newspaper read more like *The Wanderer* or the *NCR*?

The light of faith, when it is so widely refracted in the lives of the members of the community, makes sharing it difficult at best. It also makes the temptation to return to the old way of doing things, namely a catechism, somewhat enticing. But even if we submit to the temptation, the diversity will not disappear. "Who or what is a Catholic Christian?" is a crucial question in the search for a quality religious education for the 1990s. It is a question that every religious educator from bishop to parent would like to answer with certainty. But it is too soon for definitive answers. And it may be that there is no right time and never will be a right time for a definition. To be a Catholic is best described as a quest, not a destination.

Cliché Three—Values are more caught than taught.

This is translated by many religious educators of parents to mean that because parents have the primary responsibility for the education of their children and to raise them within the Catholic tradition, the parents are the primary influence upon the formation of their children's values. It is this interpretation that lies behind the decision of many priests, DREs and principals to involve parents in sacramental preparation and adult education programs. There is truth in this translation, but it is partial and, as a result, misleading. And here is the twist. The values that are caught by and taught to youngsters in today's culture come not from the parents and the Catholic community, but from the larger secular culture through the medium of the television. Parents and the Catholic Christian community are, at best, the re-shapers of the values of their children.

Are Catholics' opinions, thoughts and conversations upon current and historical events more directly affected by what is said on the McNeill-Lehrer News Hour and the Phil Donahue Show, or by what is said by the pope and the local ordinary? Are Catholics' musical tastes determined more by exposure to the constant sounds of the various radio stations and soundtracks for television shows, Broadway musicals and commercials, or by church composers and musicians? Do Catholics' images and metaphors on the meaning of life come more from the movies, or from the scriptures? Does the rhythm of life for Catholics revolve more around the celebration of cultural events, or around the celebration of the liturgical year? If a person's answers fall on the cultural side of these questions, which I am sure they must, think of how much more today's children are influenced by the curriculum of the television, because they are truly a television generation. It is estimated that the average child will spend approximately 15,000 hours in front of a television set by the time s/he reaches the age of eighteen.[11] Neil Postman, in a fascinating little book entitled *Teaching as A Conserving Activity*, argues that the "First Curriculum" in the United States is the television.[12] In his own words:

> Television is both aesthetic and (at least) quasi-religious. Because its primary form of information is the image, its style of teaching is narration. And because of that, it is concerned with showing concrete people and situations toward which one responds by either accepting or rejecting them on emotional grounds. Television teaches you to know through what you see and feel. Its epistemology begins and largely ends in the viscera. As blasphemous as it may appear to say it, television has something of the power we associate with religious communi-

cation, at least in the sense that it relies heavily on moral teachings resting on an emotional base.

Moreover, it is important to say that television commercials, which are subject to easy ridicule by those who know little about information environments, are almost never about anything trivial, especially from the point of view of youth. Mouthwash commercials are not about bad breath. They are about the need for social acceptance and, frequently, about the need to be sexually attractive. Beer commercials are almost always about the need to share the values of a peer group. An automobile commercial may be about one's need for autonomy or social status; a toilet paper commercial about one's fear of nature. Television commercials are about products only in the sense that the story of Jonah is about the anatomy of whales. To miss this point is to miss much of what the television curriculum sets out to do, for, especially in commercials, it is concerned to teach, by parable, that serious human worries are resolvable through relatively simple [and, one might add, materialistic] means and that, therefore, the resolution of anything problematic is never far away.[13]

No amount of academic complaints or "responsible" calls for TV reform can change any of the above. TV is not a school, or a book, or any curriculum other than itself. It does what its structure makes it do, and it teaches as it must. The real programmatic issue is not TV but its relationship to other systematic teachings in the information environment. The question is, to what extent can the biases of TV be balanced by the biases of other information systems....[14]

Those involved in the Catholic Church's educational and catechetical structures are responsible for one of these other information systems. The issue is how they are to exercise their responsibility effectively. I will address this in the next section.

Before I move to the second part of the paper and offer my biases and my strategies for the achievement of a quality religious education, however, let me quickly summarize what I have said up to this point. First, we live in a changed and changing church that is the only known church to today's Catholic youngsters—they have no idea of what it used to be. Secondly, there are no proven "basics" to which religious educators who are concerned about sharing the light of faith in our pluralistic world may return. Finally, parents and church leaders are at best re-shapers of their children's values.[15] So what do we do?

PART II

In this section I will state three biases that I have with regard to the church's present religious education endeavors. Each bias is followed by my suggested strategy for the achievement of a quality religious education that respects both the freedom and the dignity of all who are involved in the formal search for truth.

Bias One—We are overselling the impact that parish K-12 religious education programs can and ought to have on the religious development of participants.

If we are to bring quality to parish religious education programs in the 1990s, we need to promote more realistic outcomes—outcomes that are achievable with the educational structure that is being used. Parish religious education programs generally use a "schooling model" where students meet in classrooms with a teacher for one hour, once a week, for approximately thirty weeks a year. This amounts to 390 hours in a thirteen-year period. This is not much time— particularly when one contrasts it with the 15,000 hours in front of the television and the 11,000 hours in public school classrooms. In addition, teachers in parish programs generally are volunteers, and their teaching ability ranges from very good to poor. The chances that a child will receive consistently good catechists from one year to the next are very poor. Most parish programs use a schooling model, but with none of the supports that the school setting can offer—professional teachers, adequate class time, external rewards such as grades and a supportive learning environment.

As a result, parish programs should not be expected to, nor should they give the impression to parents that they can, achieve the same type of learning objectives that could be obtained if the children were in a formal school setting. The school and the parish religious education program are not the same type of learning environment, and they should not be considered so. Nor should they be compared one with the other. They are different, and thus their intent and their outcomes are different. Directors of religious education and their catechists need to be guided in the design of realistic objectives that flow from the strengths and limitations of the structure that they use. To accomplish this, I would suggest the following "quality-control" guidelines for consideration:

(1) *Quality parish religious education programs should have a limited number of realistic learning objectives.* It is too easy to be unrealistic in one's expectations of what can be done in the once-a-week classroom setting and in the limited time that is available. The fact that bishops, DREs, catechists and parents demand more of the structure does not mean that the structure has the capacity to meet the demand.

(2) *Quality religious education programs should design weekly learning activities that stand on their own.* Each week's learning experience should not depend upon the previous or the following week's activities. This is particularly the case with the younger children whose attention span and memory are unlikely, if not unable, to survive the seven days between classes.

(3) *Quality religious education programs should focus upon the affective not the cognitive.* This does not mean that critical thinking and the ability to articulate the reason why one would choose to be Catholic are unimportant. They are, but they also are unrealistic outcomes for a program that meets only 390 hours during the child's formative years. A quality program will attempt to insure that the learner leaves each session with a positive feeling about the experience.

(4) *Quality religious education programs should involve the parents but not be dependent upon them.* This does not mean that parents are unimportant in their child's religious education. They are, but they cannot be the key variable upon which the success of a classroom-based parish K-12 religious education depends. Each week's learning activ-

ity has to be a self-contained learning experience that can be assessed according to its own merits.

Parish programs should have a positive impact upon the lives of the participants. Religious educators are concerned with how the students will behave when they leave the classroom, that is, when the program's direct influence ceases. Catechetically speaking, they want the youngsters to continue their quest for a faith that is "living, conscious and active". Parish K-12 programs have an important role to fill, but it is a limited role at best. But this does not mean that it should not be time well spent. Each class session can have its impact—limited though it may be. Most often in a person's life it is the little things that make a difference.

Bias Two—Those who are responsible for parish religious education need to involve themselves in public schooling. Postman argues that a part of the solution to the formation of values in a media-dominated culture lies in the proper use of the nation's classrooms. Approximately seventy-nine percent of Catholic youth are being educated in public schools. These youth will spend over 11,000 hours in these schools before they graduate at age eighteen. And, according to Postman, the school's classrooms provide a viable context for the confrontation of the "first curriculum" of the television. This being the case, it seems evident to me that religious educators on both the local and national level have to take a more active role in how they influence the type of formation of values that occurs in today's public schools. As important as efforts are on the local level, they are not enough. Religious educators no longer can confine their efforts to the limited geography of the local parish community or the parochial school.

There are two additional and equally compelling reasons why any bias against involvement in public schooling must be removed. First, there is the risk of trivializing religion. If religious educators limit their efforts to the improvement and promotion of only those structures and programs that function within the parish community, participants cannot help but treat religion as something to be squeezed into one evening each week. The majority of youth and adults will continue to think of religion as something that exists on the margins of real life.

Secondly, there is the real danger that religious education efforts will not keep pace with the educational sophistication that is achieved by our youngsters in other areas of their lives. It is a fact that Catholics, in greater proportion than their number in the population would warrant, receive the best professional and academic credentials that can be acquired in American society.[16] In 1985 approximately one-third of the Fortune 500 chief executive officers were Catholic. Catholics in the United States "no longer worry about being accepted—they worry about how to lead."[17] Thus, religious educators are faced with the challenging decision of how to communicate a religious tradition that always has stressed the need for an informed faith to the best informed Catholic populations in the history of the United States. This is a new and very different type of challenge. The Catholic faith tradition needs to be conveyed in a way that appeals not only to the emotions but to the intellect. There is a need for a religious education that is not afraid of the world and pluralism but that embraces it and, at the same time, is able to critique it intelligently in light of the Catholic tradition.

On the other side of the societal coin are the children of those who are Catholic and find themselves on the margins of the culture—hispanics and blacks. They too have a huge stake in the quality of the nation's public schools, because the system does not work in their favor. The quality of public schooling for these populations is a religious education issue. National, diocesan and local religious educators need to be involved. There is no other choice. The following statement on the results of the most recent Gallup Poll on the public's attitude toward public schools illustrates the point:

> Whites in America seem convinced that, on the whole, blacks and other minority children have the same educational opportunities as whites. This conviction has not changed since 1975, when the question was first asked.... But nonwhites (who make up 14% of the sample in the current poll) have a consistently different view. A disturbing 38% see inequality

> of opportunity in education. Much of the dissatisfaction appears in larger cities, where minority populations are concentrated.[18]

So what are some practical implications of my bias in favor of involvement in public schooling? It seems to me that national organizations like the United States Catholic Conference, the National Catholic Educational Association and the National Conference of Diocesan Directors may need to make a discussion of public education a high priority and to begin now to establish structural relationships with the organizations that service the public school systems nationally. I know this is more easily said than done, especially at a time when many dioceses are experiencing financial difficulties and are making dramatic cutbacks in personnel. Yet, it seems to me that nationally the Catholic Church hardly can afford not to move in this direction.

On the diocesan and archdiocesan levels, I would recommend that religious education offices design a system by which their staff members can keep abreast of what is happening in public schooling both locally and nationally. Initially, the person who is responsible may have to be someone from outside the office and not on the payroll. In every diocese there could be someone who owns, affirms and officially critiques the structure that educates the larger portion of Catholic youth in the United States. This representative could speak forcefully for what Alfred North Whitehead sees as the seamless cloak of learning. "There is only one subject matter for education," he states, "and that is Life in all its manifestations."[19]

It may even be time for a national statement from the bishops on the role, purpose and quality of public schooling in the United States. It certainly could fit within the bishops' social justice agenda for the 1990s. The quality of public schools is a concern of more than seventy-five percent of Catholic parents in the United States, because their children are enrolled in these schools. Even the authors of the recently published *Educational Renaissance,* who uncover many positive signs in the nation's schools at the turn of the twenty-first century, begin by stating that "By and large, our schools are no longer doing their job. Not only is it possible to be graduated from high school without being able to read, write, or perform simple arithmetic, but in many parts of the United States, that is indeed the norm."[20] Imagine the sign value of a statement by the bishops.

Bias Three—The secret to a quality religious education is not to be found by looking backwards.

We presently have two generations in the church who have no personal experience of Vatican II. These are people who were not even born or who were so young when the council was held that it holds no special place as a personal referent. These people do not know the "old" church. The problem is that too many adults from the older generation, myself included, tend to define the present-day church solely in relation to a fondly remembered past. That is, the value of the church is presented by the way in which adults show how things have or have not changed since they were children or young adults. Today's young people presently offer a different challenge. They demand to be shown why it is good to be a Catholic in-and-of itself, and not in comparison to a remembered past. They have no desire to learn what it once was like, because they were not there. Besides, things have changed.

But do we have the people who can do this? Are there people who can articulate in their own words, attitudes and lifestyles an answer to the question of "Why choose to be a Catholic?"—an answer that is grounded in the tradition but speaks to the present and extends hope for the future? Catechesis is the process of initiating and socializing new and younger members into the church by expressing and conveying not only what the church thought itself to be, but also what it is in the present and what it strives to become in the future.

Practically speaking, this means that more time, effort and money must be invested on both the national and diocesan levels to improve the training of catechists and religion teachers. The *National Catechetical Directory* (*NCD*) identifies the principal elements of the Christian message that must be central in all catechesis: "the one God; Creation; Jesus Christ;

the Holy Spirit; the Church; the Sacraments; the life of grace; the moral life; Mary and the saints; and death, judgment and eternity."[21] These elements, according to the directory, "must never be overlooked or minimized, and must receive adequate and frequent emphasis."[22]

There is also a need for critical thinking, however. In catechetical circles a critical thinking approach probably is best articulated by Thomas Groome in his "shared praxis" model of Christian religious education.[23] Groome speaks of the dialectic interaction between the individual learner's story and vision and the "Story and Vision" of the Christian community. Groome's approach is appealing because it holds in healthy tension the religious quest of the individual and the time-honored traditions of the community. For any approach to religious education to be effective in the American church, however, the two foundational elements that were mentioned above—respect for religious questioning and trust in the individual's ability to arrive at reasonable answers—must not only be essential parts of the process but also must be among the intentional results that it promotes publicly.

To be open to religious inquiry requires an attitude on the part of the community and the catechist that is totally respectful of the religious quest of the learner. This attitude allows one to operate under the assumption that all people have, and need to ask, their own religious questions. This attitude of respect is based upon the realization that each individual's religious questions have a uniqueness because of the individuality of the person who asks them. A person's questions are not to be evaluated either as better or worse than someone else's questions, nor as any less important than the time-honored questions of the tradition. No question in one's search for meaning is unimportant or "dumb".

This attitude of respect for an individual's questions is necessary in a church that is marked by diversity, because diversity among sincere and believing people always results in questions. What am I to believe? Why do some in the community believe one thing and others something else? Should I go to Sunday Mass? Is birth control an acceptable option? As a woman, can I continue to serve my God and the

God of the community in a church with a male-dominated hierarchy? These are tough and very real questions for some people. In a church of diversity such questions neither can be ignored nor definitively answered.

This leads to the second essential element—trust in the individual's ability to arrive at reasonable and acceptable answers. The catechist and the catechetical environment must exude a sense of trust in the ability of people to think for themselves and to reach their own conclusions. Catechesis by definition assumes that the persons who are involved have faith. Thus, the role of the catechist and of the catechetical environment is to assist the believer in the process of informing his or her faith. Informed faith relies upon reason. The catechist and the catechetical environment are an essential part of the community's formal attempt to ground faith intellectually. Formal catechesis seeks answers to the who, what, when, where, how and why questions of faith.

The Catholic tradition has long honored the need for faith to seek understanding. What is different today is that it is no longer only priests who need and seek this understanding, but all Catholics. Educated Catholics need more than the Sunday liturgy or involvement in a parish committee or commission to maintain their faith. They need to expose their faith to the critical light of reason. Without this exposure faith is dulled, and meaningful participation in the liturgical and organizational life of the parish community becomes increasingly difficult.

All Catholics need to be affirmed in their ability to think religiously for themselves within the safety of the parish community. They need to know that the community recognizes their right to search for answers to their own religious questions. Without this recognition, both faith within the Catholic community and faith in the Catholic community are on shaky ground. The apparent question is to ask how the community can recognize a person's right to his or her own answers and yet how the community can remain faithful to the Catholic tradition. The more accurate question is to ask how the community *cannot* do this and still remain faithful to the Catholic tradition.

What knowledge, attitudes and behaviors, then, are required to be an active member of the Catholic faith community? Besides the many truths that are identified in the *NCD* as the essentials of the Christian message, I would suggest that in today's church it is imperative that catechists instill in believers the realization that inquiry is a good and a necessary part of an informed faith. Beyond fostering in believers this sense of trust in their own need and ability to ask religious questions, catechists need to develop within believers a strong confidence in their ability to find viable answers, tentative though the answers may need to be. They can do this only if they are encouraged and supported in their efforts by those who are in positions of authority. Also, there is a need for better parish structures that can support this type of critical religious education. Current K-12 parish structures do not do this.

Conclusion

David Lloyd George is quoted to have said, "Don't be afraid to take a big step if one is indicated. You can't cross a chasm in two small steps."[24] It has been my contention throughout this essay that some big steps need to be taken in parish religious education programming. If a quality religious education that respects the freedom and dignity of all is to become a reality in the Catholic Church, religious educators and church leaders need to make some dramatic paradigm shifts both in their thinking and in their actions as they plan their agendas for the 1990s and beyond. Small steps will not complete the task.

Notes

1 NCCB, *Sharing the Light of Faith* (Washington, DC: USCC, 1979) 31 [#58].

2 NCCB *Sharing* 58 [#101].

3 See Chapter 8 in NCCB, *Sharing* 99-123.

4 See Chapter 1 in NCCB, *Sharing* 7-15.

5 Joseph Berger, "5 of 7 on New York Board Support Condom Distribution in Schools," *New York Times NATIONAL* 27 September 1990, np.

6 See William D'Antonio, *et al.*, *American Catholic Laity in a Changing Church* (Kansas City, MO: Sheed & Ward, 1989).

7 David C. Leege, "Who Is a True Catholic? Social Boundaries on the Church," *NDSCPL* 12 (March 1988) 8.

8 Paul Philibert, "New Leadership for Tomorrow's Church," *The Living Light* 22 (June 1986) 306.

9 Francis D. Kelly, "A Church at Risk: Toward Balance in Catechetics," *America* 149 (October 1983) 186.

10 Padraic O'Hare, "A Church at Crisis Point: Conventional or Critical Religious Education?" *The Living Light* 20 (June 1984) 332.

11 Neil Postman, *Teaching as a Conserving Activity* (New York: Dell, 1979) 52.

12 In addition to this book, Postman has written a number of books that religious educators would be well-served to read. The following are three that I have found to be particularly provocative as a parent and as a religious educator: *Teaching as a Subversive Activity* (New York: Dell, 1969); *The Disappearance of Childhood* (New York: Delacorte, 1982); and, *Amusing Ourselves to Death* (New York: Viking Penguin, 1985).

13 Postman, *Conserving* 61.

14 Postman, *Conserving* 68.

15 Martin Marty, "This We Can Believe: A Pluralist Vision," *RelEd* 75.1 (January-February 1980) 48.

16 Andrew Greeley, *American Catholics Since the Council* (Chicago: Thomas More, 1985) 32.

17 Geoge Gallup, Jr., and James Castelli, *The American Catholic People* (Garden City, NY: Doubleday, 1987) 2.

18 Stanley M. Elam, "The 22nd Annual Gallup Poll of the Public's Attitudes Toward the Public Schools," *PDK* 72.1 (September 1990) 47.

19 Quoted in Edgar Dale, *The Educator's Quotebook* (Bloomington, IN: Phi Delta Kappa, 1984) 26.

20 Marvin Cetron and Margaret Gayle, *Educational Renaissance* (New York: St. Martin's Press, 1991) 3.

21 NCCB, *Sharing* 48 [#82].

22 NCCB, *Sharing* 101 [#1762].

23 See Thomas H. Groome, *Christian Religious Education* (San Francisco: Harper & Row, 1980).

24 Quoted in George Keller, *Academic Strategy* (Baltimore and London: The Johns Hopkins University Press, 1983) 164.

Freedom and Communication: Preaching from a Transactional Perspective

Richard C. Stern

A selection of essays on the concept of Christian freedom would seem to call for an examination of the place of communication both in the definition and in the exercise of freedom. Access to information and freedom of expression—both of which are aspects of communication—are hallmarks of the concept of freedom. The desire to communicate and the desire for freedom certainly are linked, if not nearly synonymous.

The issues of communication and who controls it are central both in movements of repression and of revolution against repression. Whether by means of incisive, intentional repression or by an insidious but gradual transfer, those who would wrest power from another have often sought first to control the channels of communication—newspapers, radio and television stations, public forums, pulpits—by means of censorship, control of editorial policy and/or restriction of the flow of information. Those who have been suppressed then have sought alternative means by which to have their beliefs communicated.

Both in a theoretical and practical way, however, the definition of communication has evolved, giving increased responsibility to the role of the listener or hearer. Yet many communicators operate as though the listener were passive in the process of communication, and thus they fail to adopt or manifest an appreciation for this augmented role. This seems particularly true in the case of the homily, the scripturally-based religious address that is presented within a liturgical setting.

Is there a perspective upon communication that would encourage and facilitate a greater role for the hearer in the homily? This is the question which motivates this essay. By means of a model of communication and the development of a continuum which depicts the range of sensitivity to listener involvement or feedback, the essay makes a prescriptive claim that homilists should move in the direction of a transactional perspective of communication.

While the importance of freedom in communication is evident in discussions of political and societal affairs, it also is present in theological discussions of freedom. For Christianity, a religion that is based upon the Word of God with the accompanying mandate to proclaim that Word through human words, freedom of communication clearly is important. Jesus bridged the Testaments with a quotation from Isaiah in Luke 4:18-19: "The Spirit of the Lord is upon me, because he has anointed me to bring good news to the poor. He has sent me to proclaim release to the captives and recovery of sight to the blind, to let the oppressed go free, to proclaim the year of the Lord's favor." The mandate to proclaim is extended to Jesus' followers when Jesus sends the twelve apostles to heal and to preach (Luke 9:2). Though each of the synoptic gospels has a record of the mission of the twelve, the call to preach is included only in Luke. In the Acts of the Apostles, Peter affirms that Jesus has "commanded us to preach to the people and to testify that he is the one ordained by God as judge of the living and the dead" (10:42).

As but one example of the link between communication and freedom, the Reformation was, in part, an issue of differences in understanding with respect to communication: communication with God, with the church and within the church. This desire for a greater freedom of communication within a religious sphere was aided by a revolution in communication media, the printing press. The desire to read, hear and study scripture in one's own language, free from the inevitable biases of another language, reflects a dimension of freedom that is related to both religion and communication. Liberation theology and feminist theology are, in part, extensions of the same fundamental issue: freedom of communication—who controls the communication, whose views are heard or ignored, whose interpretations are considered, ignored or prohibited.

The examples are many, and they are significant. Each deserves careful and thorough exploration. To focus upon a manageable topic, however, the scope needs to be narrowed considerably. For the purposes of the immediate context the discussion is limited to the relationship of freedom and communication specifically as they relate to the field of homiletics.

The interest in homiletics within the Catholic Church has grown immensely in recent years. New theories of homiletics are taught at many seminaries: narrative, inductive and phenomenological approaches serve as examples. Laity request improved homilies. This request represents not simply a demand for better quality but an underlying call for homilies that are based upon a different understanding of the purpose and place of the homily within the liturgy. In many ways the call seems to represent a request that the laity be incorporated as an active part of the homiletic process. This reflects a change in understanding not only about homilies but about how communication in general occurs. At the same time, there are important theological nuances to the change as well.

The first concern that one might reasonably have about the freedom of communication in homiletics is to ensure the freedom to preach, an issue that, in this country at least, concerns the separation of church and state as well as first amendment safeguards to the freedom of speech. The freedom to preach is an important issue with a long history. But there is another fundamental yet easily neglected matter that relates to freedom and homiletics, that is, the freedom of *hearers* as they participate in a preaching event. How does the homilist perceive the hearer? How does the homilist understand the role of the hearer? How do the hearers perceive their role in the homily? Does the hearer have any control over the creation of the homily?

This matter of the freedom of the hearer is fundamental. It is concerned with basic understandings of human communication, with ethics in human communication, even with theological anthropology, all of which would seem to undergird and precede the matter of particular religious practice and political ideology. How do people communicate with one another? How does the homily fit into this process?

If the only concern is to guarantee freedom for the one who preaches, that concern may betray a simplistic and misguided understanding of the process of human communication. Certainly, it is an important religious and political issue. In American history the right to proclaim one's religious beliefs is at the heart of one's understanding of freedom. Those who have wanted the freedom to proclaim and practice their religious beliefs, however, have not always been so eager to allow others the same freedom. The issue of freedom for the hearer, then, has theological and communicative ramifications.

How can the homilist proclaim the Word of God to hearers with an urgent, even imperative, tone, yet leave room for free response to that proclamation? An answer to this question necessarily involves the examination of conceptions of communication and preaching, the establishment of parameters for ethical preaching and, in particular, the assessment of the roles and responsibilities of the hearer, as well as of the homilist, within the process of preaching. William McElvaney has brought the issue to the very doorstep of the parish:

> What does freedom of the pulpit mean to the preacher? to the people? What are its limits? What are the responsibilities of both clergy and laity? The issue of prophetic preaching is inevitably linked with a theology of the pulpit, and I can only suggest here that it could be worthwhile for the preacher and the congregation to explore these questions together.[1]

As our understanding of human communication has evolved, our understanding of the role of the hearer has grown. This has assumed theoretical and practical importance. This evolution has been observed in recent homiletic theory. The importance of the hearer within the process of preaching has grown and is considered by some homileticians to be the point of departure as one prepares to preach. Thomas Long in *The Witness of Preaching* (1989), David Buttrick in *Homiletic* (1987), Fred Craddock in *Preaching* (1985), and *Fulfilled in Your Hearing* (1982), which is the statement by the Bishops' Committee on Priestly Life and Ministry on behalf of the National Conference of Catholic Bishops, all encourage the homilist to begin the process of homily preparation with the hearer in mind. The first three books are by noted homileticians; the last is an official statement for the American Catholic Church.

A critical matter, then, is to determine how the homilist perceives the role of the hearer in the creation of the homily. There is a range of possibilities that will be developed and explored later. For the moment, let it be sufficient to say that as a preacher one cannot delimit the perceived role of the hearer in the process of preaching to that of a passive listener without threatening the very message that one proclaims. Any delimitation of the active role of the hearer in the process of preaching may betray attitudes of sexism, racism, clericalism and a variety of other "-isms". The "bottom line", however, is that the active role of the hearer is jeopardized. Richard Lischer, in his review of an international conference on homiletics, has written, "Everyone agreed in some sense that authoritarian preaching is out and that the sermon must be a product of the *relationship* [emphasis added] between preacher and congregation."[2]

As our understanding of the role of the hearer in the process of communication and in the creation of meaning has grown, failure to allow for this can result in preaching that is less effective, even unethical. The freedom to preach also should allow for the freedom of the hearer to respond to that preaching, and in some manner to be considered a co-creator of the "preaching event". Martin Marty has labeled the hearers as "preachers-*with*" instead of the "preached-*to*".[3]

Communication Models

In order to clarify the place of homiletics in the discussion of communication and freedom, it is necessary to lay a foundation with regard to the nature of human communication. Perhaps the place to turn, then, is to a simple model of communication that originally was developed for electronic communication. In 1949 *The Mathematical Theory of Communication* was published and marked the beginning of the move to study communication as a system. Communication is defined in this essay as a dynamic, systematic process. By dynamic, it is implied that the process is ongoing, constantly changing and requires re-evaluation. By systematic, it is implied that the system is composed of components that interrelate in order to create the "end product" of the system, which in this case is communication or "shared meaning". If the system does not achieve its end, any of the components could be at fault. To see communication as a system, however, allows one to trace and avoid the repetition of communication failures. At the same time it becomes easier to explain and repeat communication successes.

This basic model appears simple enough, perhaps even commonplace. One should not be deceived by its simplicity, however. It has proven to be quite heuristic and comprehensive. There are seven elements that are involved in this model of communication: sender, receiver, message, channel, noise, frame of reference and, sometimes, feedback. Feedback is a later addition to the model. Feedback also is less certain, either because the channel of communication does not allow for two-way communication or because one simply may not be sensitive to the presence of the feedback. The model is illustrated on the following page.

The role of the sender is a fairly obvious one. The sender initiates the communication event by the development of some idea that s/he desires to transmit. The receiver is the second party in the event, that is, the recipient of the message. The receiver may be a single person or a group, either an intended or unintended recipient. Once an idea is formulated to some degree, it becomes a message that can be transmitted. The

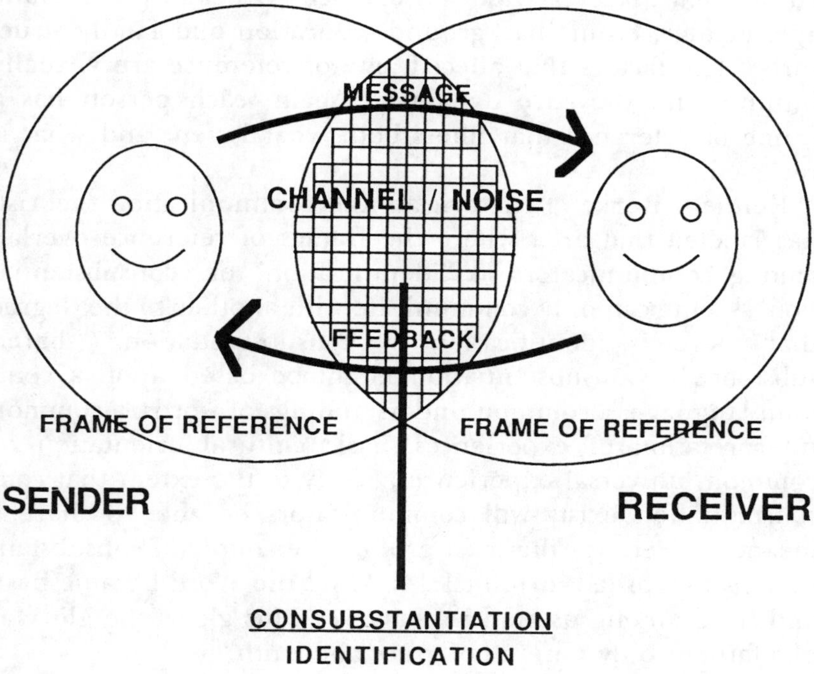

message then is transmitted through one or more channels. Hopefully, the sender chooses channels carefully, since each channel has inherent characteristics that affect the message which is transmitted. Channels may be either verbal or nonverbal.

The process of communication is complicated by the presence of noise, which may be either internal or external. External noise might include such variables as static on a telephone line, poor acoustics in a worship space, etc. Internal noise includes more cognitive and affective interferences such as prejudice, sleepiness, preoccupation with other matters, etc. Noise may interfere with communication at any point in the process.

An additional complication that is somewhat related to noise is one's frame of reference. Every person has a frame of reference. It is the collection of experiences, values, beliefs, opinions, background, biases, as well as physical abilities and limitations that make each person distinct. Other factors include age, gender, ethnic background, education and family structure. The factors that affect frame of reference are virtually infinite, and they are dynamic. Again, each person has a frame of reference that filters both what is sent and what is received.

Kenneth Burke, a rhetorician and communication theorist, has labeled that area where the frames of reference overlap among communicators as "identification" or "consubstantiation".[4] One can only communicate with another to the degree that there is identification or consubstantiation ("shared substance"). Consubstantiation might be based upon a common language, a common understandings of words, a common interpretation of experiences, basic cultural orientation or common, universal experiences. Only to the extent that consubstantiation exists will communicators be able to share a meaning. Perhaps the most profound example of consubstantiation is recorded in John 1:14: "And the Word became flesh and lived among us, and we have seen his glory, the glory as of a father's only son, full of grace and truth."

Pierre Babin, in *The New Era in Religious Communication*, also has offered a spiritual dimension to the concept. "What gives a communication a guarantee that it will last is the recognition of a shared spirit which the partners have to obey." That is to say, "the spirit recognized in each partner's own history and past commitments, the spirit seen as leading each partner to offer his or her life for the other."[5] Communication, identification and consubstantiation become virtually synonymous. Complete consubstantiation is not possible (except for the example of the Christ that is mentioned above). But Burke, in his comments about the existence of war, noted that in

> pure identification there would be no strife. Likewise, there would be no strife in absolute separateness, since opponents can join battle only through a mediatory ground that makes their communication possible, thus providing the first condition necessary for their interchange of blows. But put pure identification and division ambiguously together, so that you cannot know for certain just where one ends and the other begins, and you have the characteristic invitation for rhetoric.[6]

Burke claimed that "a doctrine of *consubstantiality*, either explicit or implicit, may be necessary to any way of life."[7] One can, of course, develop a false identification in an attempt to persuade or coerce another to a point of view or toward a particular action. This is clearly a deception and does not have a shared meaning as its goal.

The term consubstantiation has an interesting referent in eucharistic theology which has no direct relationship to this discussion. Babin, however, has offered an interesting observation with eucharistic implications. "This, then, is the revelation offered to us by Christianity: that, beyond appearances, everything is fundamentally one, the body of Christ, loved and saved by Christ."[8] He adds, "In the eyes of a Christian, what is at the origin is communion with God in the body of Christ."[9] This is consubstantiation or shared substance.

The one remaining element of the system is feedback. The sensitivity to or use of feedback in human communication occurs in a variety of ways which can be described by reference to a continuum. The continuum is depicted in the graph on the following page.

The arrows represent successive stages of one's understanding of the way in which humans communicate. As this understanding grows, "interactional" is seen to be more comprehensive than is "actional"; "transactional" is more comprehensive than "interactional". Placed in a continuum, however, the stages describe how anyone might communicate in a given situation. These terms seem to have been coined by J. Dewey and A. F. Bentley as a way to discuss educational research in their book *Knowing and the Known* (1949). Thereafter, the terms were adopted by communication studies.

As they are used in this essay, the stages or eras of understanding of communication become perspectives out of which one may operate. A person typically may operate from a single area on the continuum. Each area of the continuum, however, may be appropriate for a given communication situation.

The actional stage is the oldest level, and has been termed the "hypodermic needle theory of communication", because the meaning is injected into receivers as they hear or read the

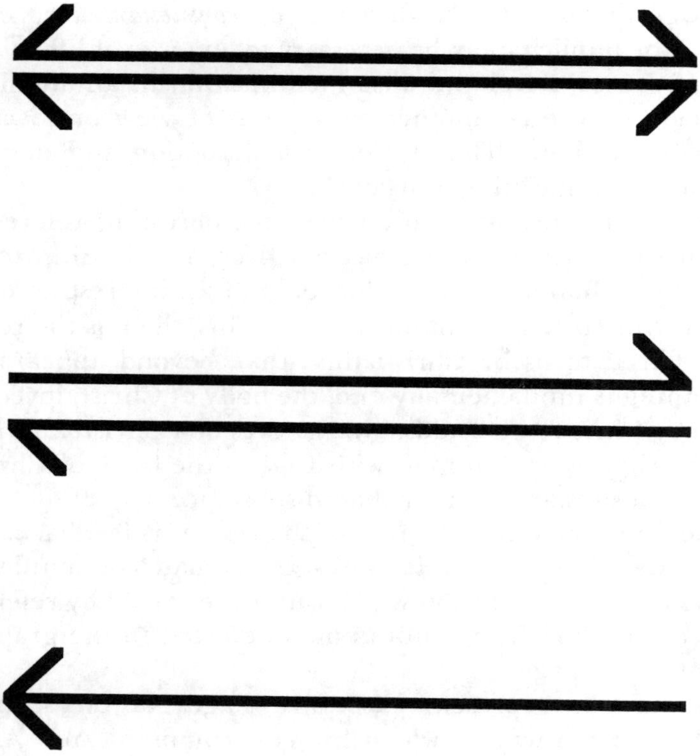

words. The key to this approach is the belief that the meaning is put into the communication by the sender and is received passively by the receiver. This is a very authoritarian style. Until quite recently this model predominated and undergirded theories of homiletics. This is not without its cost, however. The authors of *Fulfilled in Your Hearing*, the statement on homiletics by the National Conference of Catholic Bishops, have concluded:

> To preach in a way that sounds as if the preacher alone has access to the truth and knows what is best for everyone else, or that gives the impression that there are no unresolved problems or possibility for dialogue, is to preach in a way that may have been acceptable to those who viewed the church primarily in clerical terms. In a church that thinks and speaks of itself as a pilgrim people, gathered together for worship, witness, and work, such preaching will be heard only with great difficulty, if at all.[10]

Although in the actional perspective the receiver is seen as passive in the creation of meaning, there is room in this model for some adaptation to the situation of the receiver's language, culture, situation, etc. In *On Christian Doctrine*, Augustine writes, "The speaker should not consider the eloquence of his teaching [preaching] but the clarity of it."[11] He adds, "Of what use is a gold key if it will not open what we wish?"[12] The dominant emphasis in this perspective, then, is "message formation", the formation of a clear and accurate message. The communication is in the control of the sender. The obvious gap in this perspective is the lack of consideration for feedback. There is no provision by which the sender may determine the way in which the message is received. Though people continue to operate with this understanding of communication, it clearly is inadequate as a description of the whole of human communication.

When "actional communication" was seen to be an inadequate description of the way in which humans communicate, the interactional model was proposed. It has been compared to a ping-pong match. First, one communicator sends and the other receives. Then the roles are reversed. It was an improvement upon the actional approach because it *did* allow for the possibility of feedback, that is, interaction. One also might see an analogy in the stimulus-response discussions of biology and psychology. Though the interactional perspective is an improvement over the actional, it seems to oversimplify communication, thus to make each exchange too neat, discrete, isolated and self-contained. While the hearer is given an opportunity for feedback, this occurs only after the message has been delivered. Finally, this perspective fails "to provide a satisfactory theory of meaning, and of how messages from highly credible sources can provoke so many and such contradictory meanings."[13]

The third stage is the transactional perspective. While communication was seen primarily as an exchange of information in the previous two stages, there is a qualitative difference here. The process of communication is perceived to be less "deterministic and mechanical" and more "spontaneous and evolutionary".[14] "If we are truly human, communicating is receiving and transmitting a message of which we are not completely in control, because it comes from our inner depths, where the necessity and the mystery dwell."[15]

The interactional perspective is the actional perspective with a feedback loop. In "transactional communication", however, more is required. Babin has observed, "We must rehabilitate the act of receiving in communication. We do not communicate because we speak, because we listen, or because we express ourselves, but because we are receptive."[16]

There is a blend of the roles of communication, since both communicators send and receive at the same time. Babin asked if, in this new era, traditional categories of communication such as transmitter, receiver and feedback even should be considered anymore in discussions of Christian communication. Babin concluded that they can *if* "we recognize that transmitters and receivers are basically one."[17] J. G. Tilley described this blend as "a spiral of reciprocal change in feeling, attitudes, and beliefs."[18] Indeed, the sender actually may change the message as it is sent in light of feedback that is received from the receiver. There is an open acknowledgment that the meaning is created by both communicators. There is a need to be open to the receipt of feedback, which, in essence, is a requirement for flexibility, even vulnerability, that is not present in either actional or interactional communication. While this vulnerability may pose risk, the chance for communication or a shared meaning is greatest because the possibility for greater consubstantiation is increased. More to the point for this essay, the approach acknowledges the hearer as an active participant in the homiletic process, a co-creator of meaning, and gives the hearer the greater freedom in the interpretation of and response to the actual homily. Indeed, Tilley included the "perception of choice" as a necessary criterion for a transactional model of homiletics.[19]

Put into a continuum, the three stages—actional, interactional, transactional—become a range of perspectives with descriptive value. Where does a person typically operate? What perspective does a situation demand? There is also a prescriptive element to the continuum, however, in so far as one's perspective upon communication generally should gravitate toward the transactional, the most comprehensive perspective of human communication.

While not all homiletic situations may require a homily that is based upon a transactional perspective, it certainly would appear that, overall, homilies should move in that direction, since it is from this perspective that a shared meaning most likely will occur. At the very least it suggests a revision of some traditional assumptions about the role of the homily, and especially, of the hearer in the process of preaching. In addition, only from the transactional perspective does the preacher have the opportunity to *choose* whether an actional, interactional or transactional perspective would be best.

Implications for Preaching

Lest this seem too distinct (and distant) from homiletics in the Catholic Church, an examination of the statement by the National Conference of Catholic Bishops, *Fulfilled in Your Hearing*, supports the movement away from an actional understanding of homiletics and toward a transactional understanding. The statement from this document that is quoted above clearly urges a movement away from an actional perspective and toward a vision in which the entire church is perceived to be responsible for the homily, "a pilgrim people, gathered together for worship, witness, and work...."[20]

The movement toward the transactional perspective is encouraged in several ways. As was noted above, the statement begins with a consideration of the assembly. In addition, the statement notes that the "proclamation of the Word of God is the responsibility of the entire Christian community by virtue of baptism."[21] Thirdly, the homilist is seen as a "mediator of meaning" who represents "both the community and the Lord".[22] Fourthly, the homily is seen primarily to be an interpretive event. "When one hears and accepts this vision of the world, this way of interpreting reality, a response is required."[23] The fifth clue is contained in the previous quotation—the response to the message. Finally, the statement's definition clearly is transactional in spirit. The homily is defined as

> a scriptural interpretation of human existence which enables a community to recognize God's active presence, to respond to that presence in faith through liturgical word and gesture, and beyond the liturgical assembly, through a life lived in conformity with the Gospel.[24]

The sense here is that the homily is more than an explanation of a biblical passage, more than doctrinal catechesis and more than a presentation that involves the presider alone. How one defines homily, of course, is a pivotal issue, since, as Lischer has observed, "What preachers think they are doing when they preach will profoundly influence how they do it."[25] So, from both communicative and ecclesiastical perspectives, the move toward a transactional view of preaching is required.

Once this view is adopted, there are very practical implications for preaching from a transactional perspective. One already has been suggested—begin with the hearer and not the text. This does not diminish the importance of the text as the basis for the homily. What this focus suggests, however, is that the homilist needs to be clear about issues, assumptions, values, even vocabulary, before s/he approaches the text. What filters does the homilist bring to the text? It is something of a misguided myth to believe that the homilist should approach the text with a sort of scientific objectivity. To be clear about frames of reference before one encounters the text allows for a more honest exploration of the text's impact upon the hearer, and will more likely result in a homily that has impact upon the lives of the hearers. This seems to suggest that one must develop and present one's own homilies. At the very least, one must process and re-package the homily suggestions that one finds in various resources that are designed to aid the homilist through the provision of interpretive materials and stories which are intended to make the homily interesting and relevant. To use a third party's unadapted stories in order to create relevancy, however, seems contradictory to the spirit of transactional preaching.

Craddock proposes several ways in which the homilist can increase knowledge about the hearer through the use of feedback: formal (surveys), informal (observation) and empathic imagination.[26] These are all ways to increase identification with the hearer. They also are means by which the homilist can develop images and illustrations for use in the homily. They come directly from the life of the parish. Issues of confidentiality must be respected, of course.

Additionally, the hearer or assembly, since they serve as the starting point, also must be perceived as a co-creator of the homily. They are active, information-processing people who interpret not only the text but the homily. They are the side of the communication equation that ascribes primary meaning to the words of the homily that are pronounced by the homilist.

The above-mentioned methods provide the homilist with information about the situation or status of the parish prior to the homily. Other methods that are related more directly to the homily include "feed-forward" sessions: bible studies that are based upon the forthcoming texts for a Sunday's homily. They provide the occasion for the direct response of a parish with reference to their interpretation of the text, the meaning that it has for them. Feedback sessions that follow the homily offer occasions for the parish to indicate the way in which they perceived the issues that were contained within the text, or to underscore the theme(s) of the homily for parish life in the week to come. With activities like these, the homily becomes more than an isolated event within the liturgy. It becomes a way to focus one's entire catalog of ministerial activity. At the same time it offers the opportunity for more data from parishioners who both minister and are ministered to. In good transactional fashion, the roles become less distinct.

Another practical implication involves the forms that transactional homilies might take. McElvaney has suggested one possibility. "I believe it is the questioning, inquiring style that has great promise in some of our prophetic preaching. The inquiring approach lends itself to a confessional style and a mutual search rather than dogmatic coercion. Thus there is less likelihood of misusing biblical texts than otherwise might be the case."[27]

Homilies that are preached from a transactional perspective would be more evocative than didactic, more narrative and interpretive than catechetical. In his treatise on *Rhetoric*, Aristotle describes methods for the construction of an argument.

This has long been used as source material for homiletics. He also wrote the *Poetics*, however, in which he describes the way that the arts seek to imitate or re-create events in life. This latter work may provide a more suitable, at least an additional, model for transactional homilies.[28] Babin has labeled a similar approach, the "symbolic way".[29]

To preach from a transactional perspective provides both the homilist and the hearer with the greatest possible freedom, because this perspective provides the greatest opportunity for true dialogue and the greatest likelihood of shared meaning. It assumes that the hearer and homilist are co-creators of the homily, that is, that both contribute to meaning in the homily. It asserts that the hearer has an impact upon the shaping of the homily's form and content.

In *The Witness of Preaching*, Long offers a clear summary of the matter of preaching from a transactional perspective. Though he writes about the forms that a homily might take, the broader spirit of the transactional perspective is evident.

> Refining the form of a sermon is the process of thinking through *how* to present [a] claim in such a way that people can truly hear it and respond to it. This is a question of clarity, of course, but it is also a question of freedom. A sermon should present the gospel so that people can understand it, and it should also present the gospel so that people are liberated to respond to it. Sermon forms can be, if we choose, strategies for manipulation, deception, and coercion. But when they are shaped in obedience to the gospel, they become arenas for free and human decision making.[30]

Freedom and communication—these two important concepts have shared similar histories of affirmation and denial, interpretation and experience. They are concepts that have special meaning within Christianity as one perceives the call to proclaim a message of freedom and forgiveness. Yet only as one strives to secure the opportunity for all to speak and listen freely, will humanity achieve the freedom that it claims for itself.

Notes

1 William K. McElvaney, *Preaching from Camelot to Covenant* (Nashville: Abingdon, 1989) 62.

2 Richard Lischer, "Other Voices in Homiletics," *Homiletic* 16.1 (Summer 1991) 1.

3 Martin Marty, *The Word* (Philadelphia: Fortress, 1984) 79.

4 Kenneth Burke, *A Rhetoric of Motives* (Berkeley, CA: University of California Press, 1969) 20-21.

5 Pierre Babin, *The New Era in Religious Communication* (Minneapolis, MN: Fortress, 1991) 98.

6 Burke, *Rhetoric* 25.

7 Burke, *Rhetoric* 21.

8 Babin, *New Era* 72.

9 Babin, *New Era* 73.

10 NCCB, *Fulfilled in Your Hearing* (Washington, DC: USCC, 1982) 5.

11 Augustine, *On Christian Doctrine* (trans. D.W. Roberts, Jr.; Indianapolis, IN: Bobbs-Merrill, 1958) 133.

12 Augustine, *On Christian Doctrine* 136.

13 D.C. Barnlund, "Toward a Meaning-Centered Philosophy of Communication," in *Speech Communication Behavior* (eds. L.L. Barker and R.J. Kibler; Englewood Cliffs, NJ: Prentice-Hall, 1962) 71-80.

14 Barnlund, "Communication" 203.

15 Babin, *The New Era* 75.

16 Babin, *The New Era* 82.

17 Babin, *The New Era* 73.

18 J.G. Tilley, "An Analysis of Homiletics Textbooks" (MA thesis, University of North Carolina, 1983) 24.

19 Tilley, *An Analysis* 24.

20 NCCB, *Fulfilled* 5.

21 NCCB, *Fulfilled* 2.

22 NCCB, *Fulfilled* 7.

23 NCCB, *Fulfilled* 18.

24 NCCB, *Fulfilled* 29.

25 Lischer, "Other Voices" 3.

26 Craddock, *Preaching* (Nashville: Abingdon, 1985) 93-98.

27 McElvaney, *Camelot to Covenant* 65.

28 Lucy A. Rose, "Rhetoric and Poetics," paper presented at the annual convention of the Academy of Homiletics, Princeton, NJ, 4-8 December 1990, 97-110.

29 Babin, *The New Era* 146-167, 183-184.

30 Thomas G. Long, *The Witness of Preaching* (Louisville, KY: Westminster/John Knox, 1989) 113.

Collected Bibliography

Abbott, Walter M., ed. *The Documents of Vatican II*. Piscataway, NJ: American, 1966.

Adam, Adolf. *The Liturgical Year: Its History and Its Meaning after the Reform of the Liturgy*. Translated by Matthew J. O'Connell. New York: Pueblo, 1981.

Andrieu, Michel. *Les Ordines Romani du haut moyen age*. Louvain: Spicilegium Sacrum Lovaniense, 1974.

"Archives of the Congregation of the Evangelization of Peoples (Congregation of the Propaganda Fide)." University of Notre Dame Archives, microfilm.

Auchincloss, Douglas. "City of God and Man." *Time* 76 (12 December 1960) 64-70.

Augé, Matias. "Principi di interpretazione dei testi liturgici." In *Anàmnesis* 1, pp. 159-179. Edited by Salvatore Marsili. Casale Monferrato: Marietti, 1974.

Augustine. *On Christian Doctrine*. Translated by D.W. Roberts, Jr. Indianapolis, IN: Bobbs-Merrill, 1958.

——. *Saint Augustin: Expositions on the Book of Psalms*. NPNF 8. Edited by Philip Schaff. Grand Rapids, MI: Wm. B. Eerdmans, 1983.

——. *Sancti Aurelii Augustini: Enarrationes in Psalmos CI-CL*. CCL 40. Turnholt: Typographi Brepols Editores Pontificii, 1956.

Babin, Pierre. *The New Era in Religious Communication*. Minneapolis, MN: Fortress, 1991.

Baldovin, John F. *The Urban Character of Christian Worship: The Origins, Development, and Meaning of Stational Liturgy*. OCA 228. Rome: Pontificium Institutum Studiorum Orientalium, 1987.

Barnard, L.W. *Studies in the Apostolic Fathers and their Background*. New York: Schocken Books, 1966.

Barnlund, D.C. "Toward a Meaning-Centered Philosophy of Communication." In *Speech Communication Behavior*, pp. 71-80. Edited by L.L. Barker and R.J. Kibler. Englewood Cliffs, NJ: Prentice-Hall, 1962.

Barrett, C.K. "The Allegory of Abraham, Sarah, and Hagar in the Argument of Galatians." In *Rechtfertigung: Festschrift für Ernst Käsemann*, pp. 1-16. Edited by Johannes Friedrich, Wolfgang Pöhlmann and Peter Stuhlmacher. Tübingen: J.C.B. Mohr, 1976.

Baum, Gregory. *Religion and Alienation: A Theological Reading of Sociology*. New York: Paulist, 1975.

Berger, Joseph. "5 of 7 on New York Board Support Condom Distribution in Schools." *New York Times NATIONAL* 27 September 1990.

Bernabei, Nicola. *Vita del Cardinale Morone*. Modena: Tipografica Rossi, 1885.

Betz, H.D. *Galatians: A Commentary on Paul's Letter to the Churches of Galatia*. Hermenia. Philadelphia: Fortress, 1979.

Bickerman, Elias J. *The Jews in the Greek Age*. Cambridge, MA and London: Harvard University Press, 1988.

Blied, Benjamin. *Catholics and the Civil War*. Milwaukee, WI: 1945.

Boff, Leonardo. *Liberating Grace*. Translated by John Drury. Maryknoll, NY: Orbis, 1979.

Borowitz, Eugene B. "Judaism. An Overview." *Encyclopedia of Religion* 8 (1987) 127-148.

Boyer, Ernest L. *Scholarship Reconsidered: Priorities of the Professorate*. Washington, DC: The Carnegie Foundation for the Advancement of Teaching, 1990.

Brooks-Leonard, John. "Easter Vespers in Early Medieval Rome: A Critical Edition and Study." PhD dissertation. University of Notre Dame, 1988.

Brown, Raymond E., and Meier, John P. *Antioch and Rome: New Testament Cradles of Catholic Christianity*. New York and Ramsay, NJ: Paulist, 1983.

Browning, Don. *Religious Thought and Modern Psychologies*. Philadelphia: Fortress, 1987.

Bruce, F.F. *The Epistle to the Galatians*. NIGTC. Grand Rapids, MI: Wm. B. Eerdmans, 1981.

Bruylants, Placide. *Les oraisons du Missel Romain: texte et histoire*. 2 vols. Louvain: Abbaye du Mont César, 1952.

Buckel, John J. "'Curse of the Law.' An Exegetical Investigation of Galatians 3,10-14." PhD dissertation. Katholieke Universiteit Leuven, 1988.

Bugnini, Annibale. *The Reform of the Liturgy: 1948-1975*. Translated by Matthew J. O'Connell. Collegeville, MN: Liturgical, 1990.

Burghardt, Walter. "A Tribute to John Courtney Murray." *Catholic Mind* 66 (June 1968) 29-31.

Burke, Kenneth. *A Rhetoric of Motives*. Berkeley, CA: University of California Press, 1969.

Burton, Ernest. *A Critical and Exegetical Commentary on the Epistle to the Galatians*. ICC. Edinburgh: T. & T. Clark, 1980.

Buttrick, David. *Homiletic*. Philadelphia: Fortress, 1987.

Caravaglios, Maria. "A Roman Critique of the Pro-Slavery Views of Bishop Martin of Natchitoches, Louisiana." *Records of the American Catholic Historical Society of Philadelphia* 83 (1972) 67-81.

Carroll, John. *The John Carroll Papers*. 3 vols. Edited by Thomas Hanley. Notre Dame, IN: University of Notre Dame Press, 1976.

Cetron, Marvin, and Gayle, Margaret. *Educational Renaissance*. New York: St. Martin's Press, 1991.

Chavasse, Antoine. *Le sacramentaire dans le groupe dit "Gélasiens du VIIIe siècle."* 2 vols. Brussels: St-Pietersabdij Steenbrugge, 1984.

——. *Le sacramentaire gélasien*. Tournai: Desclée & Co., 1957.

Cheney, Lynne V. *Tyrannical Machines: A Report on Educational Practices Gone Wrong and Our Best Hopes for Setting Them Right*. Washington, DC: National Endowment for the Humanities, 1990.

Cogley, J. "John Courtney Murray, S.J." *America* 117 (September 1967) 220-221.

Connolly, Kathleen. "The Chicago Open-Housing Conference." In *Chicago 1966: Open-Housing Marches, Summit Negotiations, and Operation Breadbasket*, pp. 49-95. Edited by David J. Garrow. Brooklyn, NY: Carlson, 1989.

Cooney, John. *The American Pope: The Life and Times of Francis Cardinal Spellman*. New York: Times Books, 1984.

Craddock, Fred B. *Preaching*. Nashville: Abingdon, 1985.

Crews, Clyde F. *An American Holy Land: A History of the Archdiocese of Louisville*. Wilmington, DE: Michael Glazier, 1987.

Curran, Emmett. "'Splendid Poverty': Jesuit Slaveholding in Maryland, 1805-1838." In *Catholics in the Old South: Essays on Church and Culture*, pp. 125-146. Edited by Randall M.

Miller and Jon L. Wakelyn. Macon, GA: Mercer University Press, 1983.

Currier, Charles W. *Carmel in America, 1790-1890: A Centennial History of Discalced Carmelite Nuns in the United States.* Darien, IL: Carmelite Press, 1989.

Dale, Edgar. *The Educator's Quotebook.* Bloomington, IN: Phi Delta Kappa, 1984.

D'Antonio, William, *et al. American Catholic Laity in a Changing Church.* Kansas City, MO: Sheed & Ward, 1989.

Davies, W.D. "Paul and the People of Israel." In *Jewish and Pauline Studies*, pp. 123-152. Philadelphia: Fortress, 1984.

Davis, Cyprian. "Brothers and Sisters to Us: The Never-Ending Story." *America* 162 (March 1990) 319-321, 334.

——. "Four Days in Selma." *Suggested Readings* (February 1989).

——. *The History of Black Catholics in the United States.* New York: Crossroad, 1990.

DePalma, Anthony. "Catholicism is Embracing More Blacks." *New York Times* 24 January 1989, 7.

Deshusses, Jean, ed. *Le sacramentaire grégorien.* 3 vols. Fribourg: Éditions Universitaires Fribourg Suisse, 1979.

Dewey, J., and Bentley, A.F. *Knowing and the Known.* Boston: Beacon, 1949.

Dolan, Jay P. *The American Catholic Experience.* Garden City, NY: Doubleday, 1985.

Douglas, Richard M. *Jacobo Sadoleto 1477-1547.* Cambridge, MA: Harvard University Press, 1959.

Drane, John W. *Paul: Libertine or Legalist?* London: S.P.C.K., 1975.

Dulles, Avery. *A Church to Believe In: Discipleship and the Dynamics of Freedom.* New York: Crossroad, 1982.

Dumas, Alexandre, ed. *Liber Sacramentorum Gellonensis*. CCL 159. Turnhout: Brepols, 1981.

Dungan, George S. *The Epistle of Paul to the Galatians*. MNTC. London: Harper, 1934.

Ebeling, Gerhard. *The Truth of the Gospel: An Exposition of Galatians*. Philadelphia: Fortress, 1985.

Elam, Stanley M. "The 22nd Annual Gallup Poll of the Public's Attitudes Toward the Public Schools." *Phi Delta Kappan* 72.1 (September 1990) 41-55.

Ellis, John Tracy, ed. *Documents of American Catholic History*. 3 vols. Wilmington, DE: Michael Glazier, 1987.

Fenton, Joseph Clifford. "Doctrine and Tactic in Catholic Pronouncements on Church and State." *American Ecclesiastical Review* 145 (October 1961) 274.

Ford, George Barry. *A Degree of Difference*. New York: Farrar, Straus & Giroux, 1969.

Fox, Vernelle. "Substance Abuse: Mechanics and Management." Paper presented to the World Congress of Rehabilitation Medicine. Mexico City, Mexico, October 1974.

Frend, W.H.C. *Martyrdom and Persecution in the Early Church: A Study of a Conflict from the Maccabees to Donatus*. London: Basil Blackwell, 1965 (reprint edition; Ann Arbor, MI: Baker Book House, 1981).

Fuchs, Joseph. *Human Values and Christian Morality*. Dublin: Gill & Macmillan, 1970.

Fung, Ronald Y. *The Epistle to the Galatians*. NICNT. Grand Rapids, MI: Wm. B. Eerdmans, 1988.

Gallup, George, Jr., and Castelli, James. *The American Catholic People: Their Beliefs, Practices, and Values*. Garden City, NY: Doubleday, 1987.

Gannon, Michael, *Rebel Bishop: The Life and Era of Augustin Verot*. Milwaukee, WI: Bruce, 1964.

Garrow, David J. *Bearing the Cross: Martin Luther King, Jr. and the Southern Christian Leadership Conference*. New York: Random House, 1988.

——. *The F.B.I. and Martin Luther King, Jr.: From "Solo" to Memphis*. New York: W.W. Norton, 1981.

Gazzetti, Erio Eleuterio. *Il Cardinale Giovanni Morone: Patrizio Modenese*. Modena: Typographia Immacolata Concezione, 1952.

Gillett, H.M. "Loreto." *New Catholic Encyclopedia* 8 (1981) 993-994.

Grant, Robert M. *Ignatius of Antioch*. AF 4. London: Thomas Nelson & Sons, 1964.

Greeley, Andrew. *American Catholics Since the Council*. Chicago: Thomas More, 1985.

Groome, Thomas H. *Christian Religious Education*. San Francisco: Harper & Row, 1980.

Gula, Richard M. *Reason Informed by Faith: Foundations of Catholic Morality*. New York: Paulist, 1989.

Guthrie, Donald. *Galatians*. CentBNS. London: Thomas Nelson, 1969.

Häring, Bernard. *Free and Faithful in Christ*. New York: Seabury, 1978.

——. *Sin in the Secular Age*. Garden City, NY: Doubleday, 1974.

Hall, Calvin S. *A Primer of Freudian Psychology*. New York: The New American Library, 1954.

Hennesey, James. *American Catholics: A History of the Roman Catholic Community in the United States*. New York: Oxford University Press, 1981.

Higginbotham, A. Leon, Jr. *In the Matter of Color. Race and the American Legal Process: The Colonial Period*. Oxford: Oxford University Press, 1980.

Hodgson, Peter. *A New Birth of Freedom: A Theology of Bondage and Liberation*. Philadelphia: Fortress, 1976.

Jedin, Hubert. *The History of the Council of Trent*. Translated by E. Graf. St. Louis: Herder Book, 1957-1981.

Jeffers, James S. *Conflict at Rome: Social Order and Hierarchy in Early Christianity*. Minneapolis, MN: Fortress, 1991.

Jefford, Clayton. "Presbyters in the Community of the *Didache*." In *Studia Patristica* 21, pp. 122-128. Edited by Elizabeth A. Livingstone. Leuven: Peeters, 1989.

Jounel, Pierre. "Les vêpres de Paques." *La Maison-Dieu* 49 (1957) 96-111.

Kantowicz, Edward R. *Corporation Sole: Cardinal Mundelein and Chicago Catholicism*. Notre Dame, IN: University of Notre Dame Press, 1983.

Keller, George. *Academic Strategy*. Baltimore and London: The Johns Hopkins University Press, 1983.

Kelly, Francis D. "A Church at Risk: Toward Balance in Catechetics." *America* 149 (October 1983) 185-188.

Kemper, Donald J. "Catholic Integration in St. Louis, 1935-1947." *Missouri Historical Review* 73.1 (October 1978) 1-22.

Kenneally, Finbar, *et al.*, eds. *United States Documents in the Propaganda Fide Archives: A Calendar*. 11 vols. Washington, DC: Academy of American Franciscan History, 1966-1987.

Kennedy, George A. *New Testament Interpretation through Rhetorical Criticism*. Chapel Hill, NC and London: University of North Carolina Press, 1984.

Kerans, Patrick. *Sinful Social Structures*. New York: Paulist, 1974.

Krautheimer, Richard. *Corpus Basilicarum Christianarum Romae*. Vatican City: Pontificio Istituto di Archeologia Cristiana, 1937.

Lamanna, Richard A., and Coakley, Jay J. "The Catholic Church and the Negro." In *Contemporary Catholicism in the United States*, pp. 147-193. Edited by Philip Gleason. Notre Dame, IN: University of Notre Dame Press, 1969.

Lamb, Matthew. *Solidarity with Victims: Toward a Theology of Social Transformation*. New York: Crossroad, 1985.

Lambert, Rollins E. "The Negro and the Catholic Church." In *Roman Catholicism and the American Way of Life*, pp. 156-163. Edited by Thomas T. McAvoy. Notre Dame, IN: University of Notre Dame Press, 1960.

Lambrecht, Jan. "Das Gesetzverständnis bei Paulus." In *Das Gesetz im Neuen Testament*, pp. 88-127. Edited by K. Kertelge. QD 108. Freiburg: Herder, 1986.

Landers, Jane. "Black Society in Spanish St. Augustine, 1784-1821." PhD dissertation. University of Florida, 1988.

Leclercq, Henri. "Cursus." *Dictionnaire d'archéologie chrétienne et de liturgie* 3.2 (1948) 3193-3205.

Leege, David C. "Who Is a True Catholic? Social Boundaries on the Church." *Notre Dame Study of Catholic Parish Life* 12 (March 1988).

Lemann, Nicholas. *The Promised Land: The Great Black Migration and How It Changed America*. New York: Alfred A. Knopf, 1991.

Lewis, Neil A. "From Poverty to the Bench, Clarence Thomas." *New York Times* 2 July 1991, 1, 11.

Lischer, Richard. "Other Voices in Homiletics." *Homiletic* 16.1 (Summer 1991) 1-4.

Lonergan, Bernard. *Insight: A Study of Human Understanding*. London: Longmans, Green & Co., 1957 (reprint edition; New York: Harper & Row, 1978).

Long, Thomas G. *The Witness of Preaching*. Louisville, KY: Westminster/John Knox, 1989.

Lüdemann, Gerd. *Paul, Apostle to the Gentiles: Studies in Chronology*. Philadelphia: Fortress, 1984.

Lutz, H. "Morone, Giovanni." *New Catholic Encyclopedia* 9 (1981) 1150.

Lynn, Robert Wood. "Coming Over the Horizon." In *Good Stewardship: A Handbook for Seminary Trustees,* p. 58. Edited by Barbara E. Taylor and Malcolm L. Warford. Washington, DC: Association of Governing Boards, 1991.

McBrien, Richard. *Catholicism*. Minneapolis, MN: Winston, 1980.

McElroy, Robert W. *The Search for an American Public Theology: The Contribution of John Courtney Murray*. New York: Paulist, 1989.

McElvaney, William K. *Preaching from Camelot to Covenant*. Nashville: Abingdon, 1989.

Magnum Bullarium Romanum. Luxemburg: A. Chevalier, 1727.

Margolick, David. "Judge Portrayed as a Product of Ideas Clashing with Life." *New York Times* 3 July 1991, 1, 9.

Marty, Martin. "This We Can Believe: A Pluralist Vision." *Religious Education* 75.1 (January-February 1980) 37-49.

——. *The Word*. Philadelphia: Fortress, 1984.

Maxwell, John. *Slavery and the Catholic Church*. Chichester, England: Barry Rose, 1975.

Meeks, Wayne A., and Wilken, Robert L. *Jews and Christians in Antioch: In the First Four Centuries of the Common Era*. SBLSBS 13. Missoula, MT: Scholars Press, 1978.

Missale Romanum: editio typica altera. Vatican City: Libraria Editrice Vaticana, 1975.

Mohlberg, Leo Cunibert, ed. *Liber Sacramentorum Romanae Aeclesiae Ordinis Anni Circuli*. Rome: Casa Editrice Herder, 1981.

——. *Sacramentarium Veronese*. Rome: Herder Editrice e Libreria, 1978.

Morone, Gaetano. "Morone, Giovanni." *Dizionario di Erudizione Storico-Ecclesiastica* 46 (1847) 300.

Morone, Giovanni. *Il Processo Inquisitoriale del Cardinal Giovanni Morone*. Vol. 1. Edited by Massimo Firpo. Rome: Istituto Storico Italiano per L'Etat Moderna et Contemporanea, 1981.

Murray, John Courtney. "Freedom of Religion I: The Ethical Problem." *Theological Studies* 6 (June 1945) 229-286.

Myrdal, Gunnar. *An American Dilemma: The Negro Problem and American Democracy*. New York: Harper, 1944.

National Conference of Catholic Bishops. *Fulfilled in Your Hearing*. Washington, DC: United States Catholic Conference, 1982.

——. *Sharing the Light of Faith: The National Catechetical Directory for Catholics of the United States*. Washington, DC: United States Catholic Conference, 1979.

Nocent, Adrian. "Storia dei libri liturgici romani." In *Anàmnesis* 2, pp. 147-183. Edited by Salvatore Marsili. Casale Monferrato: Marietti, 1978.

Oates, Stephen B. *Let the Trumpet Sound: The Life of Martin Luther King, Jr*. New York: Harper & Row, 1982.

O'Brien, David J. *Renewal of American Catholicism*. New York: Oxford University Press, 1972.

O'Connell, Timothy. *Principles for a Catholic Morality*. San Francisco: Harper & Row, 1990.

O'Hare, Padraic. "A Church at Crisis Point: Conventional or Critical Religious Education?" *The Living Light* 20 (June 1984) 329-341.

Osborne, William A. *The Segregated Covenant: Race Relations and American Catholics*. New York: Herder & Herder, 1967.

Outler, Albert C. "Response [to the "Document on the Church" of Vatican II]." In *The Documents of Vatican II*, pp. 102-106. Edited by W.M. Abbott. Piscataway, NJ: American, 1966.

Parmet, Herbert S. *Jack: The Struggles of John F. Kennedy*. New York: Dial, 1980.

Paschini, Pio. "Morone, Giovanni." *Enciclopedia Cattolica* 8 (1948) 1422.

Pastor, Ludwig. *The History of the Popes from the Close of the Middle Ages*. Vol. 14. Edited by F. Kerr. St. Louis: B. Herder, 1923-1953.

Paulsen, Henning. *Studien zur Theologie des Ignatius von Antiochen*. FKD 29. Göttingen: Vandenhoeck & Ruprecht, 1978.

Pelotte, Donald E. *John Courtney Murray: Theologian in Conflict*. New York: Paulist, 1976.

Philibert, Paul. "New Leadership for Tomorrow's Church." *The Living Light* 22 (June 1986) 304-312.

Poole, Stafford, and Slawson, Douglas. *Church and Slave in Perry County, Missouri, 1818-1865*. Lewiston, NY: Edwin Mellen, 1986.

Postman, Neil. *Amusing Ourselves to Death*. New York: Viking Penguin, 1985.

——. *The Disappearance of Childhood*. New York: Delacorte, 1982.

——. *Teaching as a Conserving Activity*. New York: Dell, 1979.

——. *Teaching as a Subversive Activity*. New York: Dell, 1969.

Raboteau, Albert J. "Black Christianity in North America." In *The Encyclopedia of the American Religious Experience* 1, pp. 635-648. Edited by C. Lippy and P.W. Williams. New York: Charles Scribner's Sons, 1988.

—— *Slave Religion: The "Invisible Institution" in the Antebellum South*. New York: Oxford University Press, 1978.

Rahner, Karl. *Foundations of Christian Faith*. New York: Seabury, 1976 (Crossroad, 1982).

——. *Nature and Grace*. New York: Sheed & Ward, 1963.

——. *Theological Investigations*. Vol. 6. New York: Crossroad, 1982.

Reid, Daniel G., ed. *Dictionary of Christianity in America*. Downers Grove, IL: Intervarsity Press, 1990.

Rice, Madeleine Hooke. *American Catholic Opinion in the Slavery Controversy*. New York: Columbia University Press, 1944.

Ring, Nancy. "Sin and Transformation from a Systematic Perspective." *Chicago Studies* 23 (November 1984) 303-319.

Rose, Lucy A. "Rhetoric and Poetics." Paper presented at the annual convention of the Academy of Homiletics. Princeton, NJ, 4-8 December 1990.

Rynne, Xavier. *Vatican Council II*. New York: Farrar, Straus & Giroux, 1968.

Schaef, Anne Wilson. *When Society Becomes an Addict*. San Francisco: Harper & Row, 1987.

Schlesinger, Arthur M., Jr. *The Disuniting of America*. New York: Whittle Direct Books, 1991.

——. *Robert Kennedy and His Times*. Boston: Houghton Mifflin, 1978.

——. *A Thousand Days: John F. Kennedy in the White House*. New York: Crown, 1965.

Schoedel, William R. *Ignatius of Antioch: A Commentary on the Letters of Ignatius of Antioch*. Edited by Helmut Koester. Hermeneia. Philadelphia: Fortress, 1985.

Schoonenberg, Piet. *The Sin of the World: A Theological View*. Translated by Joseph Donceel. Notre Dame, IN: University of Notre Dame Press, 1965.

Schuth, Katarina. *Reason for the Hope: The Futures of Roman Catholic Theologates*. Wilmington, DE: Michael Glazier, 1989.

Seeley, David. *The Nobel Death: Graeco-Roman Martyrology and Paul's Concept of Salvation*. JNTSSup 28. Sheffield, England: Sheffield Academic Press, 1990.

Sieben, Hermann Josef. "Die Ignatianen als Briefe: Einige formkritische Bermerkungen." *Vigiliae Christianae* 32 (1978) 1-18.

Spalding, David [Thomas]. "Martin John Spalding's 'Dissertation on the American Civil War.'" *The Catholic Historical Review* 52 (1966-1967) 66-85.

Tilley, J.G. "An Analysis of Homiletics Textbooks." MA thesis. University of North Carolina, 1983.

Tracy, Robert E. *American Bishop at the Vatican Council*. New York: McGraw-Hill, 1966.

Trisco, Robert. "Reforming the Roman Curia: Emperor Ferdinand I and the Council of Trent." In *Reform and Authority in the Medieval and Reformation Church*, pp. 143-337. Edited by G.F. Lytle. Washington, DC: Catholic University of America Press, 1981.

Vagaggini, Cyprian. *Theological Dimensions of the Liturgy*. Translated by Leonard J. Doyle and W.A. Jurgens. Collegeville, MN: Liturgical, 1976.

Wachtel, Paul L. *The Poverty of Affluence*. Philadelphia: New Society, 1989.

Westermann, Claus. *Creation*. Philadelphia: Fortress, 1974.

Whalen, J.P. "Murray, John Courtney (1904-1967)." *Encyclopedic Dictionary of Religion* 2 (1979) 2461-2462.

Wilkes, Paul. "The Hands That Would Shape Our Souls." *Atlantic Monthly* (December 1990) 59-88.

Williams, S.K. *Jesus' Death as Saving Event: The Origin of a Concept*. HDR 2. Missoula, MT: Scholars Press, 1975.

Wills, Garry. *Bare Ruined Choirs: Doubt, Prophecy, and Radical Religion*. Garden City, NY: Doubleday, 1972.

Wister, Robert J. "The Teaching of Theology 1950-90: The American Catholic Experience." *America* 162 (February 1990) 88-93, 106-109.

Wofford, Harris. *Of Kennedys and Kings: Making Sense of the Sixties*. New York: Farrar, Straus & Giroux, 1980.

Yates, Robert. "St. Paul and the Law in Galatians." *Irish Theological Quarterly* 51 (1985) 105-124.

Zinn, Howard. *The Southern Mystique*. New York: Alfred A. Knopf, 1964.

Index

Ancient Sources

Old Testament

New Testament

Authors

General